1968

# AMISH SOCIETY

Revised Edition

BY
JOHN A. HOSTETLER

The Johns Hopkins Press
Baltimore and London

The Johns Hopkins Press, Baltimore, Maryland 21218
The Johns Hopkins Press Ltd., London

Standard Book Number (clothbound edition) 8018–0282–2
Standard Book Number (paperback edition) 8018–1136–8

Originally published, 1963
Second printing, 1964

Revised edition, 1968
Second printing, 1971

Johns Hopkins Paperbacks edition, 1970

TO

JOHN S. UMBLE

AND

HAROLD S. BENDER

# PREFACE

THIS BOOK DEALS WITH a segment of humanity which has chosen to live by fixed social customs within a machine civilization. The sources come not from a single Amish community but from observations drawn from many, especially the Old Order Amish communities in Pennsylvania, Ohio, Indiana, Iowa, and Ontario. This book attempts to further our knowledge of custom and conflicts, while at the same time conveying something of the nature of human experience in the Amish society.

Changes in technology are taken for granted in modern society. The determination to improve, modify, or create, gives birth to a constant flow of new inventions. The effect of machines and inventions on the social life of people in modern life is also taken as a matter of course. If a school is too small or does not meet new ideas of fire prevention, Americans build a new one. If the demand for a new consumer product is evident, a business corporation is brought into being.

But there are small groups on the modern scene that are reluctant to change with the great society. They have refused to go along with civilization. The Amish people are one example in the modern industrialized and highly mobile world of a closely integrated small society. They are a slow-changing, distinctive cultural group who place a premium on cultural stability rather than change.

In this book we look microscopically at the interaction

between a secular man-made world and a small family-like society. The American rural community generally has been radically transformed from an agrarian community to a mechanized, agricultural business. Today the Amish communities are under stress as mass technology and civilization encroach upon their way of life. The clash of technology and of "civilized ways" with "Amish ways" is apparent to the outsider, but scientists do not fully know how such ongoing conflicts affect the internal life of the group. Though a dozen or more descriptive books have been written on the Amish, little is known about individual experience, social environment, and personality needs in relation to change within a small society that is surrounded by a dominant one. The effort here is to understand custom on the one hand and change on the other.

The sequence of this book begins with the theoretical and background material and proceeds through a description of the integrated community to a discussion of the community under conflict and stress. We first observe the roots, the charter, and the basic values of the Amish by looking at the small society as a whole. How did the Amish formulate their values and group structure and how are they integrated as a group of functioning people? Once we understand what makes a people a functioning whole we are in a position to observe change and malfunctions. The second half of this volume discusses various aspects of social and cultural change and their effects on the Amish themselves.

We live in a world that is being transformed before our eyes by new inventions, new forms of communication, and new folkways. If hunger and disease are abolished by industrializing, mechanizing, and urbanizing the population of the world, is the cost not sometimes too great? What is the use of introducing a tractor or an automobile if in so doing the human qualities of *Gemeinschaft* (the natural groupings) are cut into shreds? If mankind knows how to survive in larger numbers, to prolong life, and to transform tribal communities into urban ones, what is the cost in terms of the human spirit? How much destruction of old values, of alienation of parents from children, of neighbor from neighbor, of the spirit of man from the faith of his traditional culture, must there be? How fast dare we change? These are the questions which not only the universities and the great metropolitan communities are asking, but also the small villages in Africa and Asia who are faced with a radical change from their age-old customs. This book gives no ultimate answers. But it provides a setting in which to think about technical change and human values from birth to death in one small society.

A patient who allows himself to be thoroughly examined by a skilled physician undertakes the risks of discovering his strengths and weaknesses. In the same way a society which falls into the scrutiny of scientific investigation is liable to have its internal strengths and weaknesses exposed. For any reader who may feel that one or the other has been disproportionately emphasized, the writer wishes to give assurance, especially to his Amish friends, that there has been no ill intent.

To the numerous persons who co-operated in the research and productive phase of this report, I owe sincere thanks. I have in mind those who permitted themselves to be interviewed at length as well as many informants in communities who completed assignments. A Fulbright Scholarship made possible a firsthand understanding of European Amish origins, institutions, and migrations. Grants from the American Philosophical Society and The Canada Council made possible the investigation of contemporary phases of stress and change in the United States and Canada respectively. My students in cultural anthropology at the University of Alberta assisted with the analysis of materials. Many physicians aided in several states with the section on medical behavior. Mr. Norbert Schuldes, of the University of Alberta, drew the charts and maps for the book. I thank Mr. Rae Sutherland, President of Canadian Engineering Surveys, who provided facilities for making the charts and maps. Prof. Albert F. Buffington, Professor of German, of the Pennsylvania State University, assisted me in the German, Pennsylvania German, and mixed renderings of the Amish vocabulary, and Nelson P. Springer of the Mennonite Historical Library gave bibliographical and other suggestions in the interest of accuracy.

I acknowledge the influence and intellectual nourishment of my university teachers, among them William G. Mather, M. E. John, Maurice A. Mook, Roy C. Buck, Samuel W. Blizzard, and other colleagues in the profession, including Charles P. Loomis, Robin Williams, Laura Thompson, Gertrude Huntingdon, and the late H. Richard Niebuhr.

The drawings are by Beulah Stauffer Hostetler. Their purpose is not merely to show how Amish people look to outsiders, but to convey something of their inner character. I am also indebted to my wife for her editorial assistance with the manuscript and photographs.

The revised edition of 1968 contains a new chapter on schooling, Chapter 9, and new material in Chapters 4, 6, and 14.

J. A. H.

Thing which distinguis
Amish from the popular/dominant
culture

# CONTENTS

## PART III: CHANGE AND STRESS

# INTRODUCTION

FOR ME THIS BOOK tells *the* Amish story. The story, like many others told by Americans under similar circumstances, is not without its tragic aspects. Any Amishman knows tragedy intimately either from personal experience or from the accounts of others—loved ones who have left the faith and are hence "lost," people who have been shunned or otherwise punished for doing what "outsiders" do, people who under the pressure of sanctions have lost their memories or committed suicide.

Tragedy is embodied in the belief system of the Amish, in their norms, in their sentiments, and in their group life generally. Without a universally accepted ideology, and without a highly ranked set of officials with responsibility for interpreting and perpetuating the group norms and beliefs which compose the ideology, the Amish are vulnerable both to internal and external pressures for change. This vulnerability is perhaps augmented by the heavy emphasis placed upon the individual interpretation of the Bible, the final guide for man's relation to God and man. That most compelling of goals for the Amishman, his search for the road to salvation, has led to the numberless cleavages of those small bands for whom some doctrine has primacy over ties with friends, relatives, and neighbors. The same stubborn commitment to follow God's precepts as individually interpreted, often by charismatic figures, has led to the seemingly endless formation of subsects, each with its own slightly different key to the kingdom of heaven. Cleavages of another sort occur as hundreds of Amish youth "go gay," "cut their hair," or "go English." That more have not done so is remarkable when one considers that there is more or less constant exposure to the outside world, that there is a considerable amount of interaction with outsiders which is more than casual in that it is continued over a period of time, and that there is no institutionalized and routinized set of status roles designed to effectively neutralize the appeal of the norms and values of the larger society.

The intensity with which the Amish perpetuate their separateness from the outside world is reflected in the tales of ancestral terror which comprises their martyr book: *The Bloody Theatre or Martyr's Mirror*. Those atrocities of the past, no less than the wounding schisms of the present, strike a tragic note to which no Amishman is deaf, a note which constantly admonishes him to beware of the dangers of linking himself with the outside world. The same theme in a more subtle form is made by the chanting of songs as Amishmen, wherever they are, sing from the *Ausbund*, perhaps the oldest hymnal used in this hemisphere. In the very act of singing praises to God, the author's investigations show that any given Amish group unwittingly shows how resistant to change it is. The less linked the group is to the outside world, the more its songs resemble the slow-paced Christian Medieval chants.

In nice contrast to such measures of cultural change as the tempo of church music are the more familiar indicators of technological adaptation and innovation. Few studies of technological change reveal as many important facets as the section which describes the adoption of the automobile. The sociologist interested in the impact of technological change will find here an incomparable laboratory—one which overnight catapults a people territorially limited to foot and buggy travel into a life arena suddenly expanded to include much of eastern United States. Tantalizing questions lure the intellectual curiosity as the author develops his theme. Why did the Amish during much of their early existence become the most efficient farmers in spite of a relatively high level of ignorance in other matters? Was this due to the separatism of persecution, and the ensuing *Gemeinschaft*-like pattern of interaction and communication? Or did the quest for salvation coupled with the need to prove one's diligence in husbandry and stewardship account for their remarkable achievements as farmers? How have those Amish farmers in the United States remained so prosperous, sometimes reporting the highest general farming incomes in the nation, at the same time that they have persistently eschewed the adoption of what are regarded as the necessities of modern farming, including anything but horse power for draft power? By what means were technical facilities avoided, facilities such as automobiles and tractors—especially since the Amishmen's central location has been in the heart of the most highly industrialized, commercialized, and achievement-oriented complexes of a rapidly changing nation? The answers to some of these questions are found in this book, and the scene is set to frame this knowledge in a general theory.

The author himself is not only part of the Amish story, but part of the irrevocably changing America which comes in some measure even to "separatists" such as the Amish. Born a younger child of an Amish family which was later to be excommunicated largely because of the father's alleged worldly pride in a fine registered dairy herd, he was socialized to the norm which taboos education beyond the eighth grade. He is now holder of the Ph.D. degree in sociology, a respected scholar, and teacher in a great university. Immediate members of his family still live in the heart of the Amish settlement. As I have accompanied him on visits to his Amish sisters' homes, I have been forced to ponder both the meaning of what some call the process of Americanization as well as the process of socialization by which scientists are produced. The non-Amishman such as myself comes to appreciate the warmth and sympathy of Amish familial relationships, to feel something of the anxiety lest the children be "lost" to the "outside," to understand the depth of injured sentiments in the wrenches which irretrievably remove parents, children, brothers, sisters, from full fellowship with each other. In addition, as I have worked with the author of this book I have been impressed with his relative objectivity and dedication to his science and substantive specialty no less than with his integrity as a person. The book, even as its author, rises out of Amish culture, and represents something for which Americans should be proud.

Charles P. Loomis
Michigan State University

# Part I

# FOUNDATIONS

# CHAPTER 1

# THE AMISH AS A "LITTLE" COMMUNITY

THE MERGING OF ETHNIC GROUPS and their communities into the broad stream of the American community is proceeding at an accelerated rate. Traditional, small communities, with a distinctive cultural character where life is lived in a stable human context, are disappearing from the modern world. Some are dying out slowly while most are undergoing radical changes as they come in contact with an expanding machine civilization. The social leveling of diverse peoples into a common whole produces stresses and strains upon the members of minority and majority groups alike. A variety of pressures is being exerted upon members of the traditional character-forming groups in modern life. Numerous forces are at work furthering the loss of group identity. To some people, strong community identification is regarded as both necessary and desirable for personal and community fulfillment. To others, strong attachment to an ethnic-oriented community is regarded as an obstacle to the democratic ideal. Many people have not stopped to think about the relation of the individual to his community, about the changes which are transforming traditionally stable groups into technologically efficient suburban communities.[1]

The Amish are one of many traditional, cohesive, agrarian

[1] Margaret Mead's *Culture Patterns and Technical Change* (Mentor Books, 1955) is one of several contributions on this subject. Concern over the social consequences of technical change has reached national proportions. The report of the President's Science Advisory Committee in 1962 urged behavioral scientists to measure the social impact of science on the people's daily lives (*Saturday Review*, May 5, 1962, 35).

groups whose way of life is being changed by the technology and life ways of the urban world. Strong religious convictions, the use of a distinctive language and dress, and strong patriarchal authority has helped to preserve the Amish way of life. But even these well-known means of preservation will not prevent change and the possible eventual collapse of a simple way of life. In a country like the United States no group of people is deliberately forced to change its religion, customs, or value orientations. But it is nevertheless a fact that where progress is a major goal of society, the differences among peoples tend to disappear. Different languages, races, customs, and ways of thinking usually merge into one dominant culture. The Amish, as a distinct cultural group that has been in the United States for over two centuries, still stand out sharply as a people who have maintained strong group identity.

To understand custom and conflict in Amish society we must have some bench mark with which to compare them or at least some frame of reference for thinking about them. It has been observed that small, traditional, isolated peoples, wherever we find them, have many social and psychological characteristics in common. Philosophers and scholars from Greek to modern times have observed similarities of social relation among small non-industrialized societies in contrast to the patterns of social relations that prevail in highly technological societies. Ibn Khaldun, an Arab of the twelfth century, among others, produced a classic statement of the solidarity of the small society. One of the most insightful statements of two contrasting types of societies was made by Ferdinand Toennies.[2] He designated as *Gemeinschaft* the "social order which being based upon consensus of wills rests on harmony and is developed and enobled [*sic*] by folkways, mores and religion"; he designated as *Gesellschaft* "the order which being based upon a union of rational wills rests on convention and agreement, is safeguarded by political legislation, and finds its

---

[2] See *An Arab Philosophy of History* (John Murray Company, 1950); C. P. Loomis, *Community and Society, Gemeinschaft und Gesellschaft* (East Lansing, Michigan State University Press, 1957).

ideological justification in public opinion." Many other types
have been designated as, for example, "mechanical solidarity
and organic solidarity" by Emile Durkheim, "sacred and secular" by Howard Becker, "primary and secondary" by Charles
H. Cooley, "Apollonian and Dionysian" by Ruth Benedict,
"folk and civilization" by Robert Redfield, and "familistic,
mixed, and compulsory interaction" by Pitirim Sorokin.

Anthropologists who have contrasted societies all over the
world have tended to call these semi-isolated peoples "folk societies," "primitives," or merely "simple societies." They constitute a type in contrast to industrialized, or so-called civilized
societies, as an altogether different type. The pattern variables
of Talcott Parsons are associated with the ideal types of
*Gemeinschaft-Gesellschaft* in several ways. Pattern variables
involved in instrumental action (universalism, functional speci-
ficity, affective neutrality and achievement of performance)
on the one hand, and those involved in system-integrative
action (diffuseness, particularism, ascription or quality and
affectivity) on the other, correspond with what in much sociological literature has been thought of as polar types of social
structure.[3]

The "folk" society, as conceptualized by Robert Redfield,[4]
is a small, isolated, traditional, simple, homogeneous society
where oral communication and conventionalized ways are important in integrating the whole of life. In such an ideal-type

[3] See Talcott Parsons, *The Social System* (Free Press, 1951) and also
*Working Papers in the Theory of Action* (Free Press, 1953), 207-8.

[4] Robert Redfield, "The Folk Society," *American Journal of Sociology*
(January, 1947), 293-308. An evaluation of the ideal type by Horace
Miner appears in "The Folk-Urban Continuum," *American Sociological
Review* (October, 1952), 529-37. Redfield's approach includes a theory
of culture change in that the primitive society under influence from industrialized society moves toward the urban type. Other works by this
author that stimulated a renewed anthropological interest in folk cul-
tures are: Robert Redfield, *The Little Community* (University of Chi-
cago Press, 1955); *Peasant Society and Culture* (University of Chicago
Press, 1956); *The Folk Culture of the Yucatan* (University of Chicago
Press, 1949); *Chan Kom, A Maya Village* (Carnegie Institute of Washington, 1934); *A Village That Chose Progress: Chan Kom Revisited*
(University of Chicago Press, 1950); *Tepoztlan: A Mexican Village*
(University of Chicago Press, 1930).

society, shared practical knowledge is more important than science, custom is valued more than critical knowledge, and associations are personal and emotional rather than abstract and categoric. The idea of change is uncomfortable in a folk society. Young people do what the old people did when they were young. Members communicate intimately with each other, not only by word of mouth, but also by custom and symbols that reflect a strong sense of belonging to each other. A folk society is *Gemeinschaft*-like, where there is a strong sense of "we-ness." Leadership is personal rather than institutionalized. There are no gross economic inequalities. Mutual aid is characteristic of its members. The goals of life are never stated as matters of doctrine, nor are they questioned. They are implied by the acts which make up living in a small society. Custom tends to become sacred. Behavior is strongly patterned, and acts as well as cultural objects are given symbolic meaning, often pervasively religious. Religion is diffuse and all-pervasive. Planting and harvesting is as sacred in its own way as singing and praying in the typical folk society.

Any given folk society may not have all of these characteristics. But by taking into account many folk societies all over the world, anthropologists have constructed a model with which to think about types of societies. In comparing the Amish against this model we may expect to find some of these qualities, but in different degrees. The presence or absence of these qualities in Amish society, and the effect of social change on folk characteristics, allows us to compare the known with the unknown. Progress is being made toward refining methods by which we may observe and describe folk societies in a way that is useful to social science. By using a model we can understand a given society and its changing components among a large number of complex societies in the world. This "folk" or "little community" as we will call it will be our bench mark for understanding the Amish society throughout this book.

The significance of the Amish as an intimate, face-to-face primary group has long been recognized. Charles P. Loomis was the first to conceptualize the familistic character of the

Amish in his construction of a scale in which he contrasted the Amish as a familistic *Gemeinschaft*-type system with highly rational social systems of the *Gesellschaft*-type in contemporary civilization.[5] He succeeded in illustrating relationships with degrees of measurement between the familistic and the contractual types of social systems. He showed how the Amish social system is characterized by non-rational modes of behavior such as the traditional, emotional, and sacred interrelationships. This he contrasted with the highly pragmatic relationships characteristic of a bureaucracy. Other social scientists have observed the stability [6] and personalized character of social institutions within the Amish community. Neal Gross [7] observed variables associated with isolation in Amish and non-Amish societies. These studies have done more than reiterate the commonly stressed theme that the Amish are cultural islands.

Some studies of the Amish have tended to make much of the Bible in explaining the Amish social system; that they are religiously oriented in their world outlook is correct. They are

[5] Charles P. Loomis and J. Allan Beegle, *Rural Social Systems* (Prentice-Hall, Inc., 1951), 11–30. Further refinements on the Amish as a social system appear in Charles P. Loomis, *Rural Sociology* (Prentice-Hall, Inc., 1957), and Charles P. Loomis in *Social Systems* (Van Nostrand, 1960), and in Charles P. Loomis and Zona K. Loomis, *Modern Social Theories* (Van Nostrand, 1962).

[6] Walter M. Kollmorgen, *Culture of a Contemporary Community: The Old Order Amish of Lancaster County, Pennsylvania* (Rural Life Studies No. 4, United States Department of Agriculture, 1942). While the study was being conducted under the leadership of Carl C. Taylor, Charles P. Loomis, as senior social scientist of the United States Department of Agriculture, lived a short time with an Amish family and accepted the only available role to him as an outsider, that of hired hand. See also Kollmorgen, "The Agricultural Stability of the Old Order Amish . . . ," *American Journal of Sociology* (November, 1943), 233–41, and Jane C. Getz, "The Economic Organization and Practices of the Old Order Amish of Lancaster County, Pennsylvania," *Mennonite Quarterly Review* (January, 1946), 53–80; (April, 1946), 98–127. Hereafter abbreviated *M.Q.R.*

[7] Neal Gross, "Cultural Variables in Rural Communities," *American Journal of Sociology* (March, 1948), 344–50, and "Sociological Variation in Contemporary Rural Life," *Rural Sociology* (September, 1948), 256–69.

descendants of the Bible-emphasizing Anabaptist movement of the Reformation, and much of their knowledge derives from this heritage, but some observers have tended to "read" more Bible into the Amish society than can be justified. A great many Christian groups and sects claim to base their way of life on the Bible. That the Amish make more of this theme than others has never been demonstrated. Still other observers view the Amish community largely as a sectarian society. When compared to the classic church-type of social structure the sectarian features are certainly apparent.[8] The Amish are small, a splinter group, whose members conform to traditions based upon biblical teachings, and who stress separation from the world. A mentality of separatism as well as sentiments of persecution are maintained. When asked about his distinctive traditions, an Amishman may simply reply: "This is the old way of our forefathers who lived and died in the faith. If it was good enough for them it is good enough for us." The Amish are not sectarians in that they demand others to conform to their practices, nor do they base all actions on the Bible. They are not in conflict with the great society in the same way, and with the same intensity, as are a number of other sects such as the "pessimistic or adventist" types.[9]

The several ethnographic accounts of Amish life based upon specific local communities have never been related to a unifying theory of the total society. The development of a mature social science is made possible by attending to the principles which characterize every discipline that has attained mature standing. These principles have been ignored by sociologists. Cultural anthropology as a developing science has made progress in the description, classification, and comparison of human

[8] The Amish as a sectarian society resembles that of the Old Colony Mennonites discussed in Calvin Redekop, "The Sectarian Black and White World" (Ph.D. dissertation, University of Chicago, 1959). Of interest in this connection is Bryan Wilson, "An Analysis of Sect Development," *American Journal of Sociology* (February, 1959), and Benton Johnson, "A Critical Appraisal of Church-Sect Typology," *American Sociological Review* (February, 1957).

[9] Elmer Clark, *The Small Sects in America* (Abington, 1949).

cultures, which has no counterpart in sociology. The "little community" as a model offers sound theoretical considerations begun by others, yet remains relatively free from sociological assumptions that have become doctrinaire if not sterile. I have deliberately chosen as the model the "little community" from Robert Redfield's work in preference to the concepts of "folk," "primitive," or "peasant" societies, because the latters' traditional connotations are not so aptly fitted to the subject. The little community exists as a rural subculture within the modern state and is unlike the ancient or primitive or peasant type. By "little community" I mean the folk society in the Redfield sense, and the *Gemeinschaft* features in the Toennies[10] sense. The features of this model are "distinctiveness, smallness, homogeneity, and all-providing self-sufficiency." [11] In the remainder of this chapter the main features of Amish life in terms of this model are outlined.

## Distinctiveness

The outside observer cannot help but be aware of the distinctiveness of the Amish people. All he needs to do is drive through any Amish community and observe the Amish team of horses, the carriages driving on the highway, the farm homesteads, and the dress of the people. On visiting a farm he will observe distinctions in farm implements, furniture, and books. All Old Order Amish communities are distinctive in maintaining a doctrine and practice of nonconformity to the world. These major points of the charter forbid the Amishman to engage in war, in politics, or in a business with an outsider for a partner. This belief also finds expression in the restrictions against electricity and telephones. Distinctiveness is apparent to the insider by a recognized way of life and by the many symbols of group identity: styles of clothing and grooming, a distinct language, a common occupation, intimate

[10] See p. 4.
[11] Robert Redfield, *The Little Community* (University of Chicago Press, 1950), 4.

knowledge of other members of the community, and religious ceremony and common sentiment.

Amish life is distinctive in that it is pervasively religious. The core values of the community are religious beliefs. Not only do the members worship God as they understand him through the revelation of Jesus Christ and the Bible, but patterned behavior has a religious dimension. Religion permeates daily life, agriculture, health considerations, and the application of energy to economic ends. Religious beliefs determine the conceptions of the universe, the self, and man's place in it. Religion is "an ever present dimension of experience."[12] The Amish world view recognizes a certain spiritual worth and dignity in the universe in its natural form. Religion conditions the means by which the universe is controlled and exploited. Religious considerations determine hours of work, and the daily, weekly, seasonal, and yearly rituals associated with life experience. Occupation, means and destination of travel, and choice of friends and mates are determined by religious considerations. Religious and secular attitudes are not far distant from each other. The universe includes the divine, and the Amish society is itself considered divine insofar as the Amish recognize themselves as "a chosen people of God." The Amish do not seek to master nature or to work against the elements, but to work with them. The affinity between Amish society and nature in the form of land, terrains, and vegetation is expressed in various degrees of intensity.

Religion is highly institutionalized so that one may properly speak of the Amish as a tradition-directed group. Though allusions to the Bible play an important role in determining the outlook on the world, and on life after death, these beliefs have been fused with several centuries of sectarian experience. Out of intense religious experience, societal conflict, and intimate agrarian experience, a mentality has developed that prefers the old rather than the new. While the principle seems to apply especially to religion, it has also become a generalized attitude. "The old is the best, and the new is of the devil,"

[12] Dorothy Lee, *Freedom and Culture* (Prentice-Hall, Inc., 1959), 163.

becomes a prevalent mode of thought. By living in closed communities where custom and a strong sense of togetherness prevail, an integrated way of life, a folklike culture has been formed. Continuity of conformity and custom is assured and the needs of the individual from birth to death are met within an integrated and shared system of meanings. Oral tradition, custom, and conventionality perform an important part in maintaining the group as a functioning whole. The participant believes religion and custom are inseparable. Conviction and culture are combined to produce a stable human existence.

Central to Amish life is a heritage of common sentiments. The reverence for things biblical is governed by a set of attitudes, a respect for slowness of pace, and by common expectations that have stood for generations. The worship exercises are conducted in a language (German) different from the spoken dialect. The hymnbook dates from the sixteenth century and has never undergone major revision. Other Reformation groups have changed a great deal since their origin but the Amish are a slow-changing society, still reminiscent of peasant life several centuries ago.

A great source of sacred tradition for the Amish is the suffering of the faithful, as is evident in their literature and in their oral knowledge. The enormous size of *The Bloody Theatre or Martyrs Mirror* symbolizes its importance in Amish life: the book contains 1,582 pages and measures ten by fifteen by five inches.[13] In it are the accounts of Christians who were condemned to death for their steadfast faith. There are accounts of burnings of persons, of stonings, crucifixions, live burials, suffocations, whippings, and severing of tongues, hands, feet, and ears. Many of these accounts are eyewitness descriptions with words of farewell to family and church. These testimonies are especially rich in metaphors which symbolize the battle between the carnal and spiritual world. Every Amish

---

[13] The *Bloody Theatre or Martyrs Mirror* (1660), appeared first in the Dutch language and has since been issued in German and English. The compiler was T. J. van Braght, and the most recent imprint in English was by the Mennonite Publishing House, Scottdale, Pa., in 1953.

generation is inculcated into the very real possibility of suffering as did the forefathers described in this household book. The martyr book makes vivid the reality of two spiritual powers engaged in an eternal struggle. Amish hymns tell of "the present terrible last days" in which so many false prophets and tyrants destroy unity among men and persecute the righteous.

The consciousness of difference between in-group and out-group is brought into focus by conflict of values. The Amish teach their people to assume responsibility for their aged relatives. Life insurance of any kind and the trend toward financial security run contrary to Amish values. The goals of the majority society are unacceptable to the Amish with respect to education; they would rather go to jail than send their children to consolidated high schools and thereby relieve the family from the duty to prepare the young for life.

These are some of the qualities of the little Amish community that make it distinctive. "Where the community begins and where it ends is apparent. The distinctiveness is apparent to the outside observer and is expressed in the group consciousness of the people of the community." [14] The Amish community is in some aspects a functional part of modern society but is a distinctive cultural unit within it.

## Smallness

The basic social unit of the Amish community is small. This primary, self-governing unit, wherever Amish live, is the "church district." The rules of life are determined by this local bandlike organization, which is kept small by the ceremonial functions of assembling in a single household and by the limitation imposed by horse-and-carriage travel. In most places the Amish live adjacent to non-Amish farm neighbors, but all Amish households in a geographic proximity form a district. This small unit, from thirty to forty households, is the congregation. Households take turns having biweekly religious services in their homes as there is no central building

[14] Redfield, *The Little Community*, 4.

or place set aside for ceremonial functions. Families are not prevented from migrating from one settlement to another, or from one state to another, but in so doing they affiliate with a local district. Each settlement is divided into districts, as many as needed, to keep the basic social units small and indigenous.

The district is the evaluating and decision-making social unit. The officials may informally come to an agreement on disciplinary matters, but they cannot make decisions that are binding without the consent of the assembled members. Closed member-meetings are held as needed following Sunday services. Each district has its own ordained officials and there is almost no other formal organization. The three types of clergy are bishop, minister, and deacon. Married males are selected for these positions by nominations from the local members; those nominated are voted on and the chosen serve on a lifetime, non-salaried basis. There is no formal training before or after ordination to office. The bishop has the highest and most responsible position and is elected from among the ministers who have had considerable experience in preaching. He is the chief administrator and leader of the congregation, the one who baptizes and receives new members, announces the disciplinary measures of the church, performs marriages, assists in times of ordination, and also preaches regularly. The minister is also ordained to preach. The deacon is custodian of the charities of the church, reads the Scriptures at every service, and has the delicate task of adjusting difficulties that may arise between members. Leadership is unspecialized and charismatic, that is, dependent upon spiritual guidance and inspiration. Officials are chosen from among those who have proven themselves in conforming to the values of the group. Leaders are put in office with the sanction of the Almighty and their calling is not questioned. They may not depend upon human wisdom to perform their functions in preaching, or on such helps as courses in public speaking, the exegetical tools of the trained theologian, or even upon the use of notes in delivering the sermon.

The *Regel und Ordnung* (or rules and order), which are

formulated by each district, cover the range of individual experience. In this little community, whose aim is survival by keeping the world out, there are many taboos, and material traits of culture become symbolic. Conformity to styles of dress is important. The district is the unit of personal observation and is fully representative of the whole of Amish culture.

The sanctions against those who deviate from the *Ordnung* are among the most effective means of control. The social controls are primary and are initiated by the local district. Punishment or the threat of punishment is a strong incentive for conforming to the norms. Transgressors are subject to the counsel of the entire little-church community. To be expelled or to be received back into full fellowship requires a unanimous vote. Minor offenses may be punished by making a confession to the church, provided the transgressor is not stubborn about making the confession when he is admonished. Major offenses are punishable by excommunication, which requires avoidance—the latter is called shunning, or the ban. Persons who leave the strict Old Order Amish church to join other churches are treated as apostates and must be banned. No member may knowingly eat at the table with an expelled member or have normal work or domestic relations with him.

Smallness is assured in Amish life by the multiple functions of the family within the ceremonial unit of organization. When asked about the size of his congregation an Amish bishop thinks in terms of families, not individuals. The relationships of man to man, and the persons who make up the society, are associated with genealogical position. Persons in this society have orderly kinship and coherent social connections with one another so that virtually the whole society forms a body of relatives. Outsiders who join the Amish community—although in fact very few do—tend to take on the attributes of kinship. Persons who defect from the little community, not only break with the beliefs, but also with their relatives.

Thus smallness in the Amish community is maintained by a functional unit no larger than a group of people who can know each other by name, by shared ceremonial activity, and by convention. Like the Redfield model, the Amish community "is small, so small that either it itself is the unit of personal observation or else, being somewhat larger and yet homogeneous, it provides in some part of it a unit of personal observation fully representative of the whole." [15]

## Homogeneity

The Amish community is homogeneous in the totality of its culture and psychology. Ways of thinking and behaving are much alike for all persons in corresponding positions of age and sex. "States of mind" are much alike from one generation to the next. Homogeneity is manifest in socially approved means of exploiting nature, in physical types, and in the sharing of practical knowledge. Physiological homogeneity among the Amish has been recognized by persons who associate inbreeding with facial types. The first Mennonite historian, C. Henry Smith (1875–1948), who earned a Ph.D. from the University of Chicago in 1907, was born of Amish parents and wrote in his autobiography that he was "a thoroughbred" and "full-blooded Mennonite." He says, "My ancestors were of the Mennonite faith and race. I say race deliberately; for like the Jews they had developed in the course of time not only spiritual homogeneity, but a physical solidarity as well, which, through a process of inbreeding, had accumulated many of the characteristics of a distinct human type." [16]

Psychological homogeneity finds expression through preference for traditional rather than scientific knowledge. All have the same amount of education, and the aspirations of one generation repeat those of the preceding one. Critical thought for its own sake has no function in the little community. Agri-

[15] *Ibid.,* 4.

[16] C. Henry Smith, *Mennonite Country Boy* (Faith and Life Press, 1962). Though we lack anthropological evidence of any distinct body or facial type, the homogeneity of not only religion and culture but also of inbreeding and familism has been characteristic of the Mennonite groups.

cultural lore and the farm almanacs still provide potent sources of knowledge. Science is "worldly" wisdom, although in his farming operations the Amishman cannot help being influenced by outside knowledge, and despite the fact that *Ordnung* places a limit on the kind of technology allowed, technological progress has changed some traditional Amish practices. Progressive Amish farmers have demonstrated remarkably the ability to find substitutions for things which are not allowed by the church.

Some of the most productive and stable agricultural communities in the United States are occupied by Amish farmers. Not all Amish are wealthy, and they have no great desire for wealth other than owning family-size farms. Their repulsion of trends which characterize other rural communities, such as migration to the cities, consolidation of schools, urban recreation and associations, is a function of cohesive homogeneity. Placing a high value on farming and farm-related occupations has tended to preserve a total way of life in a little community.

The homogeneous character of the Amish community can be observed in the parts which people play, the activities, and the status roles which govern life. Such functions correspond with those of the preceding generations. The infant born into an Amish home is received with joy; his given name will be similar to that of his grandparents and of his cousins, uncles, and aunts. His last name will, of course, be the same as his father's, which will be one of about forty common family names. He will grow up conforming to patterns of life like his older brothers and sisters, playing and experimenting with the things in the Amish farm environment.

The Amish boy joins the church in his late teens. Baptism is the initiation into adult Amish life. Getting baptized requires conformity to the signs and symbols of being a good Amish person. The dress and grooming, conduct and attitudes reflect the seriousness of conforming, and the applicants for baptism meet regularly with the ministers for instruction on Sundays. The vow of baptism means a life pledge to live up to the

practices of the Amish church. Each person has a vote in the
decisions made by the church, but an unmarried person's influence is limited.

Upon marriage husband and wife form a new residence,
although to some extent under the extended patrilineal character of the great household. Married sons and their wives
often take over the farm operations with the parents moving
into the grandfather house. Every couple is free to work out
its own self-sufficient economic farm unit, but all the relatives
are interested in their well-being. The husband, as the head
of the house, becomes the patriarch and the leader in public
contacts. He carries on farming and is the leader in religious
life and ceremonies. Holy Scripture informs the Amishman
that "Man was created in the image and glory of God" but
woman was made "for the glory of the man."

In the typical little community the aged are respected, and
in Amish society this respect is given biblical sanction. Growing old in Amish society is an experience that brings personally
satisfying rewards. Old people do not become an economic
liability. Wisdom accumulates with age, and with age comes
respect. Old people retain the respect of children and grandchildren. Obedience to parents is one of the most expounded
themes in Amish preaching—in family relations in particular,
and in extended kinship relations generally—so that it becomes
a sacred life principle and a means of control. Those who
honor father and mother have the biblical promise of long
life. Since the wisdom of the aged carries more weight than
the advice of the younger men, the conservation of the entire
community is assured and the religious ideals are protected
against change. The aged father and mother are content if
their children are all married in the Amish faith, if they are
all located on farms, and if they abide by the rules of the
church. They may confidently face a sober death knowing
that their children and a large group of relatives will continue
to live a stable, believing life according to the Amish pattern.
The role expectations of men and women in corresponding age
positions are much alike. In the Amish community, "the career

of one generation repeats that of the preceding. So understood, homogeneous is equivalent to slow-changing." [17]

## Self-Sufficiency

Self-sufficiency in the economic life of the Amish people is associated with agrarianism and occupations associated with nature. Closeness to the soil, to animals, to plants and to weather are consistent with their outlook on life and with limited outside contact. Tilling the soil was not a tenet in Anabaptism but emerged as one of its major values when the movement was banished to survive in hinterlands. Hard work, thrift, mutual aid, and repulsion of city ways such as leisure and non-productive spending, find support in the Bible and are emphasized in day-to-day experience. With practical knowledge and hard work, a good living can be made from the soil; and here, the Amish contend, is the only place to have family life.

Woman's sphere and work is at home, not in the factory or in a paid profession. Cooking, sewing, gardening, cleaning, white-washing of fences, tending to chickens, and helping with the milking keeps her forever occupied. Caring for the children is, of course, her principal work. She will never be a teacher outside the home, not even in her church or its formal activities. Her place in the religious life of the community is a subordinate one, though she has voting rights in congregational meetings or in nominating names for the ministry. An Amish woman's work, like the work of any American woman, is never done. But she is always with her children, and to break the monotony, there are weddings, quiltings, frolics, auction sales and Sunday services. For her satisfaction in life she turns to brightly colored flowers in the garden and in her house in the winter, to rug-making and embroidery work on quilts, pillowcases and towels, and to shelves full of colored dishes in her corner cupboard. These are her prized possessions, some the work of her hands, made not for commercial gain, but for the enjoyment of the household and her host of

[17] Redfield, *The Little Community,* 4.

relatives. Within her role as homemaker she has greater possibility of achieving status recognition than the suburban housewife: her skill, or lack of it, has direct bearing on her family's standard of living. She sews all their clothes; plants, preserves, and prepares the food her family eats, and adds beauty to life with quilts, rugs, and flowers. Canning her own food, making her chowchow, and spreading the dinner table with home prepared food, are achievements that are recognized and rewarded by her society.

The Amish community tends to be self-sufficient in its socialization and educational functions; the social needs of the individual are met within it. The Amish have no schools of higher learning, but they have built elementary schools in some places to avoid the external influence that comes with the centralized school system. As soon as the law will allow, Amish children are taken out of school for work at home. The Amish viewpoint is that "If a boy does little hard work before he is twenty-one, he probably never gets to like it afterward. In other words, he will not amount to much as a farmer." [18]

Leisure and ways of social enjoyment are met by the informal institutions within the community. The kinship duties require extensive visiting.[19] Recreation does not exist apart from meaningful social experiences, self-expression, and rites of passage within the community. Work bees, such as barn-raisings, woodcuttings, husking bees, quiltings, preparations for church services, weddings, and funerals (including casket-making), all reflect self-sufficiency. The social life of the young people is centered in the Sunday evening singing. A most important life ceremony is the wedding, which calls for a large amount of festivity, food, kinship duties, and ritual. What matters most about the prospective bride and bride-

[18] *Lancaster Intelligencer Journal* (February 19, 1931).
[19] The extraordinary Amish preoccupation with genealogy and kinship solidarity is reflected in that well over sixty family histories have been published. See "Genealogy," in *Mennonite Encyclopedia* (Vol. 2) and John A. Hostetler, *Annotated Bibliography on the Old Order Amish* (Mennonite Publishing House, 1951).

groom is not whether they come from a wealthy family, but whether they show promise of being a good farmer and a good housekeeper respectively within the bounds of the community.

In finding markets for crops and products, the little Amish community is linked with the economy of the larger industrial nation. It is not a communal society with an exclusive economic system, and ownership is not unlike the prevailing economic system in American life. Within the private enterprise system, the Amish have been able to maintain patterns of mutual aid and ways of sharing economic rewards and misfortunes. The vital linkages with outside institutions are conditioned by the distinctive core values and by the special rules which govern such relationships. By making agriculture a sacred occupation, drift toward the complex world of labor and the professions is avoided. No truck is allowed to deliver or pick up farm produce on the Lord's Day. Religion prevents members from taking an active part in activities which are beyond "necessity" on Sunday. The Amish farmers are not integrated with the farm organizations, with local political groups, or with consolidated schools.

Self-sufficiency is the Amish answer to government aid programs, such as farm subsidy and social security benefits. Amish leaders repeatedly go to Washington to seek freedom from federal aid. It is not that they object to paying taxes, though some have protested social security assessments on grounds that they are a form of insurance.[20] But they are opposed to receiving government aid of any kind, whether old age pension, farm subsidy, or compensation payments, and to having their children and grandchildren fall heir to such handouts. Before the government committees they have contended that "Old-Age Survivors Insurance is abridging and infringing to our religious freedom. Our faith has always been sufficient to meet the needs as they come. . . ."[21] In support of their firm stand they said

[20] Clarence W. Hall, "The Revolt of the 'Plain People,'" *Readers Digest* (November, 1962).

[21] From a leaflet, "Our Religious Convictions Against Social Security," April, 1960.

the Bible teaches: "But if any provide not . . . for those of his own house, he hath denied the faith, and is worse than an infidel" (I Timothy 4:8). To pay social security "tax," some Amish say, is to admit that the government has a responsibility for aged Amish members, and to admit this is to deny the faith. This would, they say, undermine their own stable community and their form of mutual aid. Amish security requires a high degree of personal relations and responsibility in times of stress, fire, sickness, old age, or death. Strictly commercial or federal means of providing for these needs are regarded as secular, if not sinful. Amish life is not segmented into cliques, clubs, or special-interest groups, but approximates a cradle-to-the-grave arrangement as an integral whole; the community "provides for all or most of the activities and needs of the people in it." [22]

We have observed the qualities of distinctiveness, smallness, homogeneity, and self-sufficiency as they apply to the Amish community. The little community is a type of human coexistence that is realized in many parts of the world. These little communities, often tribal in character, that remain around the edges of expanding civilizations are a human type. The qualities outlined by Redfield are found in different degrees in each of them. The Siriono Indians of the Bolivian forest, the Skolt Lapp community, the Nuer tribesmen of the Sudan, the Trobriand Islanders of Melanesia, or the Maya of Mexico represent different degrees of distinctiveness, smallness, homogeneity, and self-sufficiency. The Amish are not a classic folk society in the same sense as are these age-old and more completely geographically isolated, primitive types.[23] The Amish developed out of the Reformation, which in itself was a liberalizing and self-determining social movement. Another major difference is that the Amish live within the confines of a highly complex civilization and have conditioned their mode of life

[22] Redfield, *The Little Community*, 4.
[23] Elman R. Service, in *Profiles in Ethnology* (Harper and Row, 1963) has made further delineations by classifying societies into bands, tribes, chiefdoms, primitive states, and modern folk societies.

to exist as a small community within it. And, finally, the Amish way of life is permeated with the western Christian tradition and its codifications of reality that provide the members with a world view. The Amish share with many nativistic societies the affinity to nature and the soil; they meet the problems of life in conventional ways, and the whole society is familistic in its social structure. Each Amish community exhibits a local culture, though in its basic orientation it is not unlike other Amish communities. Organization, roles, authority, sanction, facility, and controls governing relations with the outside world are much alike in all Amish communities.

The way in which the little Amish community is affected by culture contact and by the ethos of an expanding technologically oriented civilization will be taken up later in this book. We turn now to (1) custom in the little community in its harmonizing and fulfilling aspects and (2) to conflicts and changes brought about by culture contact with the great society. In the terminal chapters of the book, reorganization and the future of the little community will be discussed.

# CHAPTER 2

# THE BIRTH OF THE AMISH SOCIETY

IN THE PERSPECTIVE OF TIME the Amish are older than the Industrial Revolution and were among the early settlers in colonial America. To understand Amish origins is to understand something of the nature of minority relations in the American religious heritage. The considerations that led to the formation of the Amish as a subcultural group are primarily religious, and not only religious, but sectarian. The Amish, taking their name from their leader Jakob Ammann, are the descendants of a religious division that occurred among the Swiss Anabaptists from 1693 to 1697. The Amish are direct descendants of the Swiss Anabaptists. The division which separated them from the parental group was not over fundamental Anabaptist beliefs, but about conformity to specific norms of practice. The Anabaptist movement,[1] beginning in 1525, consisted of three groupings: the Anabaptists of Holland, the Swiss Brethren, and the Hutterian Brethren of Austria. The conditions that give rise to sectarian groups are made up of many complexities, and to understand the sectarian character of the Amish we must begin with the social climate of the Reformation itself.

## The Social Climate of Reform

Fundamental changes in the dominant society are believed to be responsible for conditions that give rise to sectarian cleav-

[1] By Anabaptist we mean that movement characterized in the following sources: Harold S. Bender, "The Anabaptist Vision," *Church History* (March, 1944), and by the same author *Conrad Grebel c. 1498–1526, The Founder of the Swiss Brethren Sometimes Called Anabaptists* (Goshen, Indiana, 1950).

ages. With the impending struggle for power between the church and emerging states, many people lost faith in the traditional institutions. Intellectual unrest preceded the Reformation, and the Renaissance movement in Italy gave rise to important fermenting ideas. The prophets of a new way, like John Wycliffe in England and John Huss in Bohemia, had already set the stage for popular reform. The century-old threat of the Turks and the widespread social discontent following the Black Plague wrought dissatisfaction. Various kinds of doubts became widespread. Traders and peasants found themselves displaced from economic support by the growing commerce with other parts of the world. The journeymen and landless people without homes or masters were ready to become followers of radical religious sects.

To the common people it seemed that all ills, religious and social, were due to the established medieval Roman Catholic church. The rebellion against old systems of authority was general. Out of this discontent there developed not only new nations but also a general reorganization of religious groups ranging from the conservative or extreme "right" to the "leftist" position. The medieval Catholic church may be seen occupying the position to the "right," that is, taking a position against change. Luther and his movement, discarding some of the teachings of the Catholic church but retaining much of the customary ritual, occupied a "right central" position. The Reformed party led by Ulrich Zwingli, more liberal than Luther in doctrine but retaining the union of church and state, occupied a "left" position. Finally an extreme "leftist" position was taken by those who wanted to reform the Reformers, the Anabaptists.

The variety of religious sects existing in the sixteenth century is astonishing and demonstrates the fluidity of religious loyalty during a period of social disorganization. One source lists not only the biblical heretics, but also, among others, the Adamites, who run naked in the woods; the Free-livers, who have wives in common; the Weeping Brothers, who hold highly emotional prayer meetings; the Blood-thirsty Ones, who drink human blood; the Devil-worshippers, who praise the devil ten times daily; and the Hypocritical Ones, who are indifferent to all liturgical ceremonies.[2] Many channeled their circumstances into religious conceptions and "glorified in living loose from the world."[3]

The first widespread rebellion against the established order was the uprising of the common people culminating in the Peasants' War, in Germany. This rebellion was a political manifestation of the "leftist" position.[4] These leaders and their peasant followers hoped for deliverance from oppression. They claimed authorization from God through divine revelation to fight the army of the state and to establish the Kingdom of God on earth. The Peasants' War was the greatest mass uprising in German history, and its defeat eliminated the peasantry as a political factor for three hundred years.

The peaceful Anabaptists, however, were not interested in fighting a national battle: they wanted simply to have freedom of religion and a voluntary church. By their open debates with both Catholic theologians and the Protestant Reformers, and by their submissive and simple obedience to the Bible, it was clear that they wished to return to a primitive, early type of Christianity. Although the wrath of the Catholic church, the Reformers, and the state was against them, in the end they won for much of the modern world the separation of church and state and freedom of religion. Their beliefs as distinct from the state or territorial churches required of the individual a conscious change (rebirth) of life and intent through faith in Christ and the work of the Holy Spirit; the demand for a type of personal consciousness, which was set apart from

[2] Henry A. DeWind, "A Sixteenth Century Description of Religious Sects in Austerlitz, Moravia," *M.Q.R.* (January, 1955), 44.

[3] Franklin H. Littell, in *The Anabaptist View of the Church* (Starr King Press, Boston, 1958), provides us with a distinction between the economic and religious character of the Anabaptists. For a study of the social origins of the Anabaptists see Paul Peachey, *Die Soziale Herkunft der Schweizer Täufer* (Karlsruhe, 1954). J. Huizinga, in *The Waning of the Middle Ages* (1924) provides insights on the decline of symbolism and form.

[4] Traditionally the Zwickau prophets were classed as Anabaptists but more recent research indicates otherwise. See H. S. Bender, "The Zwickau Prophets, Thomas Müntzer and the Anabaptists," *M.Q.R.* (January, 1953); Littell, *op. cit.,* 9.

everything worldly and sinful (nonconformity); commitment to brotherly love (discipleship), which involved a sharing of material and spiritual aid; and association with a new community (brotherhood) of believers characterized by the austerity of the early Christians. They rejected as invalid infant baptism as practiced by the established state churches.

The Anabaptists' disagreement with Luther was not that he "tore down the old House, but that he built no new one in its place." Among the first Anabaptists were some of the most educated and intellectually capable people of the time, many of them former priests. Their concern was not with the correction of evil or the redress of grievances for wrongs committed against them, but with building a new fellowship after the example of the early Christians. By placing themselves under the demands of the Sermon on the Mount, they created a movement that resembled the church of the first century. They introduced a radically new ethic into a turbulent environment, living defenseless and non-resistant lives in the face of violent action. Their re-examination of the Christian faith led them to a new kind of human relation. They held that Christians should fight not with sword and gun, but "with the Cross and with sufferings."

To restore primitive Christianity the Anabaptists took literally the Sermon on the Mount as a code for Christians, they renounced oaths, reveling and drunkenness, the use of the sword whether in war or civil government, economic rewards, and personal adornment. The Hutterites went so far as to abdicate private property. The true church, Anabaptists said, should not depend on baptism administered in infancy, but on regeneration and change of character. Instead of embracing the whole of humanity, the church for them was to be a voluntary adult group of disciplined and committed people.[5]

The Reformers were disturbed to see medieval unity shat-

[5] Here the conditions were met for the development of "sect-type" in contrast to the "church-type" of social structure in Christianity as developed by Max Weber, *Gesammelte Aufsätze zur Religionssoziologie* (second edition, Tübingen, 1922), Vol. I, 150 ff., and Ernst Troeltsch, *The Social Teaching of the Christian Churches* (Macmillan, 1930).

tered by the plundering acts of the peasants and by the radical ideas of the Anabaptists. Panic evoked the military might of the combined church and state. The Anabaptists and other heretics were subjected to the death penalty and many fled. Revolting peasants and non-resistant Anabaptists alike suffered persecution and annihilation in many instances. Anabaptist activity was centered in Zurich, Switzerland, where the adherents called themselves Swiss Brethren. The movement had its counterpart in the Netherlands, where they were called "Mennists" or Mennonites after their pastor-leader Menno Simons. The name "Mennonite" was later applied generally to include descendants of both Swiss and Dutch Anabaptists.

From the Netherlands many Mennonites migrated to northern Germany, Prussia, Russia, and later to the central plains of the United States. The Mennonites who remained in their native country of the Netherlands were granted toleration after a century and became merchants and part of the well-to-do class. The Swiss Brethren suffered persecution for two more centuries; and with the original leadership gone, the succeeding generations settled into the mountainous hinterlands, pursuing an agrarian life. There they remained, conservative islands of sectarianism, and met the conditions for developing a static folk culture.[6]

It was in this setting that the Amish as a dissenting group broke from the Swiss Brethren in 1693–97 and formed a society in which custom has come to have great prominence. Before this cleavage formed among the scattered congregations of agrarian Swiss Brethren, the creative and intellectual character of Anabaptism had already vanished. Like all serious divisions, this one had its personalities and its peculiarities.[7]

[6] For the rural character of these communities see Ernst Correll, *Das Schweizerische Täufermennonitentum* (Tübingen, 1925). Also J. H. Yoder, "Mennonites in a French Almanac," *Mennonite Life* (October, 1954).

[7] Letters and documents written at the time of the controversy have been found in Amish homes and have been published on several occasions. See Milton Gascho, "The Amish Division of 1693–1697 in Switzerland and Alsace," *M.Q.R.* (October, 1937). An English translation of the

While the exact details of the division may not increase the reader's respect for sect groups, it may increase his understanding of the process by which separatist groups entrench themselves. For the reader who believes that "virtue" or "purity" can be found in going back to the origins of things, as seems to be a tendency in all sects, this account offers little evidence.

## The Founder, Jakob Ammann

Differences in religious conformity began to emerge among the Swiss Brethren late in the seventeenth century. As is often the case, the differences became focused in a controversy. The controversy centered around three specific norms of practice: the *Meidung* or shunning (also called avoidance) of excommunicated members; the excommunication of a woman who had admitted speaking a falsehood; and the saying that noble-hearted persons would be saved. The latter were the *Treuherzigen*, the noble-hearted persons or sympathizers of the Anabaptists, who shared many of their views and helped them in times of persecution but did not join the group openly. Other differences became apparent as the groups and their spokesmen took sides.

The aggressive leader of the emerging group was Jakob Ammann, an elder who lived near Erlenbach. He was a younger man than his opponent, Hans Reist, a preacher of Obertal in the Emmental congregation. Both lived in the Canton of Bern, Switzerland. The emerging Ammann group began holding communion services twice instead of the usual once each year. Their leader introduced the practice of footwashing in connection with the communion service and contended for uniformity in dress, including hats, shoes, and stockings. He taught that it was wrong to trim the beard and that persons

letters is found in *The Letters of the Amish Division*, trans. and ed. by John B. Mast (Christian J. Schlabach, publisher, Oregon City, Oregon, 1950), 120. Other sources are Delbert Gratz, "The Home of Jacob Ammann in Switzerland," *M.Q.R.* (April, 1951), 137; and articles in *The Mennonite Encyclopedia* (4 vols., Mennonite Publishing House, Scottdale, Pa., 1955-59).

who attended the state church should be excommunicated. There was contention between the leaders of the opposing sides as to who had the greater authority to set standards for the various congregations.

It does not appear that these differences are sufficiently significant to provoke a major division. Had it not been for other factors essential to the emergence of a dissenting group, the controversy might have been short-lived.

Ammann, on his own initiative, took with him two preachers and started an investigation tour of the brotherhood's congregations throughout his native Switzerland and in nearby Alsace. At each congregation the ministers were asked to state their policy with respect to the practice of *Meidung*. If the answer was affirmative, Ammann demanded their attitude on two other issues: whether noble-hearted persons would be saved, and whether persons who were guilty of telling a falsehood should be excommunicated. Ammann demanded unconditional answers, and he succeeded in polarizing the churches into opposing sides. At their first stopping place, Friedersmatt, the minister Niklaus Moser agreed to the ban, but he advised Ammann to go and see Elder Schneider. Instead the delegation went to Reutenen near the home of minister Peter Giger. Ammann called a meeting unknown to Giger until after the latter had retired for the night. When Giger arrived the meeting was about over, but Ammann and his delegation decided to continue the investigation. Niklaus Baltzi, minister at neighboring Habstetten, was summoned and accused of teaching that noble-hearted persons would be saved. Baltzi asked that the delegation be patient.

The investigating group went to Uttigen where they summoned Hans Reist to declare his position on *Meidung*. He answered, "What one eats is no sin; Christ also ate with publicans and sinners." Avoidance at the table was wrong, according to him, for it is not what goes into a man's mouth that defiles him. His answers to this and other questions were unsatisfactory to Ammann, but some who were present could not accept Amman's view of excommunication and shunning.

At their next stop, Eggiwil, Ammann was told that it would

be best if the entire ministry would assemble and decide upon a uniform practice of interpretation. He immediately took it upon himself to call a meeting of the entire Swiss ministry in Niklaus Moser's barn. But not all of the ministers were represented, and when pressed for their attitude on *Meidung*, some of them said they could not decide until after the entire ministry would meet and agree after a careful study of the Scriptures. There were no conclusions, except to call another meeting of the entire ministry. Ammann wanted the meeting in eight days, but Giger wanted it in three weeks. Meanwhile, Ammann sent two other men to Reist to ask him a second time about his stand on the *Meidung*. Reist did not answer verbally but wrote a letter stating that he could not accept the *Meidung* and asking his readers not to pay much attention to "that young fellow." From his tactics it is apparent than Hans Reist, the spokesman for the parental group, underestimated Ammann's potential strength. The parental group lacked the know-how or failed to enforce sanctions which would suppress the dissenting Ammann.

At the second meeting in Moser's barn, Hans Reist did not appear. While waiting for Reist to come, Giger recalled the Scripture: "What enters the mouth does not defile a man, but what goes out of the mouth." Ammann replied that the quotations had nothing to do with the issue. Giger quoted another: "If ye bite and devour one another, see that ye be not consumed one of another." He pleaded with Ammann not to bring about a division in the church. Meanwhile the women were instructed to go and tell Reist and others to come to the meeting, but they returned saying that it was harvest time and these men could not come. Ammann interpreted their absence as indication of their indifference.

Ammann became impatient. He then read a letter with six charges against Hans Reist and declared him excommunicated. One of the women fell on her knees and in tears begged Ammann to be patient. He turned to Moser and asked his opinion of the *Meidung*, but Moser said he could not speak for his congregation since he had not asked their opinion. Ammann turned to Giger for his opinion, but he replied that he could not give his opinion until all the ministers were present. Ammann then charged both of them with falsehood and declared them excommunicated. He next turned to Habegger, Schwartz, and Gul, and when they could not accept the *Meidung,* he excommunicated them. The meeting broke up and the Ammann party left without shaking hands. Giger pulled Ammann by the shirt sleeve saying, "Let me present my word also," but Ammann jerked his arm away and made his departure.

Ammann forbade his members to attend the service of the other group and said that Hans Reist, because he was older, claimed for himself too much authority, even though both were ordained to equal offices. He accused Reist of spiritual pride. Reist became the leader of those who opposed Ammann. Animosity ensued between Reist and Ammann and those who sided with them, as is evidenced by the vocabulary which they used. Ammann called Reist an "apostate," a "sectarian," and a "rebel." Reist labeled Ammann a "blasphemer." Other terms exchanged between them were "liars," "untruthful," "false teachers," "lying grayheads," "unbelieving people," "banished," and "the devil's servants."

Ammann continued his relentless activity, so that the dissension spread from a local region to the wider Anabaptist community. Shortly after the dramatic meeting in the barn at Eggiwil, Ammann wrote a warning letter to the Swiss ministers demanding that by a certain date they yield to his "biblical views." His ultimatum-like demands were ignored. Ammann then visited the Alsatian congregations, everywhere banning those who did not yield to his views. The division also infiltrated into the Rhineland-Palatinate, but the opposing side in southern Germany reached an agreement with Reist's supporters on a mild application of *Meidung.* They agreed that excommunicated members should not be admitted to the communion service, but they could not accept Ammann's strict position of *Meidung,* which said it should be observed between marriage partners and in eating. *Meidung* should be kept in spiritual matters, the Reist group contended, but not in everyday affairs.

Ammann had succeeded thus far in articulating differences of interpretation on the practice of *Meidung*. His authority to decide what was right was not delegated to him by an assembly or any organization. He assumed that position and proceeded by equating strictness with divine sanction. The practice of shunning excommunicated members had been included in the Schleitheim Confession of 1527 and in the Dortrecht Confession of 1632. The ban was an instrument the early Mennonites of the Netherlands used to insure the "purity" of the church. Menno Simons himself observed it as stated in I Corinthians 5:11, "if any man that is called a railer or a drunkard, or an extortioner; with such an one no not to eat." This meant that one could not eat a meal with one who had been excommunicated. If either husband or wife were excommunicated the usual relations between them were to be discontinued, and some even taught that husband and wife should separate. This ban had been a live issue among the Mennonites of Holland a century earlier and had wrought havoc to the unity of the church and split the Dutch Mennonites into many factions.

## WARNUNGSSCHRIFT VON JAKOB AMMANN

Ich, Jakob Ammann, mitsamt Dienern und Ältesten, schicken diese Schrift und soll einem jeden, es sei Weibs- oder Mannsperson, Diener oder gemeiner Jünger, allen insgemein zu wissen tun, dass ihr bis auf den 20 sten Tag Hornung [Februar] erscheinen und euch bei uns anmelden wollet, nämlich die noch durch Urteil und Rat nicht aus der Gemeine geschlossen sind, und sollt euch verantworten, ob ihr die streitigen Artikel mit uns bekennen könnt, nämlich die Ausgebannten zu meiden, und dass man die Lügner aus der Gemeinde schliessen solle und ausserbald Gottes Wort niemand selig sprechen soll, oder uns mit Gottes Wort eines andern berichten könnt, so wollen wir uns wissen lassen. So ihr auf den bestimmten Tag nicht erscheinen wollt, diese

Artikel mit uns zu bekennen, oder uns ein anderes zu zeigen aus Gottes Wort, so wollen wir euch noch einen bestimmten Tag setzen, nämlich den 7. März, euch zu verantworten, so sollt ihr mit den andern Ausgebannten nach meiner Lehr und Glauben von uns Dienern und Ältesten, und sonderlich von mir, Jakob Ammann, als sektische Menschen aus der Gemeinde Gottes geschlossene sein und gescheut und gemieden werden bis auf die Zeit eurer Bekehrung, nach laut Gottes Wort. Diese Schrift soll von einer Person zu andern geschickt werden, damit es allen kundbar werde. Anno 1693 Jahres

### JAKOB AMMANN'S WARNING MESSAGE

Together with the ministers and bishops, I, Jakob Ammann, am sending this writing to everyone who is not already expelled by judgment and counsel, both men and women, ministers and lay members, to inform you that you shall appear before us on or before February 20th to answer whether you can confess these controversial articles with us, namely: to avoid those who are expelled, and that liars shall be expelled from the church, and that no one shall be saved, apart from the Word of God. Or if you can instruct us of a better way, from the Word of God, we shall lend you our ear. If you are unable to report by this appointed date, to confess these articles with us, or to point out to us another way from the Word of God, then we shall appoint another date, namely, March 7th, on which you may present your answer. But if you fail to appear, and answer at this appointed time, then you shall according to my teaching and creed, be expelled by us ministers and elders, especially by me, Jakob Ammann, as sectarians, and shall be shunned and avoided until the time of your repentance according to the Word of God. This paper shall be sent from one person to another to make it known to all.

A.D. 1693

The dissension was bitter. According to Reist's group, Ammann made *Meidung* more important than salvation. Salvation "was sought in the *Meidung* and this made the suffering of

Jesus of no avail." The followers of Ammann were "like wolves who did not spare Christ's flock, who avoided neither lies nor deception to secure a greater following." Ammann condemned the trimming of the beard and the wearing of gay clothing, and "anyone desiring to do so," he said, "shall be justly punished." Reist said, "It is contrary to the Gospel to affix one's conscience to a pattern of the hats, clothes, stockings, shoes, or the hair of the head and to enforce such regulations with the ban." Ammann later placed most of the Palatinate ministers under the ban, including numerous persons whom he had never seen. Thus the Mennonites of Switzerland, Alsace, and southern Germany were divided into two factions. Of the sixty-nine preachers known to have taken sides in the division, twenty-seven sided with Ammann—of the total, twenty-three lived in Alsace, twenty-six in Germany, and twenty in Switzerland.

Efforts were made to reconcile the two groups, but they failed. The Amish group appeared to make such an attempt by placing themselves in a state of excommunication. They admitted that their methods were too rash and hasty, but they never surrendered the demand for *Meidung*. When the Amish were wont to be received back into fellowship, the question of the literal observance of footwashing as Ammann practiced it came up for discussion. Some of the congregations were dubious about the sincerity of the Amish attempts at reconciliation and advised against it. Animosity between the factions continued. When the Swiss Brethren and the Amish left Switzerland in large groups in 1711, they refused to enter the same ship on their voyage down the Rhine.

Material differences were not the main issue in the division but their importance increased with time. Differences in dress between Amish and Mennonites in Europe were never as obvious as today in America where the distinctive dress of the Amish symbolizes their separatism. Although the use of "hooks-and-eyes" was not the main controversy, it later symbolized the differences, for in the Palatinate, the Amish were known as *Häftler* (hook-and-eyers) and the Mennonites were the

*Knöpflers* (buttoners). Such material differences provided members with a constant stimulus for social distance and consciousness of kind.

## The Stages of Sectarian Emergence

The Amish cleavage is not unlike other social-movement patterns. Certain characteristics are common to all leaders, prophets, or founders out of which come dissenting movements. By comparing the Amish account with movement studies [8] it is possible to summarize with several hypotheses. Sectarian movements tend to emerge when the following conditions are met:

*A sectarian movement* [9] *must establish an ideology different from that of the parent group* in order to break off relations with it. Emergent beliefs tend to be selected on the basis of their differences from the parental group. They are essentially negative doctrines that state what the movement is against. The beliefs become important symbolically as signalizing their opposers. The application of *Meidung* in its strict form was important to Ammann and he succeeded in making it a major issue over which a cleavage was imminent.

[8] The origins and natural history of movements has been the concern of a number of social scientists. See Rex D. Hopper, "The Revolutionary Process: A Frame of Reference for the Study of Revolutionary Movements," in Ralph H. Turner and Lewis M. Killigan, *Collective Behavior* (Prentice-Hall, 1957), 310–19. See also "Separatist Movements," Chapter 17 in this source, and also Ralph Linton, "Nativistic Movements," *American Anthropologist* (April–June, 1943). Others are Rudolph Heberle, *Social Movements* (Appleton-Century Crofts, Inc., 1951); C. Wendell King, *Social Movements in the United States* (Random House, 1956); the Methodist Church is treated as a movement in Carl A. Dawson and Warner E. Gettys, *An Introduction to Sociology* (Ronald Press, 1948), 689–710; Eric Hoffer, *The True Believer* (Harper, 1951).

[9] By sectarian is meant a religious movement of dissent characterized by a break from the established order, tending toward perfectionism and exclusiveness from others. Continued conflict with the dominant institutions of society is often characteristic of the sectarian group. A recent summary of sectarian sociology appears in Calvin Redekop's "The Sectarian Black and White World" (Ph.D. dissertation, University of Chicago, 1959).

*The articulation of differences in belief by an enthusiastic leader claiming divine authority is an early condition necessary for the emergence of a sect.* Beliefs are always articulated by persons who manifest leadership abilities. There is evidence that Ammann was both highly articulate and aggressive. Though Ammann had two other preachers with him on his tour of investigation, he was the main spokesman and relied upon his own inspiration rather than on authority shared by others who were with him.

*A sense of urgency is vocalized by an authoritarian personality who imposes negative sanction on the opposing persons or groups.* An appeal to patience and more time for deliberation made no sense to Ammann. In his view the church was slipping farther and farther into worldliness, and no harm, in his opinion, could be done by action. The founders of such movements act on the basis of a personal, charismatic authority, and not on authority delegated by the group. Ammann could follow no middle course and he would not respond to those who fell on their knees to beg for patience.

*The goals of a sect must be specific rather than general if they are to elicit acceptance among the masses.* Ammann's goals were specific and literal rather than general and philosophical. Most social movements have both kinds, but in the initial stage goals must be explicit and specific. It is difficult to create a movement with only general goals. Enthusiasm among adherents for abstract and broad goals is hard to create and maintain. There is room for personal interpretation in broadly defined goals, but not so in specific ones. Ammann held goals that were specific and attainable, and they allowed room neither for personal deviations nor moderation.

*A sect must establish cultural separatism, involving symbolic and often material as well as ideological differences, from those of the parental group.* The symbols of separation in Ammann's group took the form of different styles of dress, grooming, and physical appearance. For him doctrinal matters had to take on visible and explicit, not just "spiritual," character. *Meidung* was not just to be practiced at the communion table, or in a spiritual way, but it had to take effect literally. Nonconformity to the world meant not only being different in thought or in the heart, but it also meant outward material earmarks of separation. Literalness [10] characterized Ammann's emphasis on establishing what he called "the old ground and foundation." The example of Jesus washing the feet of His followers was not to be taken only spiritually, but literally.

In the course of their natural history the Amish have conformed in many respects to other social movements which have at least four fundamental features in common.[11] They attempted (1) to change or keep from changing certain beliefs or practices among existing groups; (2) they appealed to the masses as a means of achieving their goals, and thereby distributed responsibility among followers and leaders according to the vision or skill of the dominant leader. This resulted in (3) a geographical scope which transcended the local community, and (4) persistence through time. The Amish achieved all of these features.

A distinctive feature of the Amish group has been the persistence of custom and its slowness to change. The rigidity with which they literally adhered to their religious practices carried over into the social and economic aspects of their culture. Whether we call this cultural inertia, cultural lag, or formalism, does not change the fact that through it we can observe how the little Amish community has remained relatively stable while the dominant society has changed radically.

The name given to the followers of Ammann in Europe was "Amish Mennonite" or "Amish." The usage of "Old Order Amish" is a later American development that came into common usage as the forces of assimilation and change began to penetrate the small communities. Those groups of Amish who kept their older customs were simply designated by the more progressives as "The Old Order."

[10] The emphasis on literalness is not only evident in the sectarian interpretation of Scripture, but also in personal ethics and orientation to life generally as has been observed by Redekop, *ibid.* In other words, sect mentality observes social reality in a black-white relationship and lacks the facility to see more than two quite opposite alternatives.

[11] C. Wendell King, *op. cit.*, 25–27.

## Extinction in Europe and Survival in America

The Amish people came to Pennsylvania from Switzerland as early as 1727. Some families may have come earlier but records of earlier arrivals are lacking. There are today no Amish in Europe who have retained the name and the principles of the original group. Their descendants in Europe have reunited with the main body of Mennonites or have lost their Amish identity. It is only in North America that the name and distinctive practices of the Amish have survived. The division was transplanted in North America, where *Meidung* continues to be practiced. Their extinction in the Old World and survival in the New is a little known story. What happened to the Amish who remained in Europe remains unknown to them but has been reasonably well documented by Mennonite historians.[12]

In Alsace most of the Anabaptist congregations followed the leadership of Jakob Ammann. Ammann himself moved to Alsace and located at Markirch in 1696. Persecution forced them to leave this area and from 1719–30 many moved to Montbéliard (Mumpelgart), then a Protestant duchy of Württemberg. Others went to Birkenhof on the Alsatian-Swiss border. Some of the Markirch Amish moved across the nearby border into Lorraine, while others moved farther into the interior of France. A small group established itself in Luxembourg. After 1815, which marked the end of the Napoleonic wars, Amish families migrated eastward and northward into Germany and to North America. Small groups had settled in Breisgau in southern Baden across the Rhine River in 1759, and in 1802 others went to southern Bavaria, near Ingolstadt, Regensburg, and Munich. The movement of Swiss families to Alsace after 1880 gradually modified the Amish characteristics of the

[12] *The Mennonite Encyclopedia*, Vols. I–IV (Scottdale, Pa., 1955–59), provides more details on European Amish settlements, Amish conferences, migrations, and doctrinal statements than can be given in this chapter.

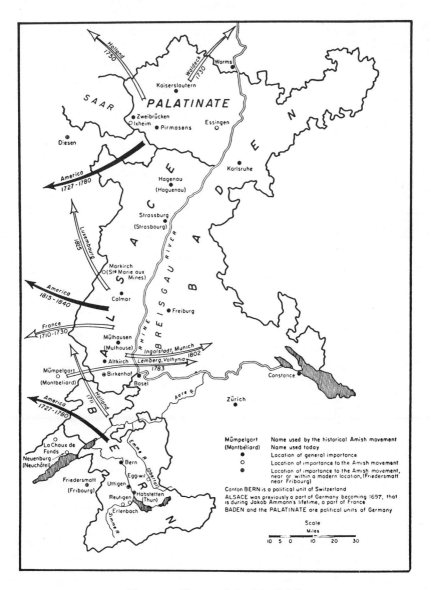

*Figure 1.* Places of Amish Origin.

Alsatian communities. A small group of Amish from Mont-béliard and from Germany moved to the Lemberg region in Galicia, Austria, and from there to Volhynia, Russia, and after 1873 they reached Kansas and South Dakota. The Alsatian and Bavarian Amish came to North America in large numbers from 1815–40 and established communities in Ontario, Illinois, and Ohio.

The Amish were not able to live in large compact settlements in Europe as they characteristically have throughout their history in America. Economic and social factors such as the scarcity of land and general intolerance against Anabaptists prevented them from forming community groupings.[13] Individuals and families who were either expelled or fled from the countries where they were persecuted accepted asylum wherever they were given it. With the exception of Alsace, the social life of the Amish was confined largely to the family and each great household became a social unit unto itself. Geographic distance made intercourse between families extremely difficult. Worship services, held in their own farm homes, were monthly or semimonthly, but always at different places. Those who lived within a short distance could attend the service, but many found it possible to come only once or twice annually. Under such conditions the scattered Amish families associated more with local non-Amish persons than with people of their own kind. The Amish who became renters or managers of large estates employed many laborers whose families also lived on the estate. The laborers, who were usually of a different religious affiliation, lived side by side with Amish families on the same estate. Although marriage with outsiders was forbidden, when necessity became too great such marriages were permitted; however, the Amish made no attempt to gain converts other than their own offspring.

With long years of suppression the descendants of the Anabaptists changed their goals into ways and means of physical survival. It was under these conditions that they learned the

[13] John A. Hostetler, "Old World Extinction and New World Survival of the Amish," *Rural Sociology* (September–December, 1955), 212–19.

disciplines of mutual aid, intensive agriculture, thrift, and toil, for which qualities they were later sought by emperors and princes for transforming wastelands into productive soils. Thus the Swiss Brethren, including the Amish, became "the quiet people of the land" and formed agrarian cultural islands lasting even to this day. Quiet passivity is more typical of the Amish than is participation in the life of the wider society outside of their immediate community. In Europe the Amish lived in Switzerland, Alsace, France, Germany, Holland, Bavaria, Galicia, and Volhynia in Russia.

In Switzerland, the homeland of Jakob Ammann, there were two groups of Amish, those in the Emme Valley and all those of the Lake Thun settlement. Ammann had been less successful in gaining followers in his homeland than in neighboring areas. It appears that during the Amish division, as early as 1696, some of the Swiss emigrated to Alsace near Markirch, and others went to the Neüchâtel, Jura region of Switzerland. The Amish founded these two other congregations, La Chaux de Fonds and Neüchâtel (Neuenburg), when there was a general emigration from the canton of Bern to the bishopric of Basel. There were still two Amish congregations in Switzerland as late as 1810, but they have gradually lost their identity. In 1886 footwashing was still practiced by these groups, but by about 1900 they no longer called themselves Amish, but a part of the Swiss Mennonite Conference. The Amish group in Basel considered itself a part of the Alsatian group. Few Amish emigrated directly from Switzerland to North America, as many of them first sought refuge in the Palatinate or other points along the Rhine River before undertaking the great venture across the Atlantic.

In southern Germany, Jakob Ammann had received very little support for his distinctive emphasis; only a small group in the vicinity of Kaiserslautern followed him. An Amish group from Alsace settled at Essingen near Landau at a later time. Although the Amish never developed large commmunities in the Palatinate, they emigrated out of the Palatinate in large numbers to other points in Germany and to North America. In 1730 a group settled in middle Germany in the Hesse-

Cassel region at Wittgenstein (later Waldeck), and in 1800 some settled in the Lahn Valley near Marburg. Small groups found their way to the vicinity of Neuwied and the Eiffel region. The groups from middle Germany, known as Hessian Amish, took voyage for North America and by 1900 all traces of the Amish had vanished. A group from Hesse located in Butler County, Ohio, beginning in 1817. The Waldeck and Marburg groups came to Somerset County, Pennslvania, and Garrett County, Maryland.

Another Amish movement from the Palatinate, along with others from Alsace-Lorraine, went to Bavaria near the towns of Ingolstadt, Regensburg, and Munich. Descendants of the Amish still live at Regensburg, but the other groups became extinct through emigration to Ontario and Illinois. The Amish who settled in Bavaria overcame many prejudices against them by diligent work and agricultural inventiveness. Because many of them were excluded from village life, they became tenants on large estates. Here they had more opportunity to experiment with new farming methods than did the peasants with their few plots of ground and their deeply regimented economic routine. Because of their nonconformity to the official state religion, they had to work harder and produce more than did non-Amish tenants. This gave them incentive to adopt new methods. Some of the descendants of the Bavarian Amish are today superior farm managers. Their distinct Amish traits were lost before the advent of the present century.

Another group from the Palatinate and from Montbéliard, France, emigrated to Galicia and to Volhynia. They were part of a larger Swiss-Mennonite movement that was attracted to these areas by liberal offers from progressive noblemen who sought their agricultural talents. Although the Amish subscribed to the Essingen discipline of 1779, they were few in numbers, and through intermarriage and close association with the Swiss Mennonites they lost most of their Amish consciousness before coming to Moundridge, Kansas, and Freeman, South Dakota.

The Amish congregation in the Palatinate maintaining distinctive habits the longest, including the practices of using lay preachers, strict shunning, footwashing, and wearing beards and hooks-and-eyes, was Ixheim, near Zweibrücken, Germany. Some of the older members practiced footwashing until 1932, but hooks-and-eyes had been discarded before 1880. The congregation also served scattered families in the Saar. The Ixheim members were long called *Häftler* (hookers) and the nearby Ernstweiler Mennonite members *Knöpfler* (buttoners), but basic consciousness of differences disappeared in the twentieth century. The two churches were officially merged in 1937, and the Ixheim meetinghouse still stands as a private dwelling.

In Alsace and Lorraine and also in the Saar region, there is today a Mennonite population of about 3,000 members, most of whom are descendants of the Amish. They are no longer Amish in name, and the original issues which separated the Amish from their parental body are forgotten. In 1819 a French newspaper reported that these people did not take civil oaths, refused military service, did not go to law, and refrained from card playing and the use of tobacco. Some of the distinctive Amish practices were still practiced in the twentieth century, but the beards, hooks, special costume, shunning, and footwashing gradually disappeared. Although optional, footwashing is still observed at Birkenhof, Diesen, and Montbéliard. The Luxembourg group practiced it until their aged bishop died in 1941.

In Holland there were two Amish congregations as a result of immigrations from Switzerland and the Palatinate about 1711. They were located near Gronigen and Kampen and took with them their distinctive rules of conduct and practices: beards, strap-instead-of-lace shoes, hooks-and-eyes, and the strict application of shunning. After a century in Holland, they were speaking the Dutch language, had lost their Amish consciousness, and were absorbed into the Dutch Mennonite churches.

The European Amish never organized a formal conference. Their association was informal, face-to-face, and based upon the issues and the attitudes that separated them from the Mennonites. The Amish endorsed the Dortrecht Confession of Faith, which had been formulated by the Dutch Mennonites in 1632. Some Alsatian Amish had adopted it in 1659, and this may have aided the cleavage between the Swiss and the Alsatian Brethren at the time of the Amish division.[14] The Amish also adopted the Elbing catechism of 1783, reprinted it at Waldeck in 1797, and they used the *Ernsthafte Christenpflicht*[15] as their prayer book as early as 1739. The Amish also reprinted the Pennsylvania, 1748 edition of *The Bloody Theatre or Martyrs Mirror* at Pirmasens, Germany, in 1780. There had been at least three general ministers' meetings in Europe for the purpose of formulating church discipline, one at Steinselz in 1752 and the others at Essingen in the years 1759 and 1779.[16]

The Amish in Europe did not develop along the lines of the folk model. They were sectarian and in their economy rural, but they were too mobile, too scattered, and too persecuted to constitute a folk culture. Their distinctiveness was factional rather than cultural, their smallness was closely associated with mobility, and their homogeneity was more like that of a first-generation social-protest movement than the later stage of institutionalization. Under these conditions they could not develop self-sufficiency. If all the Amish had remained in Europe, it is doubtful that they would have survived at all as a cultural group.

When the Amish came to America in the eighteenth century they found conditions favorable for growth and development. Land was available in unlimited quantities. They could live adjacent to each other on family farms and maintain relatively self-sufficient and closely knit communities. Under these conditions, an integrated folk culture could develop and maintain its identity. Thus the Amish survived in the New World, emerging as distinctive, small, homogeneous, and self-governing communities.

[14] Reference to the Dortrecht Confession is made on p. 49.

[15] This early Mennonite book is still the standard prayer book used by the Old Order Amish; its origin is discussed by Robert Friedmann, in *Mennonite Piety Through the Centuries* (Goshen, 1949), 189–95.

[16] *Mennonitisches Geschichtsblätter* (1938, 49).

"Human beings who do not doubt that life has a direction and a goal are not prone to despair."—Francois Mauriac. Photograph by Max Tharpe.

B. Hostetler

# Part II

# STABILITY AND FULFILLMENT

Lancaster County, Pennsylvania, farms, taken with infra red lens. The most intensive and the best-managed farm practices of all Amish communities are represented here. Photograph by Heilman.

Ohio Amish farm. General rather than specialized farming is characteristic of a way of life. Photograph by *The Budget*.

Urbanization has reduced natural isolation. Lancaster, Pennsylvania, and vicinity. Photograph by Fairchild Aerial Surveys.

"A tractor gets the work done more quickly, but horses and the love of hard work keeps us nearer to God."—Amish Bishop. Photograph by Heilman.

Small country schools are preferred. High school is not the normal experience of a child because, "It leads young people away from our way of life." Photograph by Photo Arts.

On the job learning is prized more highly than schooling or book learning. Photograph by Mennonite Community Assn.

Disaster and misfortune are met with community resources, and they are overcome by frolics or festive occasions like a barn-raising. Photograph by World Wide Photos.

The family takes time for a visit to the zoo. Photograph by *Pittsburgh Press*.

# CHAPTER 3

# THE AMISH CHARTER

WE TURN NOW to the moral principles of the contemporary Amish community. By moral we mean that which is considered right and wrong, and the principles for which life is worth living. The fundamentals of right and wrong are made relevant in the life of the society. Behavior in the Amish community is oriented to absolute values, involving a conscious belief in religious and ethical ends, entirely for their own sake, and quite independent of any external rewards. This orientation to *Wert-rational*,[1] or absolute values, requires of the individual certain unconditional demands. Regardless of any possible cost to themselves, the members are required to put into practice what is required by duty, honor, personal loyalty, and religious calling. The fundamental values and common ends of the group, recognized by the people and accepted by them, have been designated as the charter.[2] A charter need not be reduced to writing to be effective in the little community; it may be thought of as the common purpose of the community, corresponding to a desire or a set of motives embodied in tradition. Although Amish life is oriented to absolute values, there is an almost automatic reaction to habitual stimuli that guides behavior in a course which has been repeatedly followed. Behavior is traditionally oriented by belief and the habit of long experience.

The Amish view of reality is conditioned by a dualistic world view. They believe, as have many other ascetic brother-

---

[1] Max Weber, *The Theory of Social and Economic Organization*, trans. by A. M. Henderson and Talcott Parsons (The Free Press, 1947), 165.

[2] Bronislaw Malinowski, *A Scientific Theory of Culture* (University of North Carolina Press, 1944), 48, 162.

hoods, that light and truth coexist with the powers of darkness and falsehood. Purity and goodness are in conflict with impurity and evil. The rejection of the world is based upon this dualistic conception of reality and is manifest in specific life situations.[3] While the Amish share this fundamental doctrine of the two worlds with other believers, it becomes a reality to the Amish, while to many Christian people it is greatly modified.

### Separation from the World

To the Amish there is a divine spiritual reality, the Kingdom of God, and a Satanic Kingdom that dominates the present world. It is the duty of a Christian to keep himself "unspotted from the world" and separate from the desires, intent, and goals of the worldly person. Amish preaching and teaching draws upon passages from the Bible which emphasize the necessity of separation from the world. Two passages, perhaps the most often quoted, epitomize for the Amishman the message of the Bible. The first is: "Be not conformed to this world, but be ye transformed by the renewing of your mind that ye may prove what is that good and acceptable and perfect will of God." [4] This to the Amishman means among other things that one should not dress and behave like the world. The second is: "Be ye not unequally yoked together with unbelievers; for what fellowship hath righteousness with unrighteousness? and what communion hath light with darkness?" [5] This doctrine forbids the Amishman from marrying a non-Amish person or from being in business partnership with an outsider. It is applied generally to all social contacts that would involve intimate connections with persons outside the ceremonial community. This emphasis upon literalness and sepa-

---

[3] Max Weber, "On Religious Rejection of the World," *Essays in Sociology* (Oxford University Press, 1958), 323–59.

[4] Romans 12:1.

[5] II Corinthians 6:14.

rateness is compatible with the Amish view of themselves as a "chosen people" or "peculiar people." [6]

The principle of separation conditions and controls the Amishman's contact with the outside world; it colors his entire view of reality and being. Bible teaching is conditioned by the totality of the traditional way of life. Compatible with the doctrine of separation is the doctrine of non-resistance. By the precepts of Christ, the Amish are forbidden to take part in violence and war. In time of war they are conscientious objectors, basing their stand on biblical texts, such as "My kingdom is not of this world: if my kingdom were of this world, then would my servants fight." [7] The Amish have no rationale for self-defense or for defending their possessions. Like many early Anabaptists they are "defenseless Christians." Problems of hostility are met without retaliation. The Amish farmer, in difficulty with the hostile world around him, is admonished by his bishop to follow the example of Isaac: after the warring Philistines had stopped up all the wells of his father Abraham, Isaac moved to new lands and dug new wells. [8] This advice is taken literally, so that in the face of hostility, the Amish move to new locations without defending their rights.

The Amish share with the Mennonites the principles of Anabaptism as evidenced by their common endorsement of the Dortrecht Confession. [9] Both practice adult rather than infant baptism, non-resistance and refusal to bear arms, and refusal to swear an oath, and both refrain from holding public offices. Religion tends to be pervasive and associated with a

[6] This concept was present in the Old Testament in the case of the Jews (Exodus 19:5, Deuteronomy 14:2) and the Amish tend to apply the concept to themselves using New Testament passages. I Peter 2:9 and Titus 2:14. Max Weber observed that the notion of the "chosen people" comes naturally with ethnic solidarity and is a means of status differentiation ("Ethnic Groups," in *Theories of Society*, Talcott Parsons, ed. [The Free Press of Glencoe, 1961], Vol. I, 305).

[7] John 18:36.

[8] Genesis 26:15–18.

[9] Containing 18 articles, it was adopted in 1632 by the Dutch-Flemish and Frisian Mennonites as a basis of union. The text appears in John C. Wenger, *The Doctrines of the Mennonites* (Scottdale, Pa., 1958), 75.

total way of life, not a specialized activity. The Amish today differ from the Mennonites mainly in the extent to which external changes have effected the groups. The Amish are more literal in the observance of certain practices such as fasting and shunning, in practicing informal mutual aid, and in keeping the young on the farm. The Mennonites have been readier to accept changes and to incorporate them into their religious values. Mennonites are technologically modern, and they generally accept higher education. Furthermore, during the nineteenth century they founded institutions of higher education to train missionaries. Mennonites developed along the lines of modern Protestantism, while the Amish have retained literalism, limited education, and agrarianism.

The Amish are "otherworldly" minded, in contrast to the many Christian churches that are concerned with making the world a better place in which to live. The Amish show little interest in improving the world or their environment. They profess to be "strangers and pilgrims" in the present world. The Amish interpretation of salvation also differs in emphasis from much of modern fundamentalism. Belief in predestination is taboo as is also the idea of assurance of salvation. A knowledge of salvation is complete only after the individual hears the great words at the last judgment, "Come, ye blessed of my Father, inherit the kingdom prepared for you from the foundation of the world." [10] Furthermore, the commands of obedience and self-denial are given more emphasis than is the teaching on "grace through faith alone." To assert that "I know I am saved" would be obnoxious because it smacks of pride and boasting. Pride of knowledge or personal display is held to be one of the greatest of all sins. Among the highly traditional Amish, Christ becomes a *Wegweiser*, one who shows the way, and not just one who is to be worshipped for his own sake in the way that revivalists teach.

Amish preaching and moral instruction emphasize self-denial and obedience to the teaching of the Word of God, which is equated with the rules of the church. All ministers constantly

[10] Matthew 25:34.

warn their members to beware of worldliness. Long passages from the Old Testament are retold, giving prominence to crucial events in the lives of Abraham, Isaac, Jacob, Joseph, and Moses. The escape of the Israelites from Egyptian bondage and Moses's giving of the law are sermon themes; punishments meted out to the lawbreakers are emphasized. The themes: "Offenders were executed for breaking the law," and "we are not better than they," are emphatically stressed. The choice put before the congregation is to obey or die. To disobey the church is to die. To obey the church and strive for "full fellowship," that is, complete harmony with the order of the church, is to have *lebendige Hoffnung*, a living hope of salvation. An Amish person simply puts faith in God, obeys the order of the church, and patiently hopes for the best.

Separation from the world is a basic tenet of the Amish charter; yet the Amish are not highly ethnocentric in their relationships with the outside world. They accept as a matter of course other people as they are, without attempting to convert them to the Amish way of life. But for those who are born into the Amish society, the sanctions for belonging are deeply rooted in the belief in separatism.

The people of the little community have an "inside view" as well as a contrasting "outside view" of things.[11] The doctrine of separation shapes the "outside view," and in discussing further aspects of the Amish charter we turn now to the "inside view."

## The Vow of Obedience

The ceremony of baptism may be viewed as a rite of passage from youth to adulthood, but it also reveals the "inside view" of things. The meaning of baptism to the individual and the community reflects ethos. Taking the baptismal vow admits one to full fellowship in the church. When young people reach late adolescence, they are urged to become members of the church. In their sermons, ministers challenge young

[11] Robert Redfield, *The Little Community*, 80.

people to join the church. The parents are concerned that young people take this step. In most cases no overt urging by the parents is necessary, since it is normal for young people to follow the role expectation and be baptized. No young person could be married in the Amish church without first being baptized in the faith.

After the spring communion, a class of instruction is held for all those who wish to join the church. This is known as *die Gemee nooch geh*, or literally, "to follow the church." The applicants meet with the ministers on Sunday morning at worship service in the *Kämmerli*, the consultation room where the ordained customarily meet. The ministers very simply acquaint the applicants for baptism with the incidents in the Bible that suggest the right relationship with God. At the same time the *Regel und Ordnung* (rules and order) of the Amish church are explained. After six or eight periods of instruction, roughly from about May to August, a day is set for the baptismal service. The consent of the members is obtained to receive the applicants into fellowship. Baptism occurs prior to the fall *Ordnungsgemee* (preparatory service), which is followed by *Grossgemee* (communion). Great emphasis is placed upon the difficulty of walking the "straight and narrow way." The applicants are told that it is better not to make a vow than to vow and later break it; on a Saturday prior to baptism they are asked to meet with the ministers where they are given opportunity to "turn back" if they so desire. The young men are asked to promise that they will accept the duties of a minister should the lot ever fall on them. To understand not only the content of the vow, but also its setting and mood, I offer the following account of a preaching and baptismal service held in a large barn.

The service was about to begin. In the haymow of the barn, the women sat on one side and the men and boys on the other, each facing the other. Except for two long rows of benches in the middle of the barn, the seating space was almost filled. To the right, directly back of the women, alfalfa bales were stacked high. A curtain of binder canvass was tacked along the side to prevent the stubbles from scratching the women's backs and to improve the general appearance. To the left was a long grainery, on the side of which the men had hung their large-rimmed black hats.

It was a beautiful September morning. The sun shone brightly into the faces of the audience through large swinging doors, propped open at the bank of the barn. The clear blue sky and the warm sun were symbolic of the special occasion of the morning, a baptismal service. Although this was a regular worship service, it was also a meeting of special interest and anticipation to all loyal members of the church.

As the *Vorsinger* (song leader) began singing the syllables of the first song, the ministers, bishops, and deacons retired to a room in the house for consultation and to meet with the baptismal applicants for the last time. Here they would also agree on the order of the service for the day.

Between hymns there was deep silence in the audience. The aroma of the haymow, and the sounds of the birds and insects penetrated into the consciousness of the audience. The horses could be heard below, munching timothy hay. While waiting for another hymn to be announced, the farm owner as host sensed that it was getting too warm. With some difficulty, he opened a second barn door on the side where the women were seated. To facilitate a breeze he then walked to the other end of the barn floor and pushed open the roller door leading to the straw shed. Now that the ventilation was taken care of, he again took his seat near the middle of the barn floor.

After several hymns were sung by the assembly, the applicants for baptism, on this occasion six girls from ages sixteen to eighteen, came marching up the barn bank single file and took their seats in the center section near the ministers' bench. Both young and old intently watched the six young women in the bloom of youth who were ready to make their vows with God and the church, to say "no" to the world, the flesh, and the devil, and to say "yes" to Jesus Christ and his *Gemein* here on earth. Each applicant sat with bowed head, as though she were in deep meditation and prayer for the lifelong vow she was about to take. None dared to risk a glimpse at the audience or to gaze about. This was a solemn occasion. With hands folded in their laps they all sat in a straight row, their youthful, unpainted faces sombre. Their clothing was strictly uniform: black organdy caps, black dresses, white organdy capes, long white organdy aprons, black stockings, and black oxfords. Only in the materials of which the dresses were made and the color of ribbon bows at the left shoulder, faintly showing through the organdy capes, was there evidence of individual choice.

The ministers now entered. They quietly removed their hats as they entered the barn. All seven, including several visiting deacons and bishops for this special service, offered a handshake with all who were nearby as they slowly made their way to the ministers' bench. Each took his seat—the one who was to make the *Anfang* (opening address) at the head of the bench, and the bishop who was to bring the longer message next in line. As soon as the ministers were seated the assembly stopped the hymn.

Sitting silently in anticipation, the audience listened to two sermons. Two hours of intense sitting and waiting finally brought the climax of the day, as the bishop turned to the applicants with a personal admonition. The deacon left the service and returned with a small pail of water and a tin cup. The bishop reminded the applicants that the vow they were about to make would not be made to the ministers or to the church, but to God. He requested the applicants to kneel if it was still their desire to become members of the body of Christ. All six kneeled. The bishop then asked a few simple questions,[12] and each applicant answered in her turn.

[12] While baptismal questions are essentially the same in content, the wording varies. Two sets of baptismal questions appear in *Handbuch für Prediger* (Arthur, Illinois, 1950). An English translation appears in Harvey J. Miller, "Proceedings of Amish Ministers Conferences 1826–31," *M.Q.R.* (April, 1959), 141.

## THE AMISH VOW

1. Konnet ihr auch das schone Bekenntniss ablegen mit dem Kammerer von Mahrenland,* dass dir glaubet dass Jesus Christus Gottes Sohn ist? (Ya, ich glaub dass Jesus Christus Gottes Sohn ist.)

2. Erkennet ihr es auch für seine Christliche Kirche und Gemeine Gottes worunter ihr euch begebet? (Ya)

3. Saget ihr auch ab dem Teufel und der Welt mit all ihrem Abweisenden Wesen, wie auch eurem Fleisch und Blut und begehret Christum Jesum allein zu dienen der am Stamme des Kreuzes für euch gestorben ist? (Ya)

4. Versprechet ihr auch dass ihr diese Ordnungen des Herrn und der Gemeine wollet halten und helfen handhaben, der Gemeine fleissig bei-wohnen und nicht davon abweichen es gelte euch zum Leben oder zum Sterben? (Ya)

### TRANSLATION

1. Are you able to confess with the Ethiopian eunuch, that you believe that Jesus Christ is God's Son? (Answer: Yes, I believe that Jesus Christ is God's Son.)

2. Do you confess that you are uniting with the true church of the Lord? (Yes)

3. Do you renounce the devil and the world with all its wicked ways, and also your own flesh and blood, and commit yourself to serve Jesus Christ alone who died for you on the cross? (Yes)

4. Do you promise to keep the ordinances (*Ordnung*) of the Lord and the church, to faithfully observe and to help administer them, and never to depart from them so long as you shall live? (Yes)

After the applicants responded to the preliminary questions, the bishop asked the congregation to rise for prayer. He read

* The word *Mahrenland* refers to Ethiopia and not to Moravia. It must have read Moorenland originally, i.e., land of the Moors.

one of the simple and beautiful prayers in *Die ernsthafte Christenpflicht*, a prayer book of the Swiss Anabaptists.

The applicants continued kneeling when the assembly was seated. The bishop with the assistance of one of the deacons proceeded with the baptism. The deacon called for one of the older women to assist, whereupon the deacon's wife joined them. The three stood at the head of the line of applicants, while the deacon's wife untied the ribbon of the first applicant's cap and removed the cap from her head. Then the bishop laid his hands on the girl's head and said: "Auf deinen Glauben den du bekennt hast vor Gott und viele Zeugen wirst du getauft im Namen des Vaters, des Sohnes und des Heiligen Geistes, Amen." (Upon your faith, which you have confessed before God and these many witnesses, you are baptized in the name of the Father, the Son, and the Holy Spirit, Amen.) The deacon poured water into the cupped hands of the bishop and the water dripped from the head and face.

Tears fell to the floor. Overhead, the pigeons were flapping their wings as they flew from one end of the barn to the other. A gentle breeze from the open door of the straw shed brought a cloud of fine particles of chaff and dust. High in the clear blue heavens, an airplane roared in the distance, a symbol of earthly knowledge, progress, and evil.

The rite of baptism was complete. The bishop took the hand of each kneeling applicant in turn and greeted her with "In Namen des Herrn und die Gemein wird dir die Hand geboten, so steh auf." (In the name of the Lord and the Church, we extend to you the hand of fellowship, rise up.) The applicant stood up and the bishop then gave the hand of the applicant to the assisting wife who greeted the new member with the Holy Kiss. All applicants remained standing until the last one was greeted, and the bishop then asked them to be seated. A few tears were brushed aside as they began to retie their covering strings. They were now considered members of the church and would enjoy the full privileges of sisters in the *Gemein*.

The bishop took his former speaking position and admonished the congregation to be helpful to the new members. The ones baptized were instructed to be faithful to the church and to the ministry. He next related the story of the terrible idolatry (calf worship) committed by Israel while Moses was up on the mountain praying. The lesson to be learned was that young people sometimes make parties and do other sinful things while the parents are away from home. The bishop stated that if Satan can get young people, that is what he wants. He concluded the long sermon and the baptismal service with the reading of Romans 6. After taking his seat he asked the other ministers to give *Zeugnis* (testimony) to the sermon. Three of the seven ministers gave a brief statement of approval of what had been said in the sermon and a few additional comments. After four hours the service ended in the usual way, with everyone kneeling for prayer, followed by a short benediction and a hymn.

Basic to the Amish vow is the confession of Jesus Christ as the Son of God, belief in the visible church of Christ, the renunciation of the world, the devil, and one's own flesh and blood, and the confession of Jesus Christ as Lord and Savior. This is not significantly different from the requirements of Christian churches generally. What is significant is the promise to abide by orally transmitted rules not explicitly stated in the vow. The strict Amish churches include in the vow, by inference or otherwise, the promise to help maintain the *Regel und Ordnung* (rules and order) and the promise not to depart from them in life or death. "That's the way we have it in our church," explained one bishop. "It seems to me that every person should stay in the church where he is baptized. He should never leave that group if he once makes a vow. Of course, it is all right to become more religious [meaning more orthodox] but never to move closer to the world." [13] A more moderate view of the vow requires commitment to the true Church of Jesus Christ, but does not imply a lifetime commitment to the particular rules and regulations of a given district. For instance, the late Bishop John B. Peachey said, "It is not

[13] John B. Renno in a personal interview.

right to make the young people promise to stay with the *Ordnung* for life, but rather with the teachings of the Bible." [14]

## The Rules for Living

Once the individual has been baptized, he is committed to keep the *Ordnung* or the rules of the church. For a single person this means keeping one's behavior more in line with the rules than before. With marriage the individual assumes responsibility for keeping the rules as well as for "building the church," which means taking an active part in promoting the rules. The little Amish community is distinctive from other church groups in that the rules governing life are traditional ways not specified in writing. These rules can be known only by being a participant. The rules for living tend to form a body of sentiments that are essentially a list of taboos within the environment of the small Amish community.

All Amish members know the *Ordnung* of their church district and these generally remain oral and unwritten.[15] Perhaps most rules are taken for granted and it is usually those questionable or borderline issues which are specified in the *Ordnung*. These rules are repeated at the *Ordnungsgemee* just preceding communion Sunday. They must have been unanimously endorsed by the ordained body. At the members' meeting following the regular service they are presented orally, after which members are asked to give assent. If there is any change from previous practice, allowing a new innovation or adaptation, this change is not announced. The former taboo is simply not mentioned. A unanimous expression of unity and

[14] John B. Peachey in a personal interview.
[15] Some of these rules have found their way into print. See Harold S. Bender, "Some Early American Amish Mennonite Disciplines," *M.Q.R.* (April, 1934), which covers Amish conferences of 1809, 1837, and 1865. For conferences of 1779 and 1781 see *M.Q.R.* issues of April, 1937, and April, 1930; for "An Amish Bishop's Conference Epistle of 1865," see (July, 1946). Other published tracts and manuscripts are known to exist, such as the *Ordnungsbrief* of October 26, 1917. Harvey J. Miller, *op. cit.*, reports on conferences held in 1826-31 (*M.Q.R.*, April, 1959).

"peace" with the *Ordnung* makes possible the communion. But without unity there can be no communion.

The following *Ordnung*[16] of a contemporary group, published in English, appears to be representative of the Old Order Amish, except for those portions indicated by brackets. That it appears in print at all is evidence of change from the traditional practice of keeping it oral. This *Ordnung* allows a few practices not typically sanctioned by the Old Order: the giving of tithes, distribution of tracts, belief in assurance of salvation, and limited missionary activity.

### ORDNUNG OF A CHRISTIAN CHURCH

Since it is the duty of the church, especially in this day and age, to decide what is fitting and proper and also what is not fitting and proper for a Christian to do, (in points that are not clearly stated in the Bible), we have considered it needful to publish this booklet listing some rules and ordinances of a Christian Church.

We hereby confess to be of one faith with the 18 articles of Faith adopted at Dortrecht, 1632, also with nearly all if not all articles in booklet entitled "Article und Ordnung der Christlichen Gemeinde."

No ornamental bright, showy form-fitting, immodest or silk-like clothing of any kind. Colors such as bright red, orange, yellow and pink not allowed. Amish form of clothing to be followed as a general rule. Costly Sunday clothing to be discouraged. Dresses not shorter than half-way between knees and floor, nor over eight inches from floor. Longer advisable. Clothing in every way modest, serviceable and as simple as scripturally possible. Only outside pockets allowed are one on work eberhem or vomas and pockets on large overcoats. Dress shoes, if any, to be plain and black only. No high heels and pomp slippers, dress socks, if any, to be black except white for foot hygiene for both sexes. A plain, unshowy suspender without buckles.

Hat to be black with no less than 3-inch rim and not ex-

---

[16] From a tract, "Ordnung of a Christian Church," with a byline "Amish Church of Pike County, Ohio, 1950." This group has since moved to Elgin County, Ontario.

tremely high in crown. No stylish impression in any hat. No pressed trousers. No sweaters.

Prayer covering to be simple, and made to fit head. Should cover all the hair as nearly as possible and is to be worn wherever possible. [Pleating of caps to be discouraged.] No silk ribbons. Young children to dress according to the Word as well as parents. No pink or fancy baby blankets or caps.

Women to wear shawls, bonnets, and capes in public. Aprons to be worn at all times. No adorning of hair among either sex such as parting of hair among men and curling or waving among women.

A full beard should be worn among men and boys after baptism if possible. No shingled hair. Length at least halfway below tops of ears.

No decorations of any kind in buildings inside or out. No fancy yard fences. Linoleum, oilcloth, shelf and wall paper to be plain and unshowy. Over-stuffed furniture or any luxury items forbidden. No doilies or napkins. No large mirrors, (fancy glassware), statues or wall pictures for decorations.

[No embroidery work of any kind.] Curtains either dark green rollers or black cloth. No boughten dolls.

No bottle gas or high line electrical appliances.

Stoves should be black if bought new.

Weddings should be simple and without decorations. [Names not attached to gifts.]

No ornaments on buggies or harness.

Tractors to be used only for such things that can hardly be done with horses. Only either stationary engines or tractors with steel tires allowed. No airfilled rubber tires.

Farming and related occupations to be encouraged. Working in cities or factories not permissible. Boys and girls working out away from home for worldly people forbidden except in emergencies.

Worldly amusements as radios, card playing [party games], movies, fairs, etc., forbidden. [Reading, singing, tract distribution, Bible games, relief work, giving of tithes, etc., are encouraged.]

Musical instruments or different voices singing not permissible. No dirty, silly talking or sex teasing of children.

Usury forbidden in most instances. No government benefit payments or partnership in harmful associations. No insurance. No photographs.

No buying or selling of anything on Sunday. It should
be kept according to the principles of the Sabbath. [Wor-
ship of some kind every Sunday.]

[Women should spend time doing good or reading God's
Word instead of taking care of canaries, goldfish or house
flowers.]

Church confession is to be made if practical where transgression was made. If not, a written request of forgiveness
should be made to said church. All manifest sins to be
openly confessed before church before being allowed to
commune. I Tim. 5, 20. A period of time required before
taking new members into full fellowship.

Because of great falling away from sound doctrine, we
do not care to fellowship, that is hold communion, with any
churches that allow or uphold any unfruitful works of
darkness such as worldliness, fashionable attire, [bed-court-
ship, habitual smoking or drinking, old wives fables, non-
assurance of salvation, anti-missionary zeal] or anything
contrary to sound doctrine. (See Menno Simons, 1st pt.,
P. 9: – 98, and 383–385.)

The rules of the Amish church cover the whole range of
human experience. In a society where the goal is directed
toward keeping the world out, there are many taboos, and
customs become symbolic. There are variations in what is
allowed from one community to another in the United States
and Canada. Custom is regional and therefore not strictly uniform. The most universal of all Amish norms across the United
States and Canada are the following: no electricity, telephones,
central-heating systems, automobiles, or tractors with pneumatic tires; required are beards but not moustaches for all married men, long hair (which must be parted in the center, if allowed at all), hooks-and-eyes on dresscoats, and the use of
horses for farming and travel. No formal education beyond the
elementary grades is a rule of life.

The *Ordnung* is an essential part of the Amish charter. It is the way in which the moral postulates of society are expressed and carried out in life.[17] The charter is constantly subjected to forces of change, a source of conflict to be discussed later.

## The Punishment of the Disobedient

A moral principle in the little Amish community is the practice of *Bann und Meidung*. These words rendered in English mean excommunication and shunning. *Meidung* was the crucial question in the controversy that gave rise to the Amish as a sect movement in their secession from the Swiss Brethren. This doctrine [18] was intrinsic in the Anabaptist movement from its very beginning and appeared in the earliest confession of faith.[19] The Anabaptist concept of the church was that it should be a pure church of believers only; persons who fall into sin must be first excommunicated, then shunned. Menno Simons taught that the ban applies to "all—great and small, rich and poor, without any respect of persons, who once passed under the Word but have now fallen back, those living or teaching offensively in the house of the Lord—until they repent." [20] The method of dealing with a backslider is that given by Christ in Matthew 18:15–17, and "If he neglect to hear the church, let him be unto thee as a heathen man and a publican." In other words, a person who has broken his vow and will not mend his ways must be expelled just as the human body casts off an ulcer or infectious growth.[21] Through the

[17] Charles P. Loomis, *Social Systems* (Van Nostrand, 1960).

[18] See "Ban," *Mennonite Encyclopedia*, Vol. I.

[19] Not only the Schleitheim Confession of 1525 but also the Dortrecht Confession of 1632 set forth the doctrine. See J. C. Wenger, *The Doctrines of the Mennonites* (Herald Press, 1950), 69, 75.

[20] *The Complete Writings of Menno Simons* (Herald Press, 1956), 94, 961 ff. The ban is given extended treatment by Frank C. Peters, "The Ban in the Writings of Menno Simons," *M.Q.R.* (January, 1955).

[21] Other references in the Scriptures supporting the practice of shunning are: I Corinthians 5:11; Romans 16:17; II Thessalonians 3:14; Titus 3:10.

years the *Meidung* has been applied in different ways. The doctrine among the Mennonites of Holland and Switzerland was of a mild character, in which the offender was excluded from communion. But a stricter conception of the ban was advanced by Jakob Ammann. The strict interpretation requires shunning of all (1) members who leave the Amish church to join another and (2) members who marry outside the brotherhood. *Meidung* requires that members receive no favors from the excommunicated person, that they do not buy from or sell to an excommunicated person, that no member shall eat at the same table with an excommunicated person, and if the case involves husband or wife, they are to suspend their usual marital relations.[22]

The Amish make no effort to evangelize or proselyte the outsider, nor are they concerned with the redemption of the outside society to the extent that they wish to draw members from the outer society into the brotherhood. It is their primary concern to keep their own baptized members from slipping into the outer world, or into other religious groups. With greater mobility and ease of travel and communication, isolation is breaking down, and Amish solidarity is threatened by more and more of their members wanting to become like outsiders. The Amish leaders meet this threat with the ban. Members who wish to have automobiles, radios, or the usual comforts of modern living, face the threat of being excommunicated and shunned. Thus the ban is used as an instrument of discipline, not only for the drunkard or the adulterer, but for the person who transgresses the order of the church. It is a powerful instrument for keeping the church intact and for preventing members from involvement in the wider society.

The meaning of *Bann und Meidung* is made clearer if we understand how it works in life situations. Let us take the case of a young man whom we shall fictitiously name Joseph. Joseph grew up in a very strict Amish home, under the guidance of

---

[22] This literal and extreme position is still articulated by contemporary privately published writings of the Amish. *Eine Betrachtung und Erklärung über Bann und Meidung . . . 1948.*

parents who were known for their orthodoxy. He was baptized at the age of twenty. Three years after his baptism Joseph was excommunicated and shunned. Charges laid against him included the following: he had attended a revival meeting, began to chum with excommunicated persons, bought an automobile, and began to attend a Mennonite church.

Joseph was excommunicated with the counsel of the assembly and was informed in their presence. After being asked to leave the service he thought to himself: "It is strange to think that I am now to be 'mited.' I don't feel very comfortable." At home, the young man was shunned: he could no longer eat at the family table. He ate at a separate table, with the young children, or after the baptized persons were finished eating. Joseph was urged to mend his ways, to make good his broken promise. His normal work relations and conversational pattern were strained. Several times he attended preaching services with his family. Since members may not accept services, goods, or favors from excommunicated members, he could not take his sisters to church, even if he used a buggy instead of his offensive automobile, but they could drive a buggy and take him along. It was not long until Joseph accepted employment with a non-Amish person and began using his automobile for transportation to and from home. When shunned friends came to his home for conversation, Joseph's parents met them at the gate and turned them away. It was not long until father and mother asked him to leave home. He explained: "I had to move away from home or my parents could not take communion. My parents were afraid that younger persons in the family would be led astray. They didn't exactly chase me off the place, but I was no longer welcome at home."

One of the purposes of excommunication is to restore the erring member by showing him his lost condition so that he will turn to repentance. The excommunication service itself is a painful and sober procedure. John Umble's description is fitting: "The excommunication of members was an awful and solemn procedure. The members to be expelled had been notified in advance and were present. An air of tenseness filled the house. Sad-faced women wept quietly; stern men sat with faces drawn. The bishop arose; with trembling voice and with tears on his cheek he announced that the guilty parties had confessed their sin, that they were cast off from the fellowship of the church and committed to the devil and all his angels (*dem Teufel und allen seinen Engeln übergeben*). He cautioned all the members to exercise 'shunning rigorously.' " [23]

Once an individual is in a state of *Bann* (or *Bond* as the Amish call it), members are to receive no favors from him. In a very real sense he is "an outcast, rejected of God and man. His only hope is not to die before he should reinstated, lest he should be an outcast also in the world to come." [24]

Among the Amish communities today there are numerous divisions as a result of differing opinions on shunning. The moderate interpretation of the ban, taken by most of the midwestern groups, holds that moral transgressors should be excommunicated and shunned, but if the offender is restored to another Christian church of the non-resistant faith, then shunning should no longer be applied. But this, according to the adherents of the strict ban, is a departure from Jakob Ammann. In speaking of a former Amish member who joined the Mennonites a bishop told the writer: "The only way for us to lift the ban is for him to make peace with the Old Order church, going back to one of them and living his promise he made in his baptismal vow on his knees before God and the church. It does not need to be here but in any of the churches that are in peace with us." According to this view, an excommunicated person must be shunned for life unless he restores his previous relationship with the group. The ban becomes an effective means of dispensing with the offender. By shunning him in all social relations, he is given a status that minimizes the threat to other members of the community. This perpetuation of the controversy undoubtedly aids the Old Order group to remain distinct and socially isolated.

[23] John Umble, "The Amish Mennonites of Union County, Pennsylvania," *M.Q.R.* (April, 1933), 92.
[24] *Ibid.*

## Closeness to Nature

The little Amish community has a strong affinity for the soil and for nature. Unlike science, which is occupied with the theoretical reconstruction of the order of the world, the Amish view comes from direct contact with nature by the reality of work. The physical world is good, and in itself not corrupting or evil. The beautiful is apprehended in the universe, by the orderliness of the seasons, the heavens, the world of growing plants as well as the many species of animals, and by the forces of living and dying. While it is wrong to attend a show in a theater, it is not uncommon for an Amish family to visit the zoo or the circus to see the animals God has made.

The Amishman feels contact with the world through the working of his muscles and the aching of his limbs. In the little Amish community toil is proper and good, religion provides meaning, and the bonds of family and church provide human satisfaction and love.

The charter of Amish life requires members to limit their occupation to farming or closely associated activity such as operating a saw mill, carpentry, or mason work. In Europe the Amish lived in rural areas, always having a close association with the soil, so that the community was entirely agrarian in character. It is only in America that the Amish have found it necessary to make occupational regulations for protection from the influence of urbanism.

The preference for rural living is reflected in attitudes and in the informal relations of group life, rather than in an explicit dogma. For the Amish, God is manifest more in closeness to nature, in the soil and in the weather, and among plants and animals, than he is in the man-made city. Hard work, thrift, and mutual aid find sanction in the Bible.[25] The city by con-

[25] This view is treated in more detail by Walter Kollmorgen, *Culture of a Contemporary Community: The Old Order Amish of Lancaster County, Pennsylvania* (United States Department of Agriculture, 1942). Also by Jane C. Getz, *M.Q.R.* (January, 1946), 53–80, and (April, 1946), 98–127. See also Walter Kollmorgen "The Pennsylvania Farmer," in

trast is held to be the center of leisure, of non-productive spending, and often of wickedness. The Christian life, they contend, is best maintained away from the cities. God created Adam and Eve to "replenish the earth, and subdue it; and have dominion over the fish of the sea, and over the fowl of the air, and over every living thing that moveth upon the earth." [26] In the same way, man's highest place in the universe today is to care for the things of creation. One Amishman said, "The Lord told Adam to replenish the earth and to rule over the animals and the land—you can't do that in cities." Another said, "While the Lord's blessings were given to the people who remained in the country, sickness and ruination befell Sodom. Shows, dances, parties, and other temptations ruin even the good people who now live in cities. Families are small in cities; in the city you never know where your wife is, and city women can't cook. People go hungry in the cities but you will never starve if you work hard in the country." [27]

The Amish have generally prospered on the land more often than their neighbors. Lancaster County, Pennsylvania, which is the center of Amish life, has long been distinguished as the garden spot of the nation, representing an intensive kind of farming on relatively small holdings. Their success is based upon long experience with agricultural practices in the Old World and upon a philosophy of work and thrift. The older residents in Amish communities have accumulated a large amount of agricultural experience and lore reaching back to early colonial days. Some Pennsylvania landowners occupy farms that were acquired directly from William Penn or his land agent. As farms are handed down from father to son, so are the experiences and the wisdom associated with the care of livestock and farming. The Amish attribute their material success in farming to divine blessing.

The main objective of their farming, as Walter Kollmorgen

---

Ralph Wood, ed., *The Pennsylvania Germans* (Princeton University Press, 1942).

[26] Genesis 1:28.

[27] The quotations are from Getz, *op. cit.*

has pointed out, "is to accumulate sufficient means to buy enough land to keep all the children on farms. To this end the Amish work hard, produce abundantly, and save extensively." [28]

Farming constitutes a subject of Amish conversation and concern as reflected in their newspaper *The Budget*. This weekly paper, issued by a small-town, non-Amish publisher, George R. Smith of Sugarcreek, Ohio, carries news columns from almost all Amish settlements and a few Mennonite regions. The subjects discussed in this paper are the important ones for all Amish. The paper had its origin in 1890 when Amish families who moved to the newly opened state of Kansas began to publish letters in their home town newspaper. Others in the west began to write letters to the same newspaper for publication, which was then edited and owned by an Amish-Mennonite person, J. C. Miller. Ever since, *The Budget* has been a means for the Amish at various communities to keep in touch with each other. The circulation is presently over 10,000 and has been rising.

Topics customarily covered in *The Budget* are the weather, seeding, planting activity, and harvest. In springtime we read that "Farmers were busy in the fields last week." "Some corn is up." "Cattle will be on pasture soon." "Some are sowing wheat." "Wheat and alfalfa fields look nice." In summer we read that "Farmers are busy threshing oats and picking tomatoes." "People are starting to make hay and are picking strawberries." "The women are picking wild berries and putting up peas." "Most of the beans are harvested and some are beginning to pick corn." During the winter months reporters normally carry comment about livestock, sales, farm accidents, and construction work.

There are other moral directives in the little community but these form the essential core of what is viewed as right and wrong. The view of life and of man's place in the total scheme of things are determined by the sacred guides to life. These

[28] Kollmorgen, *op. cit.,* 30.

guides are: a biblical view of separation from the world, the vow of obedience, observance of the *Ordnung*, upholding the true doctrine of shunning, and living close to the God-created environment. In all of these tradition plays an important part. The people of the little Amish community tend to regard the ways of their ancestors as sacred and to believe that these time-hallowed practices should be carefully guarded.

# CHAPTER 4

# THE RESOURCES
# OF THE COMMUNITY

*The Community in Space and Time*

THE MEANING OF LIFE finds expression in the natural environment of the Amish community. The relation of the charter to nature and of toil to the harmonious working of the parts people perform are reflected in the character and ecology of the community. The relation of economics and resources to the integration of the whole symbolic system, including religion and ceremony, family life, language arts, and core values, is relevant for understanding the little community.[1] This must bring into focus such variables as space, time, ceremony, and economics.

Three distinctive ecological entities in Amish society are "settlement," "church district," and "affiliation." A settlement consists of the total aggregation of Amish families living in proximity. Of the ten settlements in the state of Pennsylvania, the largest is in Lancaster County and adjoining Chester County. This part of the state has been continuously occupied by Amish since they first settled in Pennsylvania, perhaps as

---

[1] A multidisciplinary approach to the understanding of culture has been advanced by Laura Thompson, *Toward a Science of Mankind* (Harper, 1961). In it the author develops the working hypothesis that to provide an adequate basis for the scientific investigation of mankind, the social sciences, the psychological sciences, biology, ecology, and anthropology must unite toward a new, multidisciplined understanding of whole cultures. The reader may quickly obtain an understanding of the totality of a single whole culture like the Amish by focusing on the most relevant variables.

early as 1714, but with certainty since 1727.[2] In 1767, before the Revolutionary War, the Amish spread to Somerset County in southwestern Pennsylvania. Later they migrated to other parts of the Midwest. All other settlements in Pennsylvania are small in comparison to the Lancaster area settlement: they are in central, southwestern, and northwestern areas. Eighty per cent of all Amish church districts (congregations) are in three states: Pennsylvania, Ohio, and Indiana.

The "church district" or congregation is a ceremonial unit encompassing a specific geographic area within the Amish settlement. The size of the church district is conditioned by the number of people who can meet for the preaching service in one dwelling house. The church district is a self-contained, self-governing body with ceremonial and institutional functions centering around the bimonthly preaching service. Baptisms, marriages, ordinations, and funerals are functions of the district. The bishop is the chief authority of the church district and works closely with the ministers and the deacon of his district. A bishop may have oversight of two or more districts temporarily. Other than the counsel of the older bishops, largely informal, there is no confederation which attempts to interpret policy for the church district.

Large settlements have many church districts, and the smallest settlements have at least one district. Settlements are geographically subdivided into church districts by such guidelines as roads, creeks, cable wires, or small mountain ranges. Districts on the fringe of settlements have no specific boundary line but include the most distant Amish family. Sixteen of the 36 districts in the Lancaster settlement in 1963 had boundary lines on all sides. The area

[2] The original location near Hamburg, in Berks County, became extinct after 1786 as a result of Indian attacks during the French and Indian War. An account of the Indian attack on the Hochstetler family is given in *Descendants of Jacob Hochstetler* (Elgin, Illinois, 1912). The history of these early places is documented by Grant Stoltzfus, "History of the First Amish Communities in America" (M.A. thesis, University of Pittsburgh, 1954), partially published in *M.Q.R.* (October, 1954).

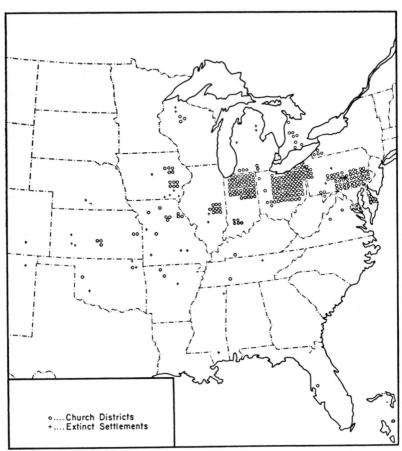

*Figure 2.* Old Order Amish Communities.

within these 16 districts ranges from 2 to 9 square miles each, with an average of 4.3 square miles. This small ceremonial unit is easily accessible by horse-and-buggy transportation. In Pennsylvania the terrain determines the many different sizes and shapes of the district. In the Midwest the districts generally run clearcut with the section roads. The 14 districts in

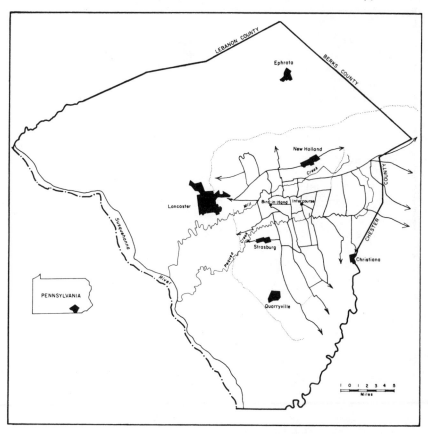

*Figure 3.* Amish Church Districts, Lancaster County, Pennsylvania. Dotted lines and arrows indicate undefined boundaries.

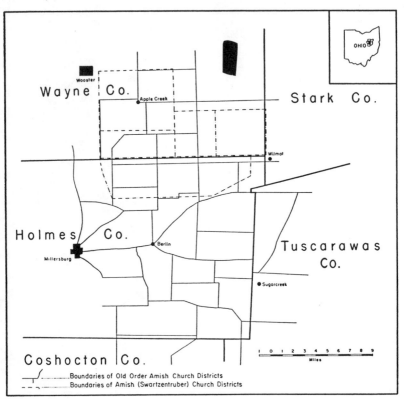

*Figure 4.* Amish Church Districts in Holmes, Wayne, Coshocton, Stark, and Tuscarawas Counties, Ohio.

Indiana with boundary lines on four sides range from 3 to 13 square miles, with an average area of 6.8 square miles per district.

Since their first Ohio settlement in Holmes County in 1807, the Amish have located in many other places in this state. Presently there are eight settlements with the largest concentration around Holmes, Wayne, and Stark counties in northeast and central Ohio. This state has had many small settlements of Amish Mennonites, who over a period of time

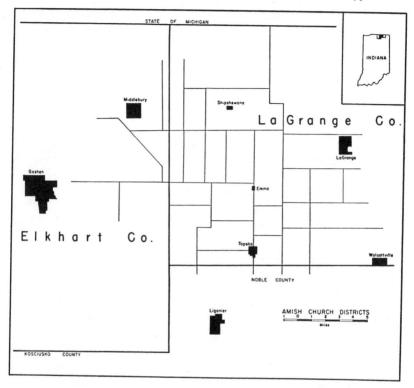

*Figure 5.* Amish Church Districts in Lagrange and Elkhart Counties, Indiana.

affiliated with the Mennonites. Still other settlements became extinct.[3] Ohio has more church districts than any other state, numbering 80 in all. Forty-seven of these are clustered in the area about Holmes County, and a settlement of 17 districts is located just east of Cleveland in the Geauga County area. The other settlements are composed chiefly of one district each except for Madison County, which has four.

[3] John Umble, "Why Congregations Die," *Mennonite Historical Bulletin* (October, 1947), and his "Factors Explaining the Disintegration of Mennonite Communities," *Proceedings . . . Conference on Mennonite Cultural Problems* (Tabor College, 1949), 113–28.

The Amish settlement in Indiana, originating from Somerset County, Pennsylvania, in 1842, has developed into a large concentration in Lagrange and Elkhart counties in the northern part of the state. This area is presently composed of 28 districts.* The second largest settlement, with nine districts, is located about 20 miles southwest in Marshall and nearby counties. There are five other Amish settlements in the state ranging from one to six districts in size.

The first Amish settlers reached Illinois in 1829; presently there are 11 districts in Moultrie and Douglass counties. The Amish settled in Iowa in 1845 and the state has two settlements with five districts in one and six in the other. Amish immigrants came direct from Germany to Ontario in 1824, and the province has several new settlements begun by settlers from the United States since 1956. There are a total of eight districts in Ontario. Kansas was reached by the Amish in 1884 and now has two small settlements with two and three districts each. The Amish came to Oklahoma in 1892 and they have two small settlements, in Custer and Choteau counties. There were Amish settlements in Michigan as early as 1900, but the Amish in that state have moved many times. At present there is a settlement of three districts in St. Joseph and Branch counties. Missouri has had a number of Amish settlements (as early as 1856) which became extinct, but in recent years the Amish have again established four small settlements there. Wisconsin, with the first Amish settlement in 1909, has three districts. Western New York has a settlement of four districts in Chautauqua County. Delaware has a settlement of five districts begun in 1915. Tennessee has one and Arkansas has two small settlements. There have been small settlements in New Mexico, Mississippi, Georgia, North Dakota, and Oregon which have not survived as Old Order Amish. The few families who tried to colonize in Mexico have returned. A group of families moved from Arkansas to British Honduras and from Orange County, Indiana to Paraguay in 1967.

The third ecological entity of the Amish community is

* The number of districts in this section is based on the 1962 survey.

"affiliation" and is based on disciplinary considerations. There may be different kinds of Old Order Amish in the same settlement. These differences are based on liberal-progressive interpretations of the *Ordnung* (discipline). Amish affiliations have their counterpart in the numerous segmentations within most Protestant denominations. Differences in affiliation are informally perpetuated and are not always observable to the outside world. The usual published lists of Amish congregations make no distinction among the different kinds of Old Order Amish. One main distinction is between the Old Order and the automobile-driving Amish, called "Beachy" Amish. But there are groups of Old Order Amish who do not associate ceremonially with other Amish, or, as the Amishman sometimes says, "They are not in fellowship with us." Full fellowship means that there is common agreement in discipline, and that ordained officials are allowed to preach in exchange visits. Some affiliations result from long-standing differences in practices, some from different emphases by the leading bishop, others from divisions. In Mifflin County, Pennsylvania, there are five affiliations of Amish from the most conservative Old School to the "Speicher" or Beachy Amish (see p. 266). In Ohio there are at least five formal and several informal affiliations of Old Order Amish, and in Iowa there are two. In the large Lancaster County settlement in Pennsylvania there was only one affiliation until 1966. Then a group of families that might normally have joined the Beachy group, because of their desire for relaxed rules on the use of telephones, electricity, and modern farm machinery, founded a separate Old Order group. The different affiliations add to the complexity of community organization, for each affiliation has its own geographic boundaries which may overlap with boundary lines of other affiliations.

The growth in the number of districts in a single Amish settlement, the Lancaster, Pennsylvania group, from 1843 to 1960 is charted chronologically (p. 78). Before 1843 there was a single Amish congregation, but in that year the group was divided into two districts called Millcreek and Pequea. Muddy Creek served as the geographic division. In 1852 the Pequea group was divided into Upper and Lower Pequea, and in 1872

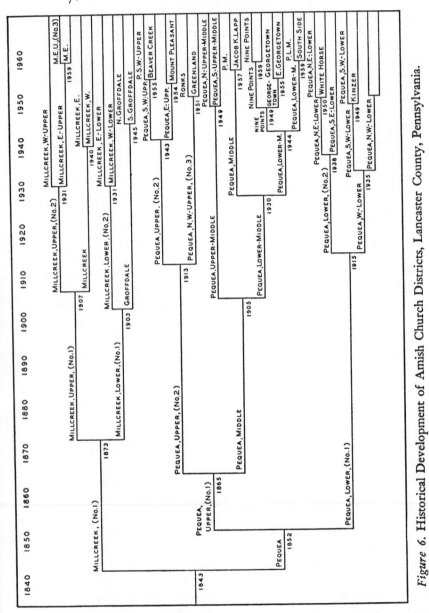

*Figure 6.* Historical Development of Amish Church Districts, Lancaster County, Pennsylvania.

Millcreek was divided into Upper and Lower Millcreek. These names are adapted from local usage indicating something of the terrain. In 1962 the entire Amish settlement had, in all, thirty-seven church districts. The nomenclature to distinguish boundaries has been expanded to include the terms "middle," "south," "north," "east," "west," and other names such as "Nine Points" or "White Horse," which are names of small villages or neighborhoods. There is a tendency in speech to designate the district by the name of the bishop in charge. These local names and usages persist in a culture that perpetuates itself primarily by oral rather than written tradition.

Table 1

Old Order Amish and Beachy Amish Population, 1961

| State | As Reported in 1962 *Mennonite Yearbook* | | Estimate of Members for Missing Data | Total OOA | Automobile or "Beachy" Amish | | Total OOA and Beachy Amish |
|---|---|---|---|---|---|---|---|
| | Districts | Members | | | Members | Churches | Members |
| Ohio | 80 | 6,808 | 52 | 6,860 | 473 | 6 | 7,333 |
| Pennsylvania | 59 | 4,889 | – | 4,889 | 781 | 6 | 5,670 |
| Indiana | 57 | 3,027 | 1,250 | 4,277 | 559 | 5 | 4,836 |
| Iowa | 11 | 794 | – | 794 | 73 | 2 | 867 |
| Illinois | 10 | 779 | – | 779 | 42 | 1 | 821 |
| Missouri | 9 | 274 | 160 | 434 | – | – | 434 |
| Ontario | 8 | 401 | 45 | 446 | 351 | 2 | 797 |
| Kansas | 5 | 177 | 100 | 277 | – | – | 277 |
| Delaware | 5 | 282 | 51 | 333 | – | – | 333 |
| Michigan | 5 | 166 | 90 | 256 | 44 | 1 | 300 |
| New York | 4 | 161 | 130 | 291 | – | – | 291 |
| Maryland | 3 | 221 | 80 | 301 | 34 | 1 | 335 |
| Wisconsin | 3 | – | 140 | 140 | – | – | 140 |
| Virginia | 2 | 131 | – | 131 | 357 | 4 | 488 |
| Oklahoma | 2 | 52 | 20 | 72 | 64 | 1 | 136 |
| Arkansas | 2 | 12 | 30 | 42 | 4 | 1 | 46 |
| Tennessee | 1 | 66 | – | 66 | – | – | 66 |
| Kentucky | 1 | 18 | – | 18 | – | – | 18 |
| Florida | 1 | – | 20 | 20 | – | – | 20 |
| Georgia | – | – | – | – | 131 | 1 | 131 |
| Totals | 268 | 18,258 | 2,168 | 20,426 | 2,913 | 31 | 23,339 |

SOURCE: *Mennonite Yearbook* (1962) and local informants.

*Population and Demography*

The Amish themselves do not need precise population figures beyond the number of families in a district, but the names of the districts and total memberships appear in the *Mennonite Yearbook and Directory*. An Amish publication, Raber's *Calendar*, lists the Amish church districts and their ordained officials. Amish persons who report their membership to the *Yearbook* often do so in round numbers, while other districts do not co-operate in providing figures. The writer has compiled, with the help of local Amish informants, estimated memberships combined with the *Yearbook* figures. Table 1 shows the number of members and districts by states for both the Old Order Amish and "Beachy Amish" congregations. Thus the Old Order in 1961 had 18,258 members in 268 districts in 19 states. The Amish population in America has increased steadily in numbers as shown by published sources. The number of Amish church districts increased from 29 in 1905 to 268 in 1961 (Table 2). The published membership figures do not

Table 2

Old Order Amish Population and Districts, 1905–60

| Year | 1905 | 1920 | 1930 | 1940 | 1950 | 1960 |
|------|------|------|------|------|------|------|
| Population | 8,200 | 13,900 | 18,500 | 25,800 | 33,000 | 43,300 |
| Districts | 43 | 83 | 110 | 154 | 197 | 258 |

SOURCE: Computed from *Mennonite Yearbook* and *Calendar*, using 168 as the mean population (see Table 3).

include the entire Amish population as the Amish practice adult baptism. This means that in any given district the population includes children below the age of baptism. There are generally more children (non-baptized persons) than baptized members in a district. In 35 districts for which we have accurate information there is an average of 79 members in a district and 89 non-members, or 168 persons per district (Table 3). Thus there are 113 non-members or children for every 100 members. If this ratio is representative for the Amish in all of North America, we may estimate that the total Old Order population in 1961 (Table 1) was 43,507. This ratio, applied to

Table 3

Ratio of Members to Non-members in 35 Amish Districts, 1960

| State | Number in Survey | Baptized Members (Mean) | Non-members (Mean) | Total Population (Mean) | Ratio: Non-members to Members |
|---|---|---|---|---|---|
| Pennsylvania | 8 | 97 | 96 | 193 | 104.1 |
| Delaware | 5 | 65 | 90 | 155 | 136.6 |
| Ohio | 10 | 78 | 115 | 193 | 147.5 |
| Indiana-Michigan | 4 | 58 | 81 | 139 | 118.8 |
| Iowa | 8 | 70 | 64 | 134 | 91.1 |
| Totals | 35 | 79 | 89 | 168 | 113.5 |

SOURCE: Amish informants in the local community.

the 1966 membership,[4] yields an estimated total population of 49,371 (based on the 1967 *Mennonite Yearbook* membership of 21,023 plus 10 per cent for missing data, as in Table 1). The number of married couples in a church district varies greatly within a settlement as well as between settlements. In Ohio the number of nuclear families in a district ranges from 25 to 58, with an average of 42.*

The Amish population growth-potential is maintained by a high rate of natural increase, that is, through large families. Studies of household size reveal that Amish households are

[4] Other estimates of the total population have been made. From a complete census of families in Crawford County, Pa., made by Prof. Maurice A. Mook, and by the writer in Mifflin County, Pa., it was learned that the offspring below baptismal age was three times the membership for a district. (Maurice A. Mook, "The Number of Amish in Pennsylvania," *Mennonite Historical Bulletin*, January, 1955). Not all of the offspring remain in the Old Order Church. In one church of two districts, the writer found that about one-third of the offspring joined a church other than the church of their parents, mostly Mennonite churches. J. A. Hostetler, "The Amish Family in Mifflin County, Pennsylvania" (M.A. thesis, The Pennsylvania State University, 1951), 209. The proportion of offspring leaving the Old Order churches varies with settlement, church district, and affiliation.

* Harold E. Cross, in a more inclusive survey in "Genetic Studies in an Amish Isolate" (Ph.D. dissertation, Johns Hopkins University, 1967, p. 47), reports that of 48 districts in Ohio he found a mean of 86 baptized members and 113 non-members per district, and a ratio of 131.3 non-members to every 100 baptized members.

larger than the national average for rural households. The average number of children per "completed" family as shown by several studies [5] is from seven to nine. The family in the United States with the largest number of living descendants, reported by a journalist, was believed to be an Amish family. When Amishman John E. Miller of Ohio died in his ninety-fifth year he was survived by five of his seven children, 61 grandchildren, 338 great-grandchildren, and six great-great grandchildren, or a total of 410 descendants. Earlier an Amishman in Indiana, Moses Borkholder (1838–1933), was reported to have 565 living descendants, according to J. C. Wenger.[6]

The age and sex composition of the Amish population is strikingly different from the rural-farm population of the United States, census of 1960. This is visually perceptible in the population pyramids (see Table 4 and the accompanying pyramids). These differences are a reflection of the social and cultural matrix of the Amish community. In comparing Amish and non-Amish populations, it will be observed that the Amish have only half the proportion of people over age sixty-five, but for persons under twenty the Amish proportions double the rural-farm population. The age distribution of a society has important bearings on economic and social problems.

The large number of Amish children are an asset to the Amish farm economy, which needs more hand labor than the farm that is operated by tractors and other machines. As long as the Amish population over age sixty-five remains relatively small, the Amish financial and social problems at retirement are less acute than in the general population. This is just one more reason why the Amish do not need the financial benefits of social security, as is the case with the general farm population of America. The presence of a large proportion of children in the farm population of America ordinarily restricts the social activities of the family or adversely affects its economic potential. But this is not true of the Amish family, as the social life and economic goals are expressed in different manner from

[5] "Birth Rate," *M.E.* Vol. I, 354. Harold Cross, *op. cit.,* 82.

[6] Glenn D. Everett, "One Man's Family," *Population Bulletin* (December, 1961), 153–69. Also John C. Wenger, *The Mennonites in Indiana and Michigan* (Herald Press, 1961), 394.

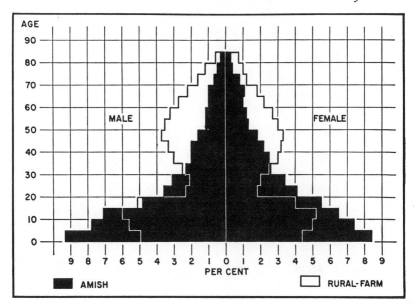

*Figure* 7. Age and Sex Distribution of Amish and Rural-Farm Population of the United States, 1960.

the American pattern. The pyramid for the Amish does not reflect the low rate of fertility during the depression, just before the sudden increase of the birth rate in 1940, as do pyramids for the general population.

The age at marriage may also affect the pyramid as early marriages are traditionally associated with large families, especially in a society where birth control is taboo. There has been a tendency to believe that Amish young people marry earlier than the non-Amish, but the facts do not support this generalization with the trend toward younger age at marriage in the United States. There is some evidence that Amish marriages occurred at a younger age several decades ago than presently. The several studies of age at marriage of the Amish show that boys marry from age 22 to 24 and girls from 20 to 22. The comparable age in the United States for men in 1955 was 22.7 and for women 20.2. The present difficulty of accumulating capital and land appears to increase the age at marriage.

Table 4

Age and Sex Distribution of Amish and Rural-Farm
Population of the United States, 1960

| Age | In Per cent Amish | | In Per cent Rural-Farm U.S. | |
|---|---|---|---|---|
| | Men | Women | Men | Women |
| 75 or over | 0.8 | 0.8 | 1.6 | 1.4 |
| 70–74 | 0.7 | 0.8 | 1.6 | 1.2 |
| 65–69 | 1.0 | 1.1 | 2.2 | 1.8 |
| 60–64 | 1.0 | 1.0 | 2.7 | 2.2 |
| 55–59 | 1.2 | 1.2 | 3.2 | 2.7 |
| 50–54 | 1.2 | 1.3 | 3.5 | 3.0 |
| 45–49 | 1.6 | 1.7 | 3.7 | 3.3 |
| 40–44 | 2.0 | 2.2 | 3.3 | 3.2 |
| 35–39 | 2.0 | 2.5 | 3.0 | 3.0 |
| 30–34 | 2.3 | 2.6 | 2.5 | 2.5 |
| 25–29 | 3.1 | 3.4 | 2.1 | 2.0 |
| 20–24 | 3.6 | 4.1 | 2.3 | 1.8 |
| 15–19 | 4.8 | 5.5 | 5.1 | 4.0 |
| 10–14 | 7.1 | 6.5 | 6.0 | 5.2 |
| 5–9 | 7.8 | 7.4 | 5.6 | 5.0 |
| Under 5 | 9.3 | 8.4 | 4.9 | 4.4 |
| Per cent | 49.5 | 50.5 | 53.3 | 46.7 |
| Number | 2,228 | 2,881 | 6,153,357 | 5,698,443 |

SOURCE: The Old Order Amish population data are based
upon 35 of a total of 268 church districts, secured from
informants in each community. The rural-farm population is taken from *United States Census of Population,
1960. General Social and Economic Characteristics,
Series PC (1)–1C.*

There are more women than men in the Amish society if
our sample is representative of the whole population. There
are 98.1 Amish males for every 100 females, again differing
from the American farm population, which in 1959 was 105.7
males per 100 females. Traditionally men have outnumbered
women in the United States, but due to the effect of the
longer life expectancy of women there are presently more
women than men (95.2 males per 100 females).[7] The ratio for

[7] *Civilian Population of the United States, Census of the United States,*
Series P-20, No. 98. January 25, 1960.

Table 5

Age at Marriage Among the Amish as Reported in Various Studies

| Investigator | Location of Community | Date of Report | Number of Marriages | Mean Age at Marriage | |
|---|---|---|---|---|---|
| | | | | Men | Women |
| Houghton | Arthur, Ill. | 1926 | 195 | 23.5 | 22.0 |
| Hostetler | Mifflin Co., Pa. | 1951 | 66 | 24.2 | 22.3 |
| Mook (unpublished) | Atlantic, Pa. | 1954 | 25 | 22.9 | 20.8 |
| Smith, Elmer | Lancaster Co., Pa. | 1961 | 500 | 22.2 | 20.8 |
| Cross | Holmes Co., Ohio | 1967 | 1887 | 23.6 | 22.5 |

SOURCE: See terminal bibliography.

the Amish appears to reflect the general trend toward longer life expectancy among women. However, it is possible that more men leave the Amish faith than women, which would reflect an imbalance in the sex ratio. The men/women ratio in the population has important implications for social relationships within the society, such as opportunities for marriage.

Reliable demographic data on Amish communities have recently been compiled in connection with genetic studies. Little was known about marriage and residence patterns until Harold Cross (1967) reported the findings of his demographic data for the Holmes County community in Ohio. Of 2,013 marriages, 26 involved partners where both had been born outside the community. There were 253 marriages where one of the mates was born outside the community: 117 men and 136 women. Although the community attracted slightly more women than men through marriage, it appears that men and women have a fairly equal chance for cross-community marriage. There is no tendency toward either patrilocal or matrilocal residence. Although most marriages occur in November, December, January, and February, there is a tendency for the wedding season to lengthen in recent decades. Of 87 remarriages, most were of men who had married single girls rather than widows. Of 792 completed families the average number of live children born per family was 6.66, which is exceeded by a related Anabaptist group, the Hutterites, with a rate of 8.76. The annual natural increase of the Amish population was found to be 3.019, or a potential doubling of the population every 23 years. By comparison, the Hutterite annual rate of natural increase (Eaton and Mayer, 1953) was 4.126, or a potential doubling of the population every 16 years. The rate of sterility among the Amish varies little from the United States population. The rate of twins born to Ohio Amish families (15.3 per 1,000 live births) and to Indiana Amish families (21.1; Juberg, 1966) is the highest of any known population.

## The Local Community and Its Functionaries

The social organization of the Amish community is centered in the church district, which is a social and ceremonial unit. As already stated, the maximum size is determined by the number of families that can be accommodated at preaching services, which are held every other Sunday in the homes of members. Households take turns (about once a year) having the preaching service. In some small districts each household will entertain the service two times in succession. Households with small dwellings, as may be the case with young couples who are renters, frequently take their turn in the summer months when the service may be held in the barn.

Each district has three kinds of clergy. Traditionally they are the *Voelliger-Diener*, minister with full powers, or bishop; *Diener zum Buch*, minister of the book, or preacher; and *Armen Diener*, minister to the poor, or deacon. These three positions in the dialect are *Vellicherdiener*, *Breddicher*, and *Armediener*. Let us now observe the organization of the district and the relation of it to the wider Amish community. The ceremonial activity itself will be discussed later.

The bishop is the leader of the congregation and its chief authority. He administers the rites of communion, baptism, marriage, excommunication, and receives "backsliding" members back into the church. He supervises the choice of ministers by lot and performs ordination services. He announces disciplinary action against violators of the church *Ordnung*.

The bishop is responsible for obtaining "the voice" or vote of the church in decision-making processes where such unanimity is required. The bishop also takes his regular turn at preaching *es schwere Deel,* or the main sermon at regular meetings for worship.

Upon his ordination, the bishop is given the following life-time charge:

> (1) So in the name of the Lord and of the church the complete ministry or bishop's office is entrusted to you (2) that you shall declare the Lord's bitter suffering and death and observe the breaking of bread and wine (3) and if there are people who wish to unite with the church then you shall teach them the Christian faith and baptize them (4) and, with the counsel of the church, you shall punish the disobedient and sinners and when they manifest repentance and conversion you shall receive them again with the counsel of the church (5) and when there are brethren and sisters in the church who wish to marry you shall unite them according to the godly ordinance (6) and you shall also ordain ministers with full authority [i.e. bishops], whenever it is necessary and requested in the church (7) and when you become old and weak you are to ordain a man after you in your place (8) and may the Lord strengthen you with his holy and good spirit through Jesus Christ Amen.[8]

There are usually two additional preachers in every district who are expected to preach when their turn comes. The bishop and preachers must be able to stand before the congregation, without notes or the aid of books, and admonish the people in the ways of God. On Sundays when there is no preaching in his own district, an ordained person may, if he wishes, visit other districts. Very frequently visiting preachers are called upon to preach if they are "in full fellowship" with the host district. Preachers also assist the bishop in distributing the wine and bread at the communion service, held twice each year. Upon the ordination of a *Breddicher,* or preacher, he is committed to the following charge:

[8] John Umble, "Amish Ordination Charges," *M.Q.R.* (October, 1939), 236.

So in the name of the Lord and of the church the ministry to the book is committed to you that you shall preach
[expound the Word], read, and pray with the church, help
protect good and help punish and prevent evil.[9]

A deacon is given the following charge at the time of his
ordination:

So in the name of the Lord and of the church the ministry to the poor is committed to you that you shall care for
widows and orphans and receive alms and give them out
with the counsel of the church and if there are brethren
and sisters who wish to enter the marriage state then you
shall serve them according to the godly order and read the
scriptures for the ministers when it is requested and shall
serve with water in the baptismal ceremony if you are requested to do so.[10]

The deacon assists regularly in the worship service by reading a chapter from the Bible. The reading is usually prefaced
by voluntary admonitions on his part. At the special service
for baptism he pours the water into the cupped hands of the
bishop over the applicant's head. He looks after the cups,
bread, and wine for the communion service, and keeps the
chalice filled during the service. He assists in the footwashing
service, which accompanies the communion, by preparing
the pails of water and the towels. He becomes a kind of
housekeeper working behind the scenes at ceremonial occasions. Two other important functions are assigned to the deacon: he is often sent by the bishop to secure information
about transgressors, and he conveys messages of excommunication. As an adjuster of difficulties between members, he has
the most difficult task of the three ordained officials. This
distasteful task is perhaps offset by the more pleasant function
of *Schtecklimann*, or go-between, in the arrangement for marriage. When a couple wishes to be married, the deacon is so
informed by the prospective bridegroom. The deacon then
inquires whether the bride's parents approve. *Wann nix im
Weg schteht* (if nothing stands in the way), he informs the
bishop, who announces the intended marriage to the congregation about two Sundays before the wedding.

[9] *Ibid.*, 237.
[10] *Ibid.*, 237.

A district is fully organized if it has persons holding all three offices. In some instances, however, a bishop must supervise two or three districts. This is usually considered a temporary arrangement until a district is large enough or the right person is found for the position. Bishops generally may not move from one district to another if there is dissatisfaction within the district. Preachers and deacons are perhaps freer to do so, but in any event, not without approval and prior consultation with the districts involved. These ordained positions are appointments for life unless persons holding them are "silenced" for misbehavior or transgression.

Each church district is a self-governing unit. There is no central organization or conference which attempts to interpret policy for the local group. The bishop is the chief authority-figure within his district. In large settlements of Amish, however, there is informal consultation among the different bishops in an area. In Lancaster County the ordained officials meet for consultation before communion in the spring and fall. In these meetings questions of discipline or causes for disunity are also dealt with. The oldest bishop generally is the one who calls these ministers' meetings and presides at them.

Each district conducts its own business and deliberations following the preaching service after the dismissal of non-members, including children. The decision-making processes are of the patriarchal-democratic type. Each district ordains its own deacon, preacher, and bishop from its own members, without a system of training or apprenticeship. Deacons and preachers are nominated from the laity by members of the congregation and ordained by lot if there are two or more names suggested for the office. A bishop is ordained from among the ordained preachers. While a bishop may exercise considerable power in making decisions, he is subject to *der Rat der Gemein* (the counsel or vote of the church). A member is excommunicated and put under the ban only by the vote of the baptized members, men and women. He is reinstated by vote. The deacon assists the poor members only when authorized by the vote of the congregation. Although the ideal of congregational rule is maintained, usually the ordained persons bring a suggested course of action to the assembly for a vote. The ordained persons meet for the *Abrot* (minister's counsel) at every preaching service during the singing of hymns by the assembly. This regular meeting of the ordained provides occasion for any of the ministers to discuss any circumstance that he feels should be brought to the attention of all. Any matter brought before the congregation must first be discussed by the ministers. Furthermore, a plan of procedure must be agreed upon by all the ministers before the problem can be brought before the members' meeting.

Any district is an integral part of the wider settlement through kinship and many informal contacts. The ten Pennsylvania settlements, for example, have a high degree of informal association. Amish families have relatives in other settlements or in neighboring districts. The great amount of visiting back and forth not only between relatives but also among friends makes a formal relation with other districts unnecessary. Some of the important life rituals, including weddings and funerals, reach across church district boundaries, as do economic and social activities such as barn-raisings and mutual aid. It would appear that ceremonial integration is centered in a district, but that kinship, social, and economic associations provide the basis of a wider community experience. The mode of travel for attending preaching services and for visiting the kinship in nearby districts is horse and buggy. But when travel of a longer distance is required as from one settlement to another, the Amish ride on trains, busses, or hire a neighbor with an automobile.

An intensive analysis of *The Budget* reveals that the Amish write more about visiting and traveling than about any other topic. Next in order are preaching services, illness, weather, accidents, and weddings. The kinship character of Amish life in all settlements provides a means of keeping in touch.

## Economics and Resources

The cultivation of the soil is a moral directive. Traditionally, family heads are farmers or are on their way to becoming farmers. Amish persons may also work as carpenters, masons, cabinetmakers, in sawmills or as blacksmiths, and to a lesser

Table 6

Per cent of Space Devoted to Subject Matter
in *The Budget,* 1960

| Subject | No. of Lines | Per cent of Space |
|---|---|---|
| Visiting | 1,170 | 25.8 |
| Travel | 532 | 11.8 |
| Preaching Service | 484 | 10.7 |
| Illness | 328 | 7.2 |
| Weather | 269 | 5.9 |
| Miscellaneous | 241 | 5.3 |
| Accidents | 198 | 4.4 |
| Weddings | 156 | 3.4 |
| Religious Discussions | 135 | 3.0 |
| Births | 129 | 2.9 |
| Funerals | 110 | 2.4 |
| Agriculture | 109 | 2.4 |
| Moving | 109 | 2.4 |
| Deaths | 105 | 2.3 |
| Health | 94 | 2.2 |
| Work, men | 53 | 1.2 |
| Work, women | 51 | 1.1 |
| Sewing, relief | 51 | 1.1 |
| Frolics | 44 | 1.0 |
| Singing | 42 | 0.9 |
| Sales | 34 | 0.8 |
| Hunting, fishing | 33 | 0.7 |
| Poetry, etc. | 29 | 0.6 |
| Bible quotations | 21 | 0.5 |
| Number of lines | 4,527 | |
| Per cent | | 100 |

SOURCE: Based on 28 issues of *The Budget* (1960),
chosen at random by taking every other issue. A
class of 28 students in anthropology undertook the
analysis by counting the number of lines given to
the 24 topics. Material that could not be classified
was placed in the miscellaneous column.

extent, in small machine shops. Outside work is accepted by
young people before marriage but is regarded as temporary.
Amish members who suffer permanent physical handicaps are
as a rule permitted marginal life-occupations not open to
others. In one such case a young man became a watch repair-
man in a small town, though he lived in the country. Working

at a feed mill, operating a limestone quarry, or taking care of a community cemetery are agriculturally related ways of making a living.

Farms are passed from one generation to the next by inheritance practices that differ little from those of other farm people. Land is always kept in the family as much as possible. A son is more likely to fall heir to the home farm than is a daughter. The older sons generally become established on farms before the father and mother are ready to retire from active life. In this way the home farm is likely to be deeded to the youngest son upon his marriage. Unmarried sons would have little chance of inheriting a farm, as marriage is considered essential to carry on the full operations of farming. Persons who remain unmarried, whether bachelors or spinsters, tend to live with their parents or their close relatives. Aging parents generally retire on the home place, in the grandfather house, retaining the right of domicile and certain other rights as long as they live.

A young Amishman who climbs the agricultural ladder rung by rung in Lancaster County begins as (1) a laborer or farm hand, (2) becomes a one-third share tenant, (3) then a one-half share tenant, and next (4) a cash tenant, and finally (5) a farm owner.[11] Amish boys do not go to high school and therefore may begin as farm hands at the age of sixteen. They may earn several hundred dollars the first year. The accumulated savings are invested in livestock or machinery. Renting usually precedes buying a farm. Amish boys also receive considerable assistance from their parents, so that many of them do secure farms in their own name not many years after they are married. Securing enough land for farming has been a continuous problem in many Amish communities, although not a serious one. With the non-Amish farm youth leaving the rural community for the city, there has been a tendency for the Amish to buy the "English" farms as they become available. The Amish have also founded new settlements when land has been difficult to obtain in the older settlements.

The Amish do not engage in farming merely for economic rewards, but they find it an occupation in which the individual

[11] Kollmorgen, *op. cit.*, 42–45.

finds fulfillment in work responsibility and in his relation with others. The Amish, generally speaking, set high standards of work for themselves. Few Amishmen will hire an outsider for farm work. Workers from the city are unacceptable to them. Outsiders, they say, "do not know enough and they don't work hard enough." When Amish boys were being drafted into conscientious objector camps in war time, the Amish said, "If we must hire outsiders, who want to work short hours and do things in a slipshod way, we'll all go broke." [12] The day begins between four and five o'clock in the morning with milking and other chores. Depending on the number of adults and the number of cows in the barn, this daily chore may take from one to two hours. Before breakfast the milk must be transported to the end of the farm lane or placed in position where the milk truck will pick it up. Breakfast may be served at five-thirty during the busy season of the year. During plowing, seeding and harvest, field work receives the major attention. In the wintertime, feeding the livestock and hauling manure become the more important tasks. The noon meal, *Middaagesse*, is served in some areas as early as eleven o'clock. After a short rest period the teams again go into the fields. Supper is served between four and five o'clock. The daily chores must then be done, if not by the working men, by the women who often help out during the busy season. This permits the men to go to the fields until dark. Bedtime comes at eight-thirty or nine o'clock.

The Amish work week comes to an abrupt end with Saturday evening. Outside of the busy season, Saturday is reserved for stable cleaning and preparing for Sunday. Only the animals and the essential routine chores are taken care of on Sunday, which is a day of rest. The major activity on Sunday may be visiting, except that on alternate Sundays the family goes to preaching service. There is no definite work cycle during the week with the exception of woman's work. Typically a woman will wash on Monday, iron on Tuesday, bake on Friday, and clean on Saturday. There are no special shopping nights, as purchases are made in the village store during the weekdays.

[12] *Ibid.*, 43.

The yearly work cycle is important. The calendar not only reflects the agricultural activities of sowing and reaping, but also the kind of leisure and the customs that tend to become associated with seasons of the year. The yearly cycle of community activity will vary from one settlement to another. The account below is based upon the Lancaster County, Pennsylvania [13] Amish and would apply generally in other areas with the exception of the raising of tobacco, which is distinctive of this Amish community.

In describing the yearly work cycle, it is convenient to begin with the calendar year. In January the few farmers who have not finished stripping tobacco finish this work. If steers are being fed, they receive considerable attention at this time so they will be ready for market whenever prices seem favorable. January, like December, is a popular month for the killing of meat animals. If the winter is mild, apple trees may be trimmed. Frequent visiting is done during this month.

In February, if there is little frost in the ground, the farmer begins to plow. Young chickens are bought from the hatchery and placed in brooders. Harnesses are mended and greased. During February and March, when the curtain for the new farming season is about to rise, farmers who wish to retire or to restrict their operations will hold farm sales. Items offered for sale are usually confined to farm machinery, stock, harnesses, household items, and stored grains and feeds, but the farm itself may also be sold. These sales are not only business occasions but also important social events, giving to men, women, and children an excellent chance for visiting. No Amish farmer misses a sale if he can help it. School teachers find it expedient to dismiss youngsters when sales take place in the neighborhood.

Many sales are attended during March even if there is no need for buying. Manure is hauled during the winter months when the ground is frozen and dry. When the ground is in the right condition, the fields are plowed. Grass fields are rolled to correct the condition of heaving, resulting from frost. Clover or alfalfa is sown in the wheat field. Liming and farrowing require the attention of some farmers during this

[13] *Ibid.*, 45–46.

month. Tobacco beds are sterilized with steam, and some vegetables are planted in the garden.

Potatoes are planted as early in April as possible. Tobacco seed is sown in the sterilized tobacco bed. Farmers who raise oats seed the crop during this month. The ground is well prepared for corn planting. The garden receives much attention and is prepared with manure from the barn.

Corn is generally planted during the first or second week of May. Toward the end of this month, the young tobacco plants are transplanted into the field. More vegetables are planted in the garden. If the growing season begins early, the cultivation of corn and potatoes is begun in the last part of the month.

The transplanting of the young tobacco plants continues until some time in early June. These plants are transplanted at intervals so that the crop matures over a period of time and can be harvested properly at the right moment. Corn and potato cultivation begins or continues, and the operation is repeated from four to six times. In addition, tobacco is cultivated about once a week. The potatoes also need to be sprayed about once a week.

In early June, alfalfa is ready for the first cutting. A week later, the mixed clover and timothy hay may be ready to cut. This crop is generally cut only once, whereas alfalfa is usually cut three times in the season. As soon as the hay is dry it is loaded with a hay loader and stored in the barn or baled in the field. None of it is stacked outside. Barley is generally ready to be harvested by the middle of June. Wheat, if it matures early, is ready to be harvested late in June. The grain is shocked in the field after it is cut so that it will dry thoroughly. After three or four days it is generally hauled into the barn where it is stored until it is threshed. Some shocked grain is threshed straight from the field. The straw, however, is nearly always stored in the barn, baled or unbaled.

In July, the cultivation of corn and potatoes continues. The whole tobacco patch is thoroughly hoed early in the month and this work engages the entire family. Wheat is generally cut between the first and tenth of July. Threshing of small grain begins in the middle of July and continues until the end of August but the threshing crew is largely self-sufficient and there is little need to exchange work with the neighbors in threshing.

August may be a slack month, and family members may visit distant relatives. Also in August tobacco cutting gets into full swing and the alfalfa is ready to be cut the second time. Some early potatoes are dug in the latter part of this month.

September and October are very busy months. In September the silos are filled and tobacco cutting and storing is completed so that it will not be injured by an early frost. During the latter half of the month the potatoes are dug and the corn is cut and shocked. Each of these tasks generally requires several days of work. Farmers begin to buy steers for winter feeding. Potato digging and marketing may well last until the middle of October. The shocked corn is picked in the field and both the corn stalks and the corn are hauled off the field.

Corn picking may continue until sometime in November. Generally the corn stalks are shredded during this month to be used as feed. Stripping of tobacco is begun. The farmer likes to pick loose stones off his field. Some meat animals are killed. December is the month for stripping tobacco, and the feeding of steers receives much attention. A good deal of butchering is done. Visiting is frequent and perhaps prolonged. Weddings are reserved with few exceptions for November and December. Thus the Amish calendar year allows little time for extended periods of absence from home and farm.

The size of Amish farms, generally speaking, is smaller than those operated by non-Amish persons.[14] The size is influenced by the limitations of horse-power farming instead of modern tractor farming, by the diversity of farming enterprises, and by the intensity of cultivation. The acreage of the average-sized Amish farm has decreased in recent years.

[14] The average size of farms in Pennsylvania (of 30 acres or more) was 116 acres in 1945, with an average of 87.4 acres in cultivation. The average number of acres in cultivation for 37 Old Order Amish farms in Mifflin County was 76. (J. A. Hostetler, "The Amish Family in Mifflin County" [Pennsylvania State University, 1951], 33.) In Lancaster County, Amish farms averaged 48 acres. (Kollmorgen, op. cit., 33). Midwest Amish farms, especially those operated by the Amish with tractors, are considerably larger.

Land prices vary a great deal in areas where the Amish are located. The land value in Lancaster County, Pennsylvania, where land sells as high as $1,500 per acre, is not at all typical of other Amish settlements. In this "garden spot" in the center of the Amish community land prices are highest. Outward from the center of the settlement land prices decrease to more nearly the prevailing level among non-Amish and non-Mennonite farmers. These extremely high prices deserve some explanation. First of all, the soil has a limestone base and is very desirable for farming. The Amish and the "plain people" generally prefer this type of soil, and when they settled in the New World, they sought this type of land. Agriculture was intensified in this southeastern Pennsylvania region with the introduction of tobacco, potatoes, and still later by tomatoes, peas, and other cash crops. Other considerations also created the conditions favorable to high land-values. The Amish are reluctant to move away from their old well-established community, which has been their homeland since they came to Pennsylvania. They are intent on living in close proximity so they can maintain their religious life and their principles of separation from the world. Their horse-and-buggy travel circumscribes the distance they can live away from other Amish people. Their simple economic needs and requirements enable them to save more of their gross income than can non-Amish farmers. The Amish have human resources, a work ethic, and a productive pace which other people are not inclined to imitate in quite the same way. Their population growth has been very substantial so that they occupy most of the farming land in the center of the settlement, which means that they have bought almost all the available non-Amish farms. A combination of these features would appear to be responsible for the high price of land.

But not all Amish settlements are alike when it comes to resourcefulness, upkeep of the soil and of equipment and buildings, and of themselves as well-groomed persons. It seems that the public image of the Amish as "picturesque Americans," or as "a solid culture that produces happiness as well as abundance," is based upon the Lancaster County group.

There are few communities of Amish, if any, that excel this group in the appearance of their farm buildings and of themselves. Other settlements that reflect very fine farm upkeep are Somerset and Mifflin counties in Pennsylvania. Settlements in the Midwest vary a great deal, from farm to farm, and from one settlement to another.

The tenancy rate appears to be higher among the Amish than among the non-Amish farmers.[15] Generally a high rate of tenancy is associated with instability and some disorganizing features of the farm community. But this is hardly the case with the Amish settlement. The rate of tenancy is kept high because young people are required to live on the farm and because they rent from their relatives in many cases. Amish farmers retire from active duty and let the young couple take over the farming operations earlier than the non-Amish population. Young couples also rent farms from outsiders until such a time as they can secure ownership.

Land use is exceedingly intensive in the most densely settled communities. All available farm land is under cultivation, and in some regions where land is unsuited for cultivation, timber is kept for a supply of lumber and firewood. The typical farm includes a large garden and a larger tract or "truck-patch" for potatoes and other vegetables for home consumption. Orchards are common. In Pennsylvania, farmers follow a four or five year rotation that includes the production of wheat, oats, corn, and hay. In some areas this plan of rotation has been modified by cash crops such as tobacco, potatoes, tomatoes, or peas. The Amish people make much use of barnyard manure, as well as lime and commercial fertilizer. Feeding livestock and cattle are outstanding features of most Amish farms in the eastern United States. Cattle feeding is carried on as much for the sake of obtaining manure as for financial profit. Hog raising is a normal activity on midwestern farms but has diminished in the eastern part of the nation. For sanitary reasons, hog raising is kept to a minimum in areas where dairy farming prevails. Farm income is supplemented by selling farm products to local and nearby city markets, especially in Pennsylvania.

[15] Kollmorgen, *op. cit.*, 29.

Favorable markets for fluid milk in some areas have modified the Amish farm in recent years. Cow stables have been remodeled and equipped to meet the demands of milk inspectors. Milk houses and cooling systems, which are operated with gasoline engines, have been installed, and a considerable number of Amish people have purchased milking machines and bulk tanks. The size of the Amish dairy herd ranges from twelve to twenty or more.

A major difficulty encountered with the commercialization of the farm has been the traditional observance of Sunday. Believing that Sunday is a holy day, a day on which there should be no business transactions, the Amish have refused to allow their milk to be picked up by trucks on Sunday. Some families solve this problem by using the weekend milkings for home consumption and by churning them into butter. One firm agreed to pick up the Sunday evening milk on Monday morning if proper cooling and storage were assured. But the large milk industries in most instances will not take on producers unless they agree to sell milk seven days per week. They will make no concession to Amish religion. This has resulted in a serious problem for the Amish. They have sought other ways to solve the problem, some by separating the milk and selling cream, and some by taking an inferior price. As a way out, the Amish have also established cheese factories in some areas.[16] In this way they have an outlet for fluid milk, and the farmers who have not modernized their barns to meet the standards of state inspectors can sell their milk to the cheese house.

Government subsidy checks for milk are refused on grounds that money not earned in honest toil cannot be accepted in good faith. Some feel that the acceptance of such checks would lead to further complicating and perhaps binding obligations to the government. These objections are sometimes publicly stated at religious gatherings, as in the case of one bishop who preached the sermon to a large community gathering at a funeral. He said: "When the last war broke out a

[16] W. R. Dilling, "Religion Boosts Domestic Swiss Cheese Output," *American Butter Review* (April, 1950).

brother from our church was asked if he received milk subsidy checks and also if he co-operated with the Triple A. He could answer with a good conscience that he did not." The preacher implied that if the "brother" had received the milk subsidy checks and co-operated with the "Triple A" he would have been obligated to help with the war effort, a practice contrary to Amish faith. The bishop added: "The less we have to do with the government the better off we are. It is much better to keep completely separate from the world."

Soil conservation practices such as contour farming and strip cropping are not generally practiced by the Amish. Such techniques were never a part of their Swiss and Palatinate agricultural background, and when contour farming was advocated by state agricultural colleges they never adopted it, but regarded it as "book farming," that is, theoretical rather than practical. The Amish are, however, equipped to restore fertility in depleted soils.

Agriculture has great significance for the Amish throughout the year as featured in *The Budget*. Although farming is invariably related to weather and natural phenomena in this newspaper, methods of farming are also discussed and shared by writers from different parts of the country. Farming among the Amish requires no books. The intellectual know-how of farming is passed on from father to son orally and remains in the head, scarcely reaching the printed page. Perhaps the only exception to this is *Baer's Almanac* and Raber's *Calendar*. Both provide zodiac information and these signs are carefully studied by some, but not by all Amish people.

# CHAPTER 5

# THE INTEGRATION
# OF THE COMMUNITY

THE AMISH COMMUNITY is a ceremonial community. Beliefs find expression in such activities as worship and prayer as conditioned by the charter. The ceremonies of the district tie all families together in a common sense of *Gemeinschaft*, where a common will becomes reality. The group sentiments exercise and support the individual member in his beliefs. Intensive participation provides the individual with a sense of order and destiny. Ceremonial participation "gives the members of the society confidence; it dispels their anxieties; it disciplines the social organization." [1] The rites associated with life such as baptism, marriage, and ordination serve to integrate personality with culture.

Belief and ritual vary greatly from one society to another but tend universally to be associated. Emile Durkheim, who made it his concern to study religion in its simplest and original forms, observed the tendency to divide reality into the sacred and the profane. [2] What becomes sacred in one society may be profane in another. He observed that religion is a vast symbolic system whose ceremonial institutions are disciplinary, integrating, and vitalizing forces. Belief and ritual have a common psychological basis. Ceremony becomes an obsessive, repetitive activity symbolizing the fundamental "needs" of the society, whether economic, social, biological, or sexual. Beliefs

[1] George C. Homans, "Anxiety and Ritual: The Theories of Malinowski and Radcliffe-Brown," *American Anthropologist*, XLIII (1941), 164–72.

[2] Emile Durkheim, *The Elementary Forms of the Religious Life* (London, 1915).

tend to legitimize and rationalize these same psychological needs. Later students of religion [3] observed how ritualistic activity affects the internal constitution of the society. The following is a discussion of the content and occasion of Amish ceremony, as well as its regularity and intensity in the total integration of the community.

### The Preaching Service

The most intense and pervasive ceremonial activity in Amish life is the preaching service held every other Sunday. The service involves most of the day, beginning in some places as early as eight in the morning and often continuing until after one o'clock. This is followed by a common meal and visiting, lasting until midafternoon.

Much preparation is necessary prior to the Sunday meeting on the part of the host household. The secular work takes on ceremonial significance as stables are emptied of manure and carpets are removed from the house. The burden of the work falls on the woman, since the house must be cleaned, the furniture rearranged, the stoves blackened, and the ornamental china washed. On Friday neighboring women come to bake pies and prepare the food which will be served after the preaching service. The man of the house secures the church benches, supervises the physical arrangements before and during the service, and performs the functions normally assumed by an usher.

Sunday is a day of anticipation in Amish society. It makes no difference whether it is a warm sunny morning or a blustery winter day; the Amish father, mother, and all the children in the family hustle around, get the cows milked, and by eight o'clock are on their way to the preaching service.

Father always drives the horse, with mother and baby beside him and the young children in the back seat. In winter, mother and baby may be tucked in the back seat of the carriage where

[3] A. R. Radcliffe-Brown, *Taboo* (The Frazer Lecture, Cambridge, 1939); B. Malinowski, *Magic, Science, and Religion* (Free Press, 1948).

the air is not so sharp and raw. The sight of a dozen carriages gathering into the long farm lane, and the sound of still other horses trotting on the hard-surface road over the hillside evokes deep sentiments among the gathering community. Neighbors and those nearby usually walk to the service. No driver would think of passing another "rig" on the way to the service.

On arriving at the place of worship, the carriages halt in the barnyard where the mother and girls dismount. Father and sons drive to a convenient stopping place where they are met by hostlers, usually sons of the host household, who help unhitch the animal and find a place for it in the stable. The horse is given hay from the supply in the barn. Meanwhile the men cluster in little groups in the stables and under the forebay of the barn, greeting each other with a handshake.

Finally the preachers observe that it is time to withdraw to the house. The men remove their heavy overcoats and hang them up in the barn, since in Amish houses there are no closets and no place to hang so many clothes. The order in which worshippers enter the house is determined by sex and age, a principle that is evident in the entire social life of the society. First the ordained men enter, followed by the oldest men. They are leisurely followed by the middle-aged. The last to enter the assembly are the unmarried boys, who come in single file according to seniority. The age grouping holds also for the meal that follows the service.

The women and girls place their shawls and bonnets in the washhouse or the woodshed. In summertime the girls remain here until it is time to gather into the assembly. In winter they gather in the kitchen. They usually take their seats before the boys come in from the barn; the latter, incidentally, in some districts remain in the barn until after the service has begun. The girls also enter single file, generally according to age, shaking hands with the ministers as they enter. The baptized single persons head the line as a rule, and a baptized person may take turns with others who have been baptized. Visiting young people who are members are frequently given the privilege of following the lead person in the procession.

Amish houses are specially built to accommodate the many people, often 200 or more, who gather for worship. The houses have wide doors, and in the eastern states, there are removable partitions so that people seated in almost any part of the main floor can observe the preacher. Each church district has benches and hymnals, which are transported from one meeting place to another. The furniture is removed or stored in such a way that rooms can be filled with benches.

The seating space consists of backless benches, which occupy the kitchen, sitting room, and main bedroom. A center row of chairs is reserved for the ordained. Older men take benches next to the wall, but the feeble ones are given rocking chairs. Chairs are frequently given to the ministers' wives and the oldest women. The preacher, who stands at the doorway between the two largest rooms, has no pulpit, but occasionally a chair upon which to lean. Women and men are seated separately, though they are not in separate rooms. Several rows of unmarried women occupy the sitting room with the men, and men who arrive late remain in the kitchen with mothers and infants. Preschool boys sit with their fathers and girls with their mothers. Infants, a month or six weeks old, are also brought to the service. While there is great emphasis on being present, personal participation is somewhat limited.

The customs and social habits of each district or ceremonial group are peculiar to that ceremonial unit. The symbols which bind a group into a unified whole differ a great deal from Pennsylvania to Iowa, and even within the state of Pennsylvania. While the order of service is almost uniform, the manner of informal behavior, and the extent to which informal behavior is institutionalized, differs. For instance, men in some districts will leave their hats on in the house until the hymn is announced. With one uniform swoop they go off, under the bench, or they are piled on empty benches, or hung on hooks. In other districts hats are taken off as the men enter the house. The boys may pile them on the porch. In some groups men leave their hats on to eat the meal, taking them off only for the silent prayer at the beginning and at the end of the meal.

The service is three or more hours long and there are a variety of activities and forms which are indicated in the following order of service.

### ORDER OF AN AMISH PREACHING SERVICE

1. Hymns (several); while the ministers retire to an upstairs room for council. The *Loblied* (*Ausbund*, p. 770) is always the second hymn.

2. *Anfang* or introductory sermon.

3. Prayer (kneeling, and in most localities silent).

4. Scripture reading by the *Armen-diener* (deacon) as audience stands.

5. *Es schwere Deel* or main sermon, concluded by the reading of a chapter from the Bible.

6. *Zeugniss,* or testimonies to the main sermon by other ministers present as requested by the one who preached. Other lay members are frequently asked to give *Zeugnis.*

7. Closing remarks by the minister who preached.

8. Prayer, all turning and kneeling while the minister reads a prayer from *Die Ernsthafte Christenpflicht.* (The prayer on page 55 is commonly used.)

9. Benediction (standing).

10. Announcements, where the next meeting will be held, and whether members should remain after dismissal for members' meeting.

11. Closing hymn.

12. Dismissal; the youngest leaving first, followed by the older ones in order of age.

After the rooms have been occupied and all are waiting for the service to begin, an elderly man announces a hymn number. The old man begins to sing what seems like a solo, but after the first syllable the whole assembly joins in unison. The *Vorsinger* or *Vorstimmer,* the one leading the singing, may be any male member who has the informal training required. He is not formally appointed, nor does he stand or sit in any special place. The *Vorsinger* continues to sing the beginning of each new line of a hymn in a shaky and trembling falsetto. Those who hear Amish singing for the first time say that it sounds like chanting or wailing. The tunes are extremely slow, with old voices joining younger ones in unison.

With the singing of the first hymn the ordained men withdraw (oldest first) to a room upstairs for *Abrot* [4] (counsel) and prayer and to arrange who shall preach the first and the main sermon. When there are applicants for baptism, they appear before the ministers upstairs. On entering, the oldest applicant says, "It is my desire to be at peace with God and the Church." Each of the others in their turn say, "That is my desire too." After instruction they are dismissed and the ordained proceed with their business.

While the preachers are in the council room, the assembly continues to sing hymns with long periods of silence between them. With a nod the elderly *Vorsinger* passes to another the responsibility for leading the next hymn, and frequently a young man is nudged by an older one to take over in the middle of a familiar hymn. Sometimes the young man loses the melody and his courage and an older member must come to his rescue.

When the preachers descend from the stairway the singing stops at the end of the verse. The preachers shake hands with latecomers and with any whom they have not greeted earlier in the morning. After they are seated one of them rises and stands between the two large rooms to deliver the first sermon. With folded hands beneath his full-grown white beard, a preacher typically begins to mumble in a low tone, gradually building up to an audible and even flow of words in mixed Pennsylvania German, German, and English.

Liebe Brüder und Schwestern und alle die womit versammelt sin, zum erschde will ich eich die Gnade Gottes winsche und die mitwirkente Graft des heiligen Geistes, un wie Petrus sagt, "Gelobet sei Gott und der Vater unsers Herrn Jesu Christi, der uns nach seiner grossen Barmherzigkeit wiedergeboren hat zu einer lebendigen Hoffnung,

[4] This is the Pennsylvania-Dutch rendering of Abrath (see *Mennonite Encyclopedia*, Vol. I, 8). The room in which the ordained meet for counsel is the *Kämmerli* (*ibid.*, M.E., Vol. III, 140).

durch die Auferstehung Jesu Christi von den Toten, zu
einem unvergänglichen und unbefleckten und unverwelk-
lichen Erbe." (I Peter 1:3–4)

*Translation:* Dear brothers and sisters and all who are assembled here, first of all I wish you the grace of God and
the accompanying power of the Holy Ghost. As Peter says,
"Blessed be the God and Father of our Lord Jesus Christ,
which according to his abundant mercy hath begotten us
again unto a lively hope by the resurrection of Jesus Christ
from the dead, to an inheritance incorruptible, and unde-
filed, and that fadeth not away, reserved in heaven for you."
(I Peter 1:3f.)

In a typical opening sermon, the minister reminds the congregation of the purpose of their meeting—to listen once again
to the Word of God. He brings to the attention of all some
scriptural teachings, pointing out the importance of obeying
the commandments. For instance, he admonishes the worship-
per: ". . . schaffet, das ihr selig werdet, mit Furcht und Zit-
tern" (Work out your own salvation with fear and trembling.
—Philemon 2:12). This is a favorite quotation. Before bringing his half-hour introduction to a close, he mentions the importance of prayer and trust in God. Appreciation for freedom of worship is typically expressed. After a few words of
apology for his weakness he informs the congregation that he
does not wish to take the allotted time away from the brother
who is to bring the main message, in these words: "Auch ich
will die Zeit net lang verbrauche in meine grosse Armut und
Schwachheit und die Zeit wegnehme von der Bruder wo es
schwere Deel hat." He asks the hearers to pray for the minister
who is to bring the main message and quotes a favorite verse:
"Kommt, lasst uns anbeten, und knieen, und niederfallen vor
dem Herrn, der uns gemacht hat. Denn er ist unser Gott, und
wir das Volk seiner Weide, und Schafe seiner Hand. Heute, so
ihr seine Stimme horet, so verstocket euer Herz nicht. [For
translation, see Psalms 95:6–8.] Und wann dir einig sind lasset
uns bede." (If you are all agreed let us pray.) All kneel together for a season of silent prayer.

The signal to rise from prayer may not be apparent to the visitor. When the preacher feels there has been enough time allotted for individual prayer, he gets up from his knees. Others who hear his foot scraping on the floor as he arises know that it is time to stand.

All remain standing while the deacon reads a chapter. Before doing so he takes the liberty to make several remarks and admonishes the congregation to be obedient to the Lord. The entire chapter is read in a singsong, chantlike fashion. After the last verse of the chapter the deacon concludes: "So weit hat die Schrift sich erstreckt" (thus far extendeth the Scripture), and all are seated.

Now the time has come for the main sermon, which in this instance is delivered by a visiting bishop. He begins with the usual greeting: "Gnade sei mit euch und Friede von Gott unser Vater. Wir sin schon viel-feldich vermanhnt wore auf dem meiget Stund bei dem Bruder." (Grace be with you and peace from God our father. We have been admonished many times this morning hour by the brother.) He reminds his hearers of the importance of obedience to the vow of baptism, of obedience to the Bible and parents. *Das alt Gebrauch*, equivalent to "the old way of life," sums up a major aspect of moral emphasis. This phrase embodies the principle of separation from the world, the *Regel und Ordnung* (rules and discipline) of the church, and the idea of strangers and pilgrims in an evil world. Innovations which are unacceptable are labeled *eppes Neies* (something new) and are met with the force of *das alt Gebrauch*.

The sermon delivery falls into a stylized pattern, somewhat chanted, with voice raised to a rather high pitch; at the end of each phrase the voice suddenly drops. Babies who fall asleep in their mothers arms are carried, sometimes directly in front of the preacher, into the next room and up the stairway where three or more may sleep on the same bed. Other children lean on the arm of the parent, or pass the time with a handkerchief, making such objects as "mice" or "twin babies in a cradle." In the kitchen the mothers are nursing their new babies. Not only do the babies tire; the singsong sermon, the

*Figure 8.* Intonation of an Amish Sermon. Adapted from J. W. Frey in *Pennsylvania Songs and Legends*, George Korson, ed. (University of Pennsylvania Press, 1949). Used with permission.

stuffy atmosphere and warmth of the packed room frequently put many of the hardworking men to sleep. Some who appear to be sleeping are just changing their posture, since there is no back rest.

The service is orderly, well mannered, and reverent. On rare occasions humorous incidents occur, like the forgetful mother who put her baby to sleep and upon descending from the stairway had the baby's little white cap on her own head.

Meanwhile, as the preacher goes on with his singsong sermon, the backless benches seem to get harder and harder. The children begin to get restless. The mother of the house may pass a dish of crackers and cookies to all the mothers and fathers having youngsters at their side. The dish is passed down the aisle, across, and over to the next room so that no child misses this treat. Moments later a glass of water is passed for the same youngsters. The long sermon has just started and there will be at least two more hours of sitting still. The host of the house may bring a glass of water for the preacher.

The preacher relates first the Old Testament story from Adam to Abraham, and second from John the Baptist to the end of Paul's missionary journeys. The earnestness with which he speaks produces drops of sweat on his face so that every few minutes it is necessary to reach to his inside coat pocket and draw out a handkerchief to wipe his forehead. He holds the white handkerchief in his hand and waves it through the air as he illustrates points of scripture.

He concludes the long sermon with the reading of a chapter, but interrupts himself with comments. Altogether the sermon takes one hour and a half. With a long sigh the preacher sits down and then asks other ordained men to give *Zeugnis* (testimony) to the message and to "bring anything up which should have been said," or to correct any mistakes. Those offering comments (ranging from three to ten minutes) remain seated.

The first speaker heartily approved of the day's sermon, and (since this was a baptismal service) he wished for the newly baptized members a rich spiritual nature (*geistliche Natur*). Furthermore, he said that he hoped they would keep their promises to the end. The church has received a fresh growth (*frischer Graft*) with the new members. "Ich hoff sie kenne aushalde bis ein glickseliges Ende." (I hope they will be able to endure to their redemption.) A second said he was entirely in harmony with what had been done and that he with his great weakness could add nothing better to what had already been said. He added, "Ich will schweigge." (I will keep silent.) The third testimony included the request for prayer. He reminded the younger members that the time would soon come when major church responsibilities would be upon their shoulders. In tears and heaviness of heart the speaker said it was only a short time ago when it was his privilege to sit in the audience and listen. Now he was being called upon to preach, and he asked the members to pray for the ordained persons.

After the testimonies are completed the main preacher stands to his feet for some closing remarks. He is thankful that the sermon can be taken as God's word and he further admonishes the congregation to give the praise to God and not to man, in these words: "Ich feel dankbar dass die Lehr hat erkannt sei kenne fer Gottes Wort. Gewet Gott die Ehr nicht Mensche." He thanks the congregation for being quiet and attentive. As a guest, he admonishes all to be obedient to the home ministry, and in speaking to the ministry he advises them to visit other districts. This, he said, strengthens and builds up the church. He asks the congregation to kneel for closing prayer. Except for three or four mothers who are holding sleeping babies, all kneel while the minister reads in chant style from the prayer book.

When the minister is through chanting the long prayer everyone rises for the benediction, which he repeats from memory:

> Zuletzt, liebe Brüder, freuet euch, seid vollkommnen, trostet euch, habt einerlei Sinn, seid friedsam; so wird Gott der Liebe und des Friedens mit euch sein, grüsset euch unter einander mit dem heiligen Kuss. Es grüssen euch alle Heiligen. (II Corinthians 13:11–12)
>
> So befehle ich noch mich, mit euch, Gott und seiner Gnadenhand an, dass er uns walte in dem seligmachenden Glauben erhalten, darinnen stärken, leiten und bewahren bis an ein seliges Ende, und das alles durch Jesum Christum, Amen.

> *Translation:* Finally, dear Brethren, rejoice, be perfect, be comforted and be of one mind; be peaceful, and the God of love and peace shall be with you. Greet each other with the Holy Kiss. You are greeted by all the saints.
>
> So I submit myself, with you, to God and his gracious hand, that He please to keep us in the saving faith, to strengthen us in it, to guide and lead us until a blessed end; and all this through Jesus Christ. Amen.

Just as the speaker repeated the words *"Jesum Christum"* at the very last, all bowed both knees in complete uniformity. This genuflection may come as a big surprise to the visitor, but to the member it is an intense experience indicating full obedience and reverence. It symbolizes unanimity with the group before departure.

When the assembly is seated, the deacon announces the place of the next meeting. In the event that business pertaining to discipline or church problems is to be taken up, the deacon also asks that members remain seated after the singing of the closing hymn with the phrase: "Was Brüder und Schwechdre sin, solle wennich schtill sitze bleiwe." On such occasions, all the unbaptized boys and girls are dismissed.

When there is no members' meeting the congregation is dismissed with the close of the hymn. The youngest leave the service first as both men and women march out separately.

The men remove some of the benches through a window and the door to make room for tables, which are formed by setting benches together. Soon the women and girls have set the tables with *Schnitz* pies, bread, butter, jam, pickles, red beets, and coffee—always a standard menu that varies slightly with local custom. Each place setting consists only of a knife, cup and saucer. The pies are baked firm enough so that each person can cut his own piece and eat it while holding it in the hand. This meal is not supposed to be a feast, but just a "piece" to hold one over until he returns home. The ordained, regardless of their age, always eat at the first sitting and visitors are often asked to come to the first table. Otherwise age determines who should come to the table. It is usually necessary to set the tables three or four times, with the boys and girls and children eating last. When preaching was held in my home my brother and I hid some "half-moon pies" in the barn (with mother's permission) and with our best buddies ate them right after the dismissal.

From one to four o'clock in the afternoon is spent in conversation about religion and other matters of mutual interest. To rush away from the service or immediately following the meal is considered somewhat rude. The men congregate informally about the house or barn. In some of the larger districts there are well-developed age-interest groups that function after church, so that young men scarcely converse with older men.

Status among the young men is attained either by showing

special interest in the church and Amish religion or by the opposite, namely, being a nonconformist to the established religious folkways and mores. All young people tend to show their loyalty to leaders of one or the other of the two informal polarized groups. Interest in religious matters is manifest in a variety of ways, chief of which is obedience to parents. Other means of gaining good standing are: being punctual in attending services, listening to the preacher instead of sleeping, helping to sing, showing some initiative in maintaining a conversation with older and more serious-minded men, having a hairline beyond questionable length, and being neat in appearance with no ornamentation. On the other hand, those who gain status by being nonconformists do precisely the opposite.

The afternoon fellowship is broken up by three or four o'clock when many families load into their buggies to go home and do the evening chores. Young people who are not needed to help with chores may go to a friend's home until the evening singing, which takes place at the same farm where the preaching was held. Friends and neighbors numbering as high as fifty are often invited to remain for the evening meal at the place of preaching. The meal is favored with many deserts and extra preparations which have been carried out the previous week.

## The Ceremonial Calendar

Ceremony is governed by the days of the week, by seasons, and by the calendar. Baptism comes only once each year preceding the fall communion service. Weddings are held in November and December. Council meetings and communion are held twice each year, spring and fall. A preaching service is, of course, held every second Sunday. Rites not governed by the seasons are ordinations to office and funerals.

Scriptures read at the Amish preachings follow a seasonal pattern. The register of Scriptures begins at Christmas time with the birth of Christ and concludes with the New Testament account of the judgment and end of the world. There are Scripture selections for sowing and harvesting. Selections from the hymnal (*Ausbund*) are integrated with the register of Scripture and hymns. Slight differences can be observed by comparing the register used in Pennsylvania with that in Ohio, Indiana, Illinois, and Iowa.[5] In midwestern communities a second hymnal is used, the so-called "Baer" or *Eine unpartei-ische Liedersammlung* and also the "Guengerich" hymnal, a revision of the same book but bearing a similar title. The order of service and ceremony is the same. The "Baer" edition is popularly known as *Es dinn Bichli* (the thin booklet), in contrast with *das dicke Buch* (*Ausbund*). It is also used in the singings by the young people.

There are two kinds of Sundays among the Amish; those observed by going to preaching as described above, and the "off" Sundays observed by staying at home or visiting the relatives.

*Gemeesunndaag*, or church Sunday, structures the life of the individual. Individual desire must conform to group expectations. There are no alternatives but to do the usual milking and feeding in the morning and prepare to go to preaching service. No member is allowed to stay at home unless he is sick or manifests severe symptoms of illness. Father harnesses the horse before breakfast, but hitches up the horse as the family is about ready to leave the house. A young man old enough to "run around" (being of courting age) has his own "rig," a one-seated buggy, topless in Pennsylvania but not so in Indiana and Iowa. If he has sisters of courting age he will take them along to preaching in his buggy. To be old enough, or to have the permission of parents to attend the Sunday-evening singing, becomes the cherished goal of adolescents. Upon returning home the Amish family spends the remainder of the day doing the usual farm chores and the evening in leisure. From the standpoint of the adolescent and the child, Sunday is an intense, rigorous experience.

[5] Registers have been published on many occasions. Aside from pamphlets and those published by J. A. Raber in his *Der Neue Amerikanische Calendar*, a few have appeared in the *M.Q.R.* (January, 1941), and in Joseph Yoder, *Amische Lieder* (1942).

The off Sunday is a more pleasant experience for the adolescent, since time is spent in a much more informal manner. This Sunday is a relief from the long, preaching Sunday. Of course, it is permissible to attend preaching in another district if the family or part of the family wishes to do so. It is not compulsory, though preachers more frequently than lay families tend to visit districts other than their own.

In Iowa and Indiana among some districts the alternate Sundays are spent in Sunday school during the summer months. The adoption of this custom in the Midwest is legitimized by the Old Order Amish in some areas. It represents a departure from the Amish tradition in the eastern states. The Sunday school is held in an abandoned school house. Attendance is voluntary, and no lunch is served. The school elects its own lay leaders, a superintendent and an assistant, who in turn appoint teachers for the classes. The teachers of the classes stand up and see that the group takes turns in reading assigned passages from the German Bible. A major function of the school is to learn the German language. Teachers in the classes make little or no comment. The interpretation is left to the general superintendent and the preachers in the general assembly. Young children are given rewards for completing reading assignments at the end of the school year. Each family generally returns home after the school, which lasts from about nine-thirty to noon. Young people of "running around" age may gather with "the crowd" in a home. Here a lunch is served and the afternoon is spent in visiting and in the enjoyment of each other's company. It is also here where the young people will join to go to the evening singing.

Families who have no Sunday school to attend enjoy spending the day at home. After a week of hard work in the field, a day of rest is welcome. When the farm chores are done, the family may dress in clean clothes and spend the time reading and learning the German language. Some families set a regular time for gathering around the family table with German Bibles and primers. Mothers frequently read Bible stories to the youngest children, in English as well as in German.

The young man usually catches up on sleep lost the previous

night, for he may stay at his girl friend's home during the "wee hours" of Sunday morning. But Saturday-evening courtship is restricted (traditionally) to every other Saturday on those weekends when the girl has an off Sunday.

This day is also made delightful with a delicious noon meal at home in an environment that is more relaxed than the weekday meals. The afternoon may be spent in sitting in the living room. Young people especially like to catch up on sleep after a Saturday-night date. Yet an attitude of reverence prevails. No loud noise is permitted on the farm. The use of a hammer or other tools is forbidden to Amish boys on Sunday, though cracking of hickory nuts was tolerated among the children in my home. No whistling was allowed in my home on Sunday. Children may invite other Amish children to their home, or ask to play at the home of another family. Playing in haystacks and in and out of the barn, or hiking, are also common. Occasionally the parents may go visiting old or sick people, thus leaving the children at home alone. In our home it was special to have visiting playmates and even more special to be left at home without the parents. Though fishing was forbidden, hiking to the top of the mountain or wading in the creek was not. We played many games and enjoyed these long periods of uninterrupted play when parents let us alone. It was seldom that we got into real mischief, though things did happen that could not have taken place when adults were about: harnessing up the neighbor's cow, teasing the rooster or the ram, or going to the village dump where we got into old automobiles, occupied some of our time. In the dump we learned how to shift gears, even though we could not get the motor to run. Our parents took some misbehavior in stride and were satisfied to leave us alone at home if one or two of the group appeared reasonably responsible.

Families who go visiting on Sunday have the enjoyment of their own age group. It is customary to arrive at the friend's house in the forenoon, often an hour before lunch. Three or four families may be present for the occasion. The men unhitch their horses and have much to talk about as they find their way to the house where the women have been preparing a long table with delicious foods. The sitting room is often full of people seated in a circle, until the women call the men to dinner. Men gather around the table first, as women stand back and later fill any unoccupied seats. A second seating is often necessary. The highlight of the day of visiting is the noon meal. Outdoor picnics or eating in cafeteria style, practiced by some of the midwestern families, is not considered good hospitality by the most formal Amish groups. The afternoon is spent in talking in the living room, where the men are joined by the women after the dishes are done. Again, in the afternoon, candy or popcorn may be passed around the circle. The Amish are good conversationalists. Topics discussed are the weather, crops, machines, sickness, recent events in the secular world, moving, farm transactions, journeys taken, and sometimes allegedly true stories that have happened in the past but are often bordering on the mysterious. The women may vacillate between listening to the talk of the men and engaging in their own topics of interest, such as sewing, quilt patterns, household hints, and diagnosis and treatment of illness. In late afternoon children's play is interrupted as the family gathers its little ones into the buggy to go home and do the chores.

It is customary to visit relatives without invitation. The mother of every home knows that having Sunday guests is normal, and she will be prepared for any eventuality. There may be short visits after the preaching on Sunday, especially to those who are ill. Sunday-evening visits to nearby Amish neighbors are common. My own family often got into the buggy after supper on Sunday evening and drove to the neighbor's place. If they were not at home we drove to another home. Visitors from distant states may circulate in one settlement among many families during the course of a week or two. Of all topics discussed in the weekly Amish newspaper the largest proportion of space, as already noted, is given to visiting.

Special days observed as holidays are: Christmas, Good

Friday, Easter, Ascension Day, Pentecost, and Thanksgiving Day. The intensity with which they are observed differs among Amish communities, especially for the last two mentioned holidays. National holidays are not observed in the same way as are the Amish religious holidays, and were it not for the calendar, the Amish would be unaware of many of the "worldly" holidays such as Memorial Day, Independence Day, Labor Day, and Armistice Day. Amish preachings are sometimes held on weekdays to accommodate visiting preachers from great distances. Weddings provide additional holidays; not only the wedding day itself, which by tradition is on a Tuesday or a Thursday, but also the day of preparation preceding the wedding and the day of cleaning up after it.

Amish holidays are observed not by having preaching or any kind of formal assembly, but by refraining from normal work and spending the day much like the "home" Sunday. But there are exceptions, since customs vary from one region to another. As in the greater society, Christmas is probably the most celebrated holiday. Christmas is a family and kinship, rather than a ceremonial, holiday. Unlike the American society, which has made it both a ceremonial occasion and a secular celebration, the Amish observe it in their own way without a Christmas tree and without Santa Claus. However, children are exposed to such influences through the public school and some Amish parents come to the annual Christmas program at the school. Some Amish have adopted the practice of drawing names among themselves for buying presents. Before retiring on Christmas Eve in my home, each child set a dish at his place at the table. The parents filled the dishes with many kinds of candy and nuts after the children were asleep. Children who wanted a specific toy usually got it, but toys were generally simple and inexpensive. On Christmas Day it is customary for the relatives of the husband (or the wife) to meet for a delicious meal. If the family is too large, one year the wife's siblings are invited and the next year the husband's. Two-day observance of Christmas by some of the Amish groups is a survival of European custom. Some observe

New Year's Day by visiting. Old Christmas or second Christmas, on January 6, otherwise known as Epiphany, is observed by the older Amish people in Pennsylvania and in some other settlements.

Fasting is observed before the spring and fall communion. Good Friday is a fast day. Easter, like Christmas, is observed for two days in some areas. There is no special celebration on Easter, but some practices among the children are survivals of ancient European customs. For two or three weeks before Easter, children sometimes go to the hen house daily and get a few eggs to hide in a secret place in the barn. On Easter morning the eggs are brought to the house to see who has collected the most. Colored Easter eggs are common. Some are permitted to eat as many eggs as they wish on Sunday morning. Ascension Day is observed as a day of rest or visiting, but on this day young people, or even families, go out into the woods for picnics and the boys may go fishing. Young men gather together for a ball game in the Midwest. On weekday holidays hunting is generally not taboo, but such prohibitions vary with regional folkways and mores. Good Friday was never observed very strictly in my family in Pennsylvania, but when we moved to Iowa our neighbors were greatly perturbed when my father did field work on that day.

We have now reviewed the Amish ceremonial year, its liturgical features as carried out by the community and the way the calendar affects the life of the individual. In the little Amish community Sundays are regarded as holy days and are observed with more reverence than any sacred days during the week. The communion service, which is the most sacred of all district-wide ceremonies in the little community, is discussed next.

## Communion and Footwashing

The district is bonded together not only by the habitual preaching services, but also by the important semiannual communion and its associated ceremonies. First there is the *Att-*

*nungsgemee* (preparatory service or earlier known in high German as *Ordnungsgemeinde*), and the *Grossgemee* (communion service, or *Abendmahl, Nachtmahl,* or *Liebesmahl*). Communion service is held twice each year among the Amish, and it will be remembered that the frequency of this service was one of the points on which Jakob Ammann differed from the Swiss Brethren, who held communion but once each year.

Communion binds the Amish members within a district together with sacred ties. Communion symbolizes the unity of the church, and for a district not to have communion means that there has been serious difficulty in getting unanimous opinion on important issues. Communion means entering into the experience of the suffering and death of Jesus Christ, and to emerge with gratitude and remembrance for his death.

The personal examination process begins prior to or with the *Attnungsgemee* (preparatory service), held two weeks before communion. Every member must be present. The service usually takes most of the day, as the sermons are longer than usual, and the meeting does not dismiss until late afternoon. At this service the ministers present their views on the *Attnung* (*Ordnung,* in high German) and mention practices which are forbidden or discouraged. Each member is asked whether he is in agreement with the *Ordnung,* whether he is at peace with the brotherhood, and whether anything "stands in the way" of entering into the communion service. Faults are confessed and adjustments are made between members who have differences to settle.

Great emphasis is placed on the importance of individual preparation for this holy service. No person is to partake unworthily or with hate in his heart. The Scripture is made plain to all: "For let a man examine himself, and so let him eat of that bread, and drink of that cup. For he that eateth and drinketh unworthily, eateth and drinketh damnation to himself." (I Corinthians 11:28)

Members who are known to be guilty of minor offenses but who do not confess are punished by "getting set back from communion," meaning they cannot participate in the communion ceremony. Those who have been excommunicated are sometimes taken back into the fellowship at this service by kneeling and acknowledging their faults and receiving the right hand of fellowship of the bishop. This service is therefore of utmost importance for evaluating personal behavior, of achieving unanimity of opinion, and of bringing deviating persons into conformity.

Another form of introspection prior to communion is fasting, which consists of eating no breakfast and by spending the morning in quiet meditation. Fast day is generally on Good Friday in the spring, and in the fall on *Michaelstag* or St. Michael's Day, on October 11.

Children typically do not attend the strenuous *Attnungsgemee* and *Grossgemee*, as they are all-day affairs, and much of the meeting must be closed to non-members and children. The Amish children look forward to these occasions because they may spend the whole day with children of the neighborhood and be free from adult supervision. The children of several families may come together where they are supervised by the single unbaptized persons. Parents also look forward to these occasions because it is a change from the usual routine. For some parents, it requires getting up earlier to allow time to take the children to another home before going to the service. For others it means leaving some of the morning farm chores with the older children. The younger ones do not need to be dressed for church. The parents enjoy the liberty of attending services without squirming youngsters by their side. Every church member anticipates the quietness of this most holy occasion (communion) without the children. The Amish church is, after all, Anabaptist, that is, an adult affair. It is not for children and certainly not for entertainment.

Both *Attnungsgemee* and *Grossgemee* are all-day meetings and are attended by guest ministers and bishops. They are frequently needed to help preach the specially demanding long sermons on these occasions. Besides, the presence of guest ministers provides emotional support to the local group. If there is to be a vote taken for an ordination, it is usually done in connection with the preparatory service. But it is the sermons on these two all-day meetings which test the physical endurance and capacity of the ones preaching. The sermons preached at these occasions are known as the *Altväter-Geschichten* (the history of the old fathers or patriarchs) and must cover the biblical history from the creation story to the suffering of Christ. The purpose is to relate both the good and the bad in the characters as lessons for today. The second sermon on these two occasions is usually the longer, lasting sometimes about three hours. At the communion a bishop usually ends his discourse with *das Leiden Christi* (the suffering of Christ). He is in charge of breaking the bread and passing the cup with the help of other ordained men.

The long sermon continues over the noon hour as members leave the assembly without any particular order and find their way to another part of the house to eat at the table. In some settlements eating is done by standing at a table on these special occasions. Those who have eaten return to the service so that everyone but the main preacher has been out to lunch. (He generally eats an early lunch.)

Near the end of the long sermon two ministers leave and bring bread and wine. While they cut the loaf on a table by the bishop's side, he talks about the origin of bread (and wine), the sowing, harvesting, milling, and baking processes. He rehearses the growth of the grapes, the need for pruning, and the purifying of the wine. The meanings are, of course, symbolic for the life of the people of God. The bread is always home-baked, made by the hostess. The wine has been made by the wife of the bishop.

In breaking the ceremonial bread after concluding the sermon, the bishop receives a slice of bread from the deacon and asks the members to stand for prayer. All remain standing while the bishop and one of the ministers distribute the bread to each member. Each member bows his knees in reverence, places the bread in his mouth, and is seated. The same procedure is followed with the cup, which is filled with home-made wine, or in some communities with grape juice. After the bread and wine have been passed the bishop proceeds by asking for *Zeugnis* in the usual manner, and then with prayer.

Following the prayer a minister reads the account of the washing of the disciples' feet (John 13), while the deacon and lay members bring in towels and pails of water. The bishop admonishes members not to be partial but to wash the feet of the person nearest. Stooping, not kneeling, is required of the one who is doing the washing. A hymn is announced and the men begin to remove their shoes and stockings and to wash feet in pairs. Women follow the same pattern in a different room. After each pair has finished they clasp hands, kiss each other and the oldest says *Da Herr sei mit uns* (the Lord be with us) and the other responds *Amen, zum Frieda* (Amen, in peace). The Holy Kiss, as in the early primitive church, is a symbol of love and fellowship between believers; it is withheld in the case of transgressors. The kiss is also exchanged between ordained men as they meet each Sunday for preaching, but is practiced less among the laymen.[6] After all have washed feet the service concludes with a hymn. As they leave the service, members contribute to the *Armengelt* (the poor fund of the district), which is the final act in the communion service. Each person places his contribution into the hand of the deacon, who immediately places it into his pocket.

## Music and Integration

Group singing is a type of symbolic integration almost entirely overlooked by social scientists.[7] In Amish life no other ritual has so much sustained emotional appeal as does participation in singing. For the student of human society the hymns of the Old Order Amish constitute a fascinating study in cultural diffusion and folklore, but to the Amish the singing of

[6] See *Mennonite Encyclopedia*, Vol. III, 180–85.
[7] For a psychological approach see Roland L. Warren, "German Parteilieder and Christian Hymns as Instruments of Social Control," *Journal of Abnormal and Social Psychology*, Vol. 38 (1943), 96–100. Also Max Weber, *Rational and Social Foundations of Music* (1958).

them evokes the deepest emotion of the human spirit. Singing is a source of emotional support and reflects the content and psychology of a culture. Integration of culture is evident in both the content of the music and the manner of singing.

The text of the hymns appear in a hymnal called the *Ausbund*, a term referring to excellence of selection.[8] The first known edition in Europe appeared in 1564, while in America it was first printed at Germantown in 1742. This book has 140 hymns and 812 pages of verse, but no musical notations. Since the tunes are orally transmitted from one generation to the next, this has led students of music to regard it as folk music.[9] The Amish *Vorsinger* sets the pitch and sings the first syllable of each line. On the second syllable the whole congregation joins in unison for the rest of the line. Helpful hints for singing the music are offered by J. W. Frey: "The last syllable of a line is cut short abruptly, and there is a brief pause until the *Vorsinger* begins the next line alone, and so on. The hymns move along at an extremely slow rate, and everyone seems to know or feel where the succeeding note is. Although we do not speak of division into bars of this type of music, there is a noticeable pulse or beat between phrases, and the thesis and arsis of every line are quite clearly defined. Those who sing out of tune are younger members who have not yet mastered the melodies, or persons who have no musical ear. The *Vorsinger* need not be one special person; after a period of silence between hymns, any member of the congregation, if moved by the spirit, may announce the number of a hymn and proceed to commence each line, thus setting the pitch."[10]

The most familiar Amish hymn, the *Lobelied* or *'S Lobg'sang* is reproduced here as it is sung by a group in Iowa. Joseph W. Yoder reduced to scores the tunes used by the Mifflin County, Pa., Amish.[11] This hymn is always sung as the second hymn in

    [8] "Ausbund," *M.E.*, Vol. I, 191.
    [9] J. W. Frey, "Amish Hymns as Folk Music," in G. Korson, *Pennsylvania Songs and Legends* (University of Pennsylvania Press, 1949), 129–62. John Umble, "The Old Order Amish, Their Hymns and Hymn Tunes," *The Journal of American Folklore*, III (1939), 82–95.
    [10] Frey, *op. cit.*, 142.
    [11] Joseph W. Yoder, *Amische Lieder* (Yoder Publishing Co., 1942).

every Amish district. Frey says, "Remember that the division into bars does not indicate an equal number of counts in each measure in the conventional manner. It merely shows a sort of break between each musical syllable or phrase. At normal rate, it takes about thirty seconds to sing any one of these lines." To sing all four verses takes twenty minutes in some of the most conservative Amish communities, while in some places it is sung in eleven minutes. Amish music reflects culture, and the speed of singing can be positively correlated with a degree of assimilation.

These slow tunes are believed by some to have their origin in the Gregorian chant or plain song, "which was probably the only form of church music in existence down to the Reformation. They are practically impossible to represent by musical notation with regular divisions, since the rhythm of Gregorian chants is not subject to the laws of modern measure—that is, with uniform isochronous measures. It is curious that these tunes (tones or modes) originally composed for the singing of liturgical Latin based on the Latin accent should have been adapted by the early Amish martyrs to their own peculiar Swiss-German dialect. It is also something of a miracle that these tunes have been passed down among the Amish from generation to generation for more than 250 years solely from mouth to ear!" [12]

George Pullen Jackson,[13] on the other hand, has matched Amish tunes with old German folk songs, in an attempt to show that the Amish tunes have their origin in both European and American folk tunes. Each Amish hymn has a headline indicating the tune to be used. The fusion of the secular tunes with sacred hymns is manifest in some of these headlines. The *Lobelied* for example is sung to the tune *Aus tiefer Not schrei*

[12] Frey, *op. cit.,* 141.
[13] George Pullen Jackson, "The American Amish Sing Medieval Folk Tunes Today," *Southern Folklore Quarterly,* X (June, 1945), 151–57; "The Strange Music of the Old Order Amish," *The Musical Quarterly,* XXXI (July, 1945), 275–88. See also Charles Burkhart, "The Music of the Old Order Amish and the Old Colony Mennonites: A Contemporary Monodic Practice" (M.A. thesis, Colorado College, 1952), and Rupert K. Hohmann, "The Church Music of the Old Order Amish of the United States" (Ph.D. dissertation, Northwestern University, 1959).

*ich zu Dir*, which corresponds to the secular tune "There Went a Maiden with a Jug."

Yoder's purpose in reducing the music to scales was to produce a book which the Amish would adopt as their own, to aid them in singing the tunes uniformly. It is not surprising that they rejected such progressive methods, even though Yoder published instructions for reading music in his book. Furthermore, the Amish are too reluctant to part with their old hymnbook or their old way of singing. Nevertheless, the musicians and folklorists have much to say in praise of Mr. Yoder for preserving a knowledge of Amish music.

### 'S Lobg'sang
### (The Hymn of Praise)

*Figure 9.* 'S *Lobg'sang.* Courtesy of George Korson (ed.), *Pennsylvania Songs and Legends* (The Johns Hopkins Press, 1960), p. 143. Used with permission.

The texts of the hymns were written as poems and testimonials of Anabaptist prisoners while confined in the great castle at Passau, Bavaria, which still stands. The story they tell is of sorrow and trials in this life and of ultimate victory for the faithful. The text reflects deep humiliation and an over-whelming sense of dependence upon God as the deliverer. A dominant theme running through all of them is one of great sorrow and deep loneliness, of protest against the world of wickedness. However, no despair is exhibited: rather triumph and an unspeakable conviction that God will not forsake his own but lead them through sorrow to everlasting life.

One hymn continues in a solemn doleful mood for seventy-one stanzas, in the last of which God is praised for having sent a Savior to cleanse man of his sins. "Many more of the hymns go on at great length about the wickedness of worldliness. It is small wonder then that humility is an Amish virtue, and pride is considered the cardinal sin. Each time an Amishman sings these hymns he reminds himself that it is worldly and sinful to be proud, to have any likeness made of himself, to have a whipsocket or dashboard on his buggy, or to display or even own any fancy gadgets on his farm." [14]

The slow tunes or *langsam Weis*, as the Amish call them, are characteristic of all the tunes they use in worship. They do not use notes but assume that the congregation should learn them by memory as is the case with the folk music. It is this slowness which prompted Yoder to assume that they are de-rived from the Gregorian chant. However, it would appear that Jackson's observations would aptly apply, that "in un-controlled group singing each tune is dragged out, which leads to all kinds of strange ornamentation foreign to the original tune." [15]

The tunes of the young people at the Sunday-evening sing-ing are the "fast tunes." These tunes are used with the *Un-partheyisches Gesang-Buch* (Non-denominational songbook) and in the *dinn Bichli* (the thin book), called *Liedersammlung*.

[14] Frey, *op. cit.*, 145–46.

[15] Robert Friedmann, "Ausbund," *M.E.*, Vol. I, 191. Several Amish hymns (from Iowa and Indiana) were recorded by Alan Lomax and John Umble in 1938 and filed in the Archives of American Folk Song in the Library of Congress.

These German hymns are sung to the tunes of popular Gospel songs, though the Amish sing them *a cappella* and in unison and much more slowly than they are sung in English. Examples of these follow: *Wo ist Jesus, mein Verlangen*, is "What a Friend We Have in Jesus"; *Du unbegreiflich hochstes Gut*, is "Sweet Hour of Prayer"; and *Herr Jesu Christ, dich zu uns wend*, is "He Leadeth Me." In many places the young people at their singing will switch to the English language for the last half of the evening "singing." These faster tunes are also sung at the wedding table, but for barn games, an altogether different type of song is used.

About the only property owned by an Amish church district, aside from church benches, are the hymnbooks. They are kept in a special wooden box and are passed on from one household to the next where preaching is to be held. The books are under the trusteeship of the deacon and are distributed by him at the preaching service. The Lancaster County Amish own the plates to the *Ausbund* and for other German books, and when a new supply of hymnals is needed, they take the plates to a print shop. They also supply copies to other Amish districts in North America.

The articulation of the Amish community displays many facets of a stable, slow-changing society. Its integrative features conform to the model of the little community discussed in the first chapter. Sowing and harvesting activity is reflected in the ceremonial calendar of the community. Individual experience is combined with the experience of others in ceremony. Yet there appears to be a balance between formal and informal associations, between ceremony and kinship duties. The individual learns the entire culture pattern of his community and not a fragment of it. What one man learns differs little from the learning of other men. The institutions are simple rather than complex. The assembly of the Amish does not require much involvement in the affairs of this world, either in special equipment or buildings, or in capital investment. The ceremonial considerations transcend the life of the individual. The attitudes, ideas, and habits of the individual are shaped by the ongoing institutional ways from the formative years throughout adulthood.

We may observe that there is general consistency among the various institutions. Persons given authority are not demanding contradictory behavior. What parents expect of the child conforms to the expectations of the church. Family sentiments and values are closely integrated with those of the religious community. The numerous religiously sanctioned ceremonies are consistent with the Amish world view of reality. The Amish community has remained informal, small, and face-to-face and requires a very minimum of formal controls. Under these conditions little bureaucratic organization is needed for the maintenance of the society.

# CHAPTER 6

# THE SYMBOLIC COMMUNITY

THE AMISH COMMUNITY is a multibonded community. The members are held together not by a single interest but by many symbolic ties which they have in common. The ecologic and ceremonial functions are bounded by the limits of horse-and-buggy travel. But there exists also a symbolic community made up of many social rules for living and a culture that has set definite boundaries. A member of the Amish faith is bound to the norms and practices of his social group. He is a member of the in-group or *unser Satt Leit* (our sort of people) and is marked by certain symbols. The out-group is *anner Satt Leit* (other sorts of people), who are distinguished by their symbols. This sharp line of distinction gives rise to a general principle by which in-groups tend to stereotype out-groups, and any threat from an out-group tends to intensify the cohesion of the in-group.[1]

Before observing in detail the intimately shared activities which make the Amish community a multibonded one, it is well to note the over-all complexity of these ties. Language provides a guide to a social reality that is different from that of other people. All new members with rare exceptions are offspring and they are assimilated gradually by a majority of the old members. Physical property, including farms that were the abodes of the forefathers, and preference for certain soils and topography come to have sentimental attachment. Common traditions and ideals which have been revered by the whole community from generation to generation embody the expectations of all. All relatives are Amish or of Amish descent. There are formal church rules that guide the members in their

[1] Robert Bierstedt, *The Social Order* (1957), 268.

conduct with each other and with outsiders. The specialists, the lifetime ordained persons, carry on the functions of the church and enable it to act as a unit in maintaining separation from the world. The size of each church district is kept to a minimum, enabling it to function as a small, intimate, and informally controlled group, whereas largeness would make consensus more difficult. There are special means to resist shock such as mutual aid in times of fire, death, and sickness. The life of the community is prolonged because the basic needs of the individual are met from the cradle to the grave. The Amish baby grows up strongly attached to those of his kind and remains indifferent to contacts outside his culture. The tendency to symbolize all of life provides a basis for action in meeting the future. It assures internal unity and community longevity.

## Symbols, Convention, and Tradition

Symbols form an important maintenance function in everyday life. The symbols are different from the non-Amish or "English" symbols. In the world around them, the Amish see the symbols of worldly civilization. They are such objects as the cathedral, the skyscraper, the modernistically designed automobile and house, the television set, the missile, and modern ways of clothing the body. To the Amishman these symbols represent the world. They are a reminder of danger to him and are to be avoided.

The Amish have their own symbolism which provides a basis for common consciousness and a common course of action.[2] We may hypothesize that in a simple society like the Amish the people themselves become symbolic, and not their achievements as in world civilization. The horse and buggy, the beard of the married man, and the styles of dress—all take

[2] The importance of symbolism for the human society has been restated in a fruitful discussion by Susanne K. Langer, *Philosophy in a New Key: A Study in the Symbolism of Reason, Rite and Art* (Harvard University Press, 1960).

on symbolic meaning. All Amish know that this is the accepted way of doing things, and symbolism becomes an effective means of social control as the nonconformist can quickly be detected from the conformist. Symbols which are universal in all Amish communities include the following: hooks-and-eyes on the Sunday coat and vest of all men, trouser styles that have no fly-closing but a flap that buttons along the waist, wide-brimmed black-felt hats for men, white organdy caps for women, plain rather than patterned or striped dresses for women, uncut hair for women, and long hair cut in bangs for men. All these symbols together constitute a world of social reality, a way of life that teaches how people should live and what they should imitate.

An illustration of convention which is symbolic is the way courtesy is expressed among the Amish. Acts rather than words perform this function. In a small society where convention is understood few words are needed between actor and alter to make meanings precise. Words of courtesy, as expressed by the English-speaking world, are conspicuously absent among members of the Amish family and community. The dialect contains few if any words of endearment between husband and wife, but young people of courting age frequently employ English words of endearment. Amish parents who hear "English" couples exchange words like "honey" and "sweetheart" have remarked that such a relationship is probably anything but "sweet." There are no words in the Amish spoken language that correspond to "pardon me" or "excuse me." Children might use such English terms in their play but persistence in using them in family relationships would not be approved. They would be accused of trying to be "society" persons. "Oops" is sometimes used to indicate that a certain act was not intentional. "Please" and "thank you" are not a part of table manners nor a part of everyday conversation, but children are taught to say *Denki* (thank you) and *Willkomm* (you are welcome) when giving or receiving gifts on special occasions.

Acts of politeness are much more characteristic than words.

The wife may brush the husband's hat on Sunday morning before he gets around to it. The act requires no "thank you." If the husband is thoughtful he will carry the toddler, help his wife into the carriage, and tuck the blankets around her. Belching is a normal occurrence around the dinner table and conceived as a sign of good appetite with no thought of discourtesy. A boy who was chewing his food vigorously at the breakfast table was greeted by his older brother with the words: "Fer was machst so wiescht?" (Why do you make so ugly?) The boy did not reply but modified his behavior. However, in the presence of English people the Amish will adopt the polite language of the outsider. An Amish woman walking along a village sidewalk who approached a woman washing her sidewalk said "pardon me" as she stepped over the washed part of the sidewalk.

Symbolism in Amish life performs the functions of communication. When much of life is governed by symbols, fewer words are needed for communication. The conspicuous absence of words of courtesy in the Amish dialect would appear to be a function of the importance of symbols, making such words unnecessary. Like dress patterns, the speech habits have also been preserved in the New World. Polite language in Medieval Europe was characteristic of the nobility and not of the peasant groups. Actions among the Amish speak louder than words of courtesy. Acts and intentions are understood, while words of courtesy which might be adopted from the English language would not be understood. The large number of symbols which function within the Amish society aid the growing Amish child to find his place within the family, the community, and within the world of the Amish people.

## The Language of Dress

Anything that can be perceived through the senses can be symbolized, and in Amish society styles of dressing become very important as symbols of group identity. The garb not only admits the individual to full fellowship but also clarifies his role and status within his society.

The hat, for example, distinguishes the Amishman from the outsider and also symbolizes his role within his social structure. When the two-year-old boy discards a dress and begins wearing trousers for the first time, he also receives a stiff jet-black hat with three or more inches of brim. Hat manufacturers produce at least twenty-eight different sizes and a dozen different styles of Amish hats. The bridegroom in Pennsylvania gets a telescopic hat that is worn during the early married years. The hat is distinguished by a permanent crease around the top of the crown. Grandfather's hat has a four-inch crown and a four-inch brim. The bishop's hat has a four- and one-half-inch crown, slightly rounded, and a wide seam around the brim. A hat which has a flatter crown is worn by the rank and file of Amish fathers. The outsider may never notice these differences, or if he does he may regard them as accidental. But to the Amish these symbols indicate whether people are fulfilling the expectations of the group. A young man who wears a hat with a brim that is too narrow is liable for sanction. The very strict Amish congregations can be distinguished from the more progressive ones by the width of the brim and the band around the crown. Thus when the writer's family moved from Pennsylvania to Iowa, one of the first adaptations to make was to take out the scissors and cut off some of the brim. This made my brothers and myself more acceptable to the new community of Amish. At the same time the act symbolized other adaptations that had to be made to adjust to a more "westernized" group of Old Order Amish.

The Amishman has two kinds of coats. Their function is not only keeping the body warm; there is a proper time and place to wear these coats. A vest is also worn under the Sunday dress coat. A wamus or ordinary coat can be a Sunday dress coat or a work coat, and the *Mutze* is always worn to preaching service after baptism. The male member may appear in full dress with a wamus when he goes to town or to visit relatives on Sunday, but for preaching he will wear the *Mutze*. This garment is longer than the ordinary coat and has a split tail. All three of these garments fasten with hooks-and-eyes. Buttons are permitted on work coats in some communities and appear to be the first step of departure from the stricter norms. All of these garments, as with Amish costume in general, were common in Europe among the rural people.[3] The Amish merely retained them by convention. Traits of culture once secular in Europe have been retained by the closed Amish community where they become sacred.[4]

The dress of women is more colorful than that of the men, as variation in color is permitted so long as it is a solid color and without pattern. One-piece dresses are made from traditional patterns. Over the bodice an Amish woman wears what she calls a *Halsduch*, which is similar to what plain-dressing Mennonite groups call a "cape." The name for this in the Palatinate was *Bruschttuch* (breast cloth). The *Halsduch* consists of a triangular piece of cloth about thirty inches long. The apex is fastened at the back and the two long ends go over the shoulder, and after embracing the front, are pinned around the waist. These garments also distinguish married women from the unmarried and the old from the young. Girls wear white organdy capes and white aprons for preaching services, but married women wear aprons and capes that match the color of the dress. These garments are fastened to their dresses by numerous straight pins.

One of the most highly symbolic of all garments among the women is the *Kapp* or head cap worn by every woman and even by infants. Girls from about age twelve to marriage wear a black cap for Sunday dress and a white cap at home. After marriage a white cap is always worn. The size, style, and color of caps varies slightly with regions and with degrees of orthodoxy in a single community. The fine pleats ironed into some of these caps requires hours of tedious work. The specific way in which they are made, including the width of the

---

[3] Palatinate costume is well documented in Karl August Becker, *Die Volkstrachten der Pfalz* (Kaiserslautern, 1952), which makes possible comparisons with contemporary Amish dress.

[4] The "processes by which societies are tightened, hardened, reintegrated, restored" and by which the secular is made sacred are discussed by Howard Becker, "Normative Reactions to Normlessness," *American Sociological Review* (December, 1960). The historical processes in the history of the Amish are full of such examples.

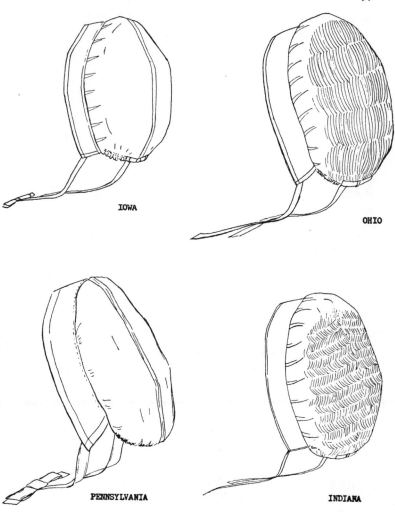

IOWA

OHIO

PENNSYLVANIA

INDIANA

*Figure 10.* Regional Styles of the Old Order Amish *Kapp.*

*fedderdeel* (front part) and the *hinnerdeel* (back part), and the width of the pleats and seams are sacred symbols of the community. Though this headpiece has undergone some changes in detail, the present Amish cap is essentially the same

as that worn by the Palatine women of earlier centuries.[5]
Among most American Mennonites of Swiss-German origin
the cap has become a "prayer cap" or "veiling" required of
women "when praying or prophesying." (I Corinthians 11:5)

These few illustrations of Amish dress could be supported
with still many others. But this is sufficient to indicate how
dress styles serve as symbols for a group. The symbols function very effectively in maintaining separatism and continuity.
The language of dress forms a common understanding and
mutual appreciation among those who share the same traditions and expectations. Dress keeps the insider separate from
the world and also keeps the outsider out. These shared con-
ventions are given sacred sanction and biblical justification:
*unser Satt Leit* (our sort of people) are distinguishable from
*englische Leit* (English people) or *anner Satt Leit* (other
people). The attempts by theatricals to reproduce the dress of
the Amish never quite measure up to the authentic. They
appear ludicrous if not hilarious to the Amish.

### The Language of Speech

The Amish community is also a speech community. Language provides familiarity in which individuals find common
grounds for understanding. Although the Amish came from
Switzerland, from Alsace and Lorraine in France, and from
the Rhineland of Germany, yet their conversational speech is
remarkably uniform. The reason for this is that they came
from the same (Allemanic) dialect-speaking area. Some of the
Alsatian Amish could speak French when they arrived in
America and a few French words have been incorporated into
their dialect which is Pennsylvania Dutch (or German).
Dutch in this instance is a usage from "Deutsch" meaning
German, and not the language of the Netherlands. The four
districts of Amish in Adams County, Indiana, around Berne,
speak a Swiss dialect, but it poses no real barrier for interaction with other Amish. An Amish person traveling from

[5] Karl Becker, *op. cit.,* 118.

Pennsylvania through the midwestern states on a kinship visit can speak his own familiar dialect and be understood.

Linguists have observed that the Amish are trilingual, that is, they can speak three somewhat distinctive yet intermixed tongues.[6] These are: Pennsylvania Dutch, High German, and English. The usage of three distinctive tongues, rather than one or two languages, lends itself to social isolation in that there are speech groupings within the community. Roles and functions tend to organize around each language; thus when speaking English the Amishman tends to think and behave like the English-speaking person.

Pennsylvania Dutch is the familiar tongue of children at home and in informal conversation. It is the mother tongue of children born to Amish parents. Professor Albert Buffington has made it clear that this speech is not a "garbled English" or "corrupted German in the mouths of ignorant people who speak with a heavy accent," but a distinct dialect of the German language.[7] The dialect resembles the Palatine German folk speech. It is, of course, spoken by many Pennsylvania Dutch people who are not Amish.

The second language of the growing Amish child is English. A child is introduced to English when he attends school; as he learns it he also learns that his non-Amish playmates are "English" or *Englischer* in the dialect. They are *anner Satt Leit* (the other sort of people). Amish children learn to speak the two languages without difficulty and without noticeable accent. Upon entering school the child frequently has no English vocabulary, but he readily learns his second language.

English is used when speaking with non-Amish persons in town, at school, or when talking to an "English" visitor or

[6] J. W. Frey, "Amish Triple-Talk," *American Speech* (April, 1945), 84–98, and by the same author "Amish Hymns as Folk Music," in *Pennsylvania Songs and Legends* (University of Pennsylvania Press, 1949), 129–62. A linguistic study of one community appears in Alfred L. Shoemaker, "Studies on the Pennsylvania German Dialect of the Amish Community in Arthur, Illinois" (Ph.D. dissertation, University of Illinois, 1932).

[7] Albert F. Buffington, "Pennsylvania German: Its Relation to Other German Dialects," *American Speech* (December, 1939), 276–86.

salesman. Thus Amishmen employ the English language on "forced" occasions. An Amish person may shift his conversation from the dialect to English, or from English to the dialect, whichever he finds most convenient for the situation. An outsider as a guest at an Amish table may find that dialect chatter prevails at one end of the table, while one or two members of the family keep the general conversation in English for the benefit of the guest. Frey has described the Amish use of English as "American English built on a framework of Pennsylvania Dutch language patterns and interjected continually with whole or part loan-translations from the dialect." [8] The Amish generally experience little difficulty in speaking correct English.

High German, or more precisely "Amish High German," is used exclusively for the preaching service and at formal ceremonial occasions. An Amish person does not converse in High German and most Amish adults know High German only passively, and then only as quoted from the Bible. The ordained officials must know the High German well enough to preach and quote Bible verses. The prayers read from the prayer book, and the hymns sung from several hymnals are in German. High German is taught to the children in the family by parents in the evening, or every two weeks on Sunday when there is no preaching service. German or "Dutch school" is held for several weeks in the winter for Amish youth of courtship age and is accompanied by spelling bees. The school is taught by an older person, a minister or a lay member with natural teaching skills.

It is the religious exercises which require the High German but even here we find that the sermons are intermixed with dialect and with some English words. Passages are memorized from *s'Teschdement* (the New Testament) and from the whole of the *Biewel* (the Bible). English loan-words occur frequently in the dialect with a German prefix and suffix, which is also the case with High German. The endings that have been weakened or dropped altogether in the dialect are

8 J. W. Frey, *Pennsylvania Songs and Legends*, 136.

frequently retained in the High German. The *umlaut*, as ö or ü, is not pronounced with the rounding of the lips as in modern New High German. Thus *fröhlich* (joyous) is pronounced *freehlich*. A passing knowledge of High German is thus preserved by its use and association with ceremonial functions.

The Amish nomenclature denoting an outsider as an *Englischer* has symbolic meaning. Such a general term means that he may be Methodist, Baptist, Lutheran, or anything but Amish. The Mennonites are not classed as English. Since the Mennonites are only a step removed from the Amish they are *Mennischte* and not really as "English" as other people. On the other hand a person of Catholic affiliation is called a *Gedolischer* (from the German word *Katholischer*). Outsiders who are neighbors of the Amish people often refer to the Amish as "The Dutch."

Conversation in the dialect becomes an especially important function of community life as the Amish are very sociable and hospitable people. It was noted earlier that the Amish devote more space to the subject of visiting in their weekly newspaper than to any other topic. Visits to the homes, preaching services, particularly before and after the service, funerals, weddings, sales, quiltings, barn-raisings, frolics of various kinds, sewings, singings, and Sunday visiting are all occasions for conversing at length.

In the little homogeneous community conversational speech must find ways of differentiating between people with the same last name, and in many cases with the same first name also. There are 162 Miller family names on the rural mail routes at Kalona, Iowa. One carrier has on his route 44 Miller families, 33 Yoder families, 15 Gingerich families. Under such conditions the importance of a middle initial or even a nickname becomes crucial. To keep the mails straight the carrier must "read between the lines" on the addresses, keep a knowledge of relatives and family history, and keep a fair check on the location of the friends of the family. Family names occurring most frequently in the ministers' lists in Pennsylvania are Stoltzfus, Byler (or Beiler), Fisher, and Lapp; in Ohio,

Miller, Yoder, Troyer, and Hershberger; and in Indiana, Miller, Bontrager, Yoder, and Swartz.

It is an established principle that any subject which becomes important in a given society will have many words to differentiate between categories of meaning. The Eskimos have not one word for snow, but over thirty, which distinguish what kind of snow. The Trobriand Islanders who depend upon yams for their livelihood, have many words for yam, indicating precisely what kind of yam. In the little Amish community the subject of differentiation is persons. Nicknaming is common to all Amish settlements and speech develops means for differentiating between very similar names.

In a study of nicknames among the Amish, Maurice Mook states that "nicknaming runs rife, almost as an onomastic necessity, and it is easily obvious to all observers that the Amish employ more nicknames than their non-Amish neighbors . . . I feel free to aver that the incidence of Amish nicknames may exceed that for any other group for which we have an adequate knowledge of names." [9] Name differentiation is achieved by abbreviation, by using physical traits of the person, by individual preferences or habits, by a humorous happening, by the practice of matronymic and patronymic naming of children, by use of a middle initial and a unique enunciation of the first name and the initial, by occupation, and by place of residence. Solomon becomes Sol, and Benjamin becomes Ben. Chubby Jonas, Curly John, and Shorty Abner are indicative of physical traits. Applebutter John, Butter Abe, and Toothpick John derive from eating preferences and habits. Gravy Dan stuck with one Amishman when he poured gravy instead of cream into his coffee at a threshing dinner table. Nancy John and Nancy Jake are named after their mother's first name. Auctioneers at sales are careful to distinguish between Ben Z., Ike Z., or Sam Z., so there will be no confusion as to who is the purchaser. Jockey Joe is a horse trader, Chicken Elam operates a chicken farm, and Chickie Dan works for him.

[9] Maurice A. Mook, "Nicknames Among the Amish," *Mennonite Life* (July, 1961).

Gap Dave, Gap Elam, and Gap Joe live near a village named Gap. When my own family moved from Pennsylvania to Iowa my father was known as "Pennsylvania Joe" to distinguish him from other family heads with the same name. Peach Orchard Mike distinguished one Mike from others in Mifflin County. Nicknames are used in the speech community and seldom appear in writing.

## Unpretentious Knowledge

Like other societies, the Amish perpetuate a core of knowledge that is conducive to their survival. Knowledge is limited on the one hand by what may be imported from the outside, and on the other by taboos within the society. Two sources of knowledge are pertinent to the Amish: practical agrarian skills and a knowledge of Christianity as interpreted by the Amish. The preference for useful or practical knowledge, a feature the Amish have in common with many folk societies, contrasts sharply with the emphasis on speculative, abstract, or modern scientific knowledge. Book learning (also called chair-mindedness) is held in suspicion. How to plow a straight furrow is more important to the Amish boy than knowing the spatial relationships of geometry. Practical knowledge is acquired in the most effective way known to man, by an apprentice-like system that permits learning by informal participation in the rewards of work and in the goals of the society. What is believed to be of utmost importance, co-operation with other human beings and learning to like work, they acquire informally by working with others in the family and community and not by attending school. There is an unvarnished disinterest in theoretical questions.

The Bible, as understood and interpreted by the Amish people, is an important source of knowledge, for it forms a basis of tne ethic that compels them to live as they do. This ethic is transmitted by the family and the church, and reinforced in the ritual of community life. No successfully socialized Amish person seeks individuality or prominence by intellectual invention or discovery; rather he seeks the shared wisdom that comes from spiritual communion and identification with his brothers. Individuality tends toward high-mindedness, self-praise, and pride. High-mindedness is specifically forbidden in the Bible (II Tim. 3:4) and in the Amish context is associated with higher education. "Self-praise stinks," is a common Amish saying.

"The Amish," wrote one Amish leader, "are very much interested in teaching their children the three basic parts of learning: reading, writing, and arithmetic. We feel that they can develop their minds better by working with their parents and by experience, than from books and the influence that surroundings of a college education would give them. We do not despise those who are capable of going through college . . . as the world has need of people like these. We feel that anyone who is capable of making a decent living, helping his neighbors in need, raising a family that will be an asset to the community, and living at peace with God and his fellow men has attained about the most practical and best education there is to get. So, really, we do not disdain a good education. What worth is an education if we do not have peace with God? What is education worth to us if we can't control our children?" [10]

After the elementary grades the children are given work on the family farm. The emphasis on work as a form of discipline and as a means to preparation for adult life underlies all Amish thought: "Our people are engaged in some form of agriculture and we feel positive that as farmers we are better off with only a common school education. Education does not build muscle like tilling the soil in the open field and sunshine with lots of hard work. If a boy does little hard work before he is twenty-one, he probably never gets to like it afterward. In other words, he will not amount to much as a farmer." [11]

The Amish opposition to consolidation of schools and to high school attendance has become widely known in America (see Chapter 9). An Amish father who was summoned before

[10] Quoted in J. Martin Stroup, *The Amish of the Kishacoquillas Valley.* Mifflin County Historical Society, Lewistown, Pa., 1965.
[11] *Lancaster Intelligencer Journal* (February 19, 1931).

a court for violating the school attendance law said: "We teach our children not to smoke or use profane language and do such things as that. I know most of the high school pupils smoke cigarettes and many girls I guess too. . . . It is better to have them at home. . . ." [12]

The Amish do not want their children exposed to the "wisdom of the world," for they are repeatedly taught in the sermons that "the wisdom of the world is foolishness with God" (I Cor. 3:19). The "world" is educated, and to the Amishman "worldly education" leads to sinfulness and moral corruption. To the Amishman, the highest of all educated people are the scientists who have invented the theory of evolution and who have made bombs to destroy the world. Such ends are held to be contradictory to the teaching of the Bible.

The practice of limiting formal schooling and of not permitting the young to enter public high schools or colleges limits the amount of exposure to knowledge and reduces alternate courses of action.[13] The practice of disciplining members who do not abide by this rule, coupled with positive rewards for practical knowledge, are effective means of maintaining the boundaries of the society.

## Mutual Aid and Generosity

Intense interrelationship in the little homogeneous community makes members feel responsible for the welfare of each other. Although the aid is often a form of economic sharing, the feelings are the result of intense social concern. While the Amish do not practice complete "community of goods" as do their Anabaptist cousins, the Hutterites, they find many ways to come to the aid of each other within a capitalistic society.[14]

[12] Enos Mast in Thomas F. Lansberry et al., Record. Superior Court of Pennsylvania, Western District (April Term, 1949), 104a.

[13] Wilbert E. Moore and Melvin M. Tumin, "Some Social Functions of Ignorance," American Sociological Review (December, 1949), 787-95.

[14] Joseph Winfield Fretz, in his dissertation Mennonite Mutual Aid (University of Chicago, 1941), discusses the doctrine and practice of mutual aid among all Mennonite groups. Melvin Gingerich discusses "Amish Aid Plans" in detail in the Mennonite Encyclopedia, Vol. I, 89.

Perhaps the most dramatic form of mutual aid is the barn-raising. But there are many additional neighborly associations that result in exchange of services including sawing and cutting wood, erecting milk houses or remodeling buildings, painting, fencing, and butchering. Among the women there are quiltings, sewings, and house-cleaning activities. Baking, cleaning, and preparing both house and barn for the preaching service often evokes the help of neighbors or relatives. When the unexpected happens such as a death, an accident, or illness, the community comes to the rescue to take care of the farm chores, to harvest the crops, or to care for the children. The lending of money to the young farmer who is just getting started is often done without interest. When there is a fire, the Amish have their own system of insurance by assessing each household when needed. They avoid commercial insurance wherever possible.

Security is therefore assured to the Amish individual by the concern of the whole community. If a member is sick, in distress, or is incapacitated, the community knows about it. While the Scriptures admonish the believer to do good to all men, the Amish are especially serious about the advice with respect to their own "household of faith." [15] The care of the aged has never become a problem with the Amish. Old people retire on the farm. Many Amish farms have two household units, one for the grandparents and another for the young farming couple with children. The older people are often supplied with products from the farm and their needs remain simple.

We have now observed some of the ways in which the Amish community remains a multibonded social unit. Their charter, which is rooted in the Bible and in Anabaptism, outlines the ideology of the society and sets limits within which persons may express their behavior. The ecological community, the limited need for outside consumer goods, and the ceremonial integration are in keeping with the symbolic expectations. Tradition and experience tend to become highly symbolic in structural acts such as a shared style of dress, language, limited education, and mutual-aid practices. Still other

[15] Galatians 6:10.

shared relations could be discussed such as rural residence, occupational homogeneity, and the smallness of the population. The Amish are successful in repelling trends which character- ize the American rural community. Some of these trends are migration to the cities, consolidation of schools, greater de- pendence on government, urban recreation, general seculariza- tion, and urban associations. They have diverted these trends not only by the substitutionary forms of intense sharing but also by meeting the social needs of the individual. It is a society which provides for the symbolic needs of the people in a cradle-to-grave arrangement.

Without symbols, social sentiments could have only a pre- carious existence.[16] Emblems are necessary if a society is to become conscious of itself. They are indispensable for assuring the continuation of the group. Of course the Amish have no flag, motto, or totem pole, but they live by many emblems of the group. Their emblems are not rooted in the vegetable and animal world but in religious concepts expressed in specific ways of dressing and grooming. The emblem expresses the social unity in a material form. It clarifies the sentiment a society has of itself. Individual consciousness, if left alone, can have no real communion. Internal states can only be expressed by means of signs, words, gestures, or acts. It is only as the individual reacts to the community emblem that he informs himself of his own appearance or position. The signs expressing the common sentiments are themselves fused into a single bond of identification. It is this that informs individuals that they are in harmony and are conscious of their moral unity. Al- though the internal quality of community may be perceptible, as Max Weber has observed, the outward conspicuous differ- ences always emerge, and they often persist even after the community has disappeared. People are not born with homo- geneous mental states, but they become so as they come in contact with corresponding representations. The emblems of the group in the little Amish community are multiple. They are indispensable for the integration of the society.

---

[16] Emile Durkheim, *The Elementary Forms of Religious Life*, *op. cit.*, cited from "On Communal Ritual," in *Theories of Society*, 230-31; for Max Weber's observations see the same source, pages 305-9.

# CHAPTER 7

# THE FAMILY SYSTEM

No SOCIAL GROUP is more intimate, informal, and primary than the family. Infants are born into a family; they do not join a family. The family is a closed system in many respects, for in it the basic wishes and needs of its members are expressed. The home is the place where individual interests first collide with group interests. Here members of a family vacillate between their own will and those of others, a process which has been called antagonistic co-operation.[1] Procreation, protection, and training are accomplished in most societies in the family. Much could be related about the Amish family, but we shall examine only selected aspects dealing with function and form.

## Married-Pair Living

Family organization among the Amish has always been strictly monogamous and patriarchal rather than matriarchal. Over-all authority tends to belong to the father, with varying degrees of modification and application in specific families. Patriarchal authority is illustrated in many daily functions. A family of ten was seated about the table. When the husband took the pie, he cut one large piece for himself, one of a smaller size for his wife, and then divided the balance among the eight children. The illustration is not necessarily typical.

Co-operation between husband and wife prevails in differing degrees, depending somewhat on the make-up of the personalities and their adjustment. The line of authority is not rigid, however, as another example will indicate. A man and his wife called at the home of a neighbor to see a bed which was for

[1] William G. Sumner, *Folkways* (Ginn and Co., 1906), 345.

sale. He remained seated in the buggy while she entered the house and inspected the bed. Undecided, and not willing to commit herself without the encouragement of her husband, she called him. After both looked at the bed and pondered over the price, she said, "What do you think?" He replied, "You are the boss of the house." After a few gestures which indicated that she approved of the purchase, he wrote out a check for the amount.

The wife is often consulted when family problems arise, and she exercises her powers in rearing children, but her husband's word is regarded as final in domestic matters. This conforms to the biblical standard: "The head of the woman is the man."[2] God created woman as a helper for man; she is her husband's helper but not his equal. An Amish woman knows what is expected of her in the home, and her attitude is normally one of willing submission. This is not suggesting that there are no exceptions, for the writer has known families where the wife exerts influence out of proportion to the usual pattern. In real practice, the farm is the Amishman's kingdom, and his wife is his general manager of household affairs.

Property, whether household goods or farm equipment, is spoken of as "ours" within the family. In actuality, however, any transaction involving the sale or purchase of property is made through the husband, or has his approval. Farms are usually owned jointly by husband and wife to insure legal ownership in case of the death of the husband. In public affairs men are regarded as more fit for leadership than women. Banking, writing checks, and depositing money are the business of the husband. Women as well as men bid for household items at public sales. The experienced housewife generally has the authority to make decisions pertaining to the house, but husband and wife usually confer with each other before making any large purchases, and the considerate husband will consult his wife before purchasing any household item. The wife generally has a purse of her own which is replenished periodically by her husband for the purchase of household supplies, gro-

[2] I Corinthians 11:3.

ceries, and clothing. When her supply of money is exhausted, she asks for more.

Major household expenses or anticipated medical expenditures are usually discussed mutually, and if the wife decides she would like to patronize a certain doctor, her husband is likely to consent. The husband, on the other hand, may purchase farm equipment or livestock without seeking the advice of his wife. The wife sometimes may keep the income from eggs sold.

The extent to which the farmer aids his wife in household tasks is nominal. Of course, he helps on special occasions such as butchering and cooking apple butter, but does not help in the routine preparation of food or washing dishes. At weddings, the men serve as cooks and table waiters with their wives. Guests at an Amish table are often addressed by the husband: "Now just reach and help yourselves."

The wife's duties include care of the children, cooking and cleaning, preparation of produce for market, making clothes for the family, preserving food, and gardening. Women and adolescent girls frequently help with the harvest of crops, especially cornhusking. In one family each of the older girls manages a team of horses during the summer months. They plow the fields, cultivate the soil, and do the work of adult males. This is exceptional, however, since women are not generally called upon to help with the heavier jobs in farming. It is the woman who sees that the fences, posts, grape arbors, and frequently the trees about the farm buildings are whitewashed in the spring. The appearance of the lawn and the area surrounding the house is largely the responsibility of the wife, and she feels obligated to keep the inside as well as the outside clean and neat in appearance.

The wife aids the husband in work not usually considered household tasks more than the husband helps his wife in household work. While the men and carpenters were remodeling the barn, in anticipation of the oldest son's marriage, the mother of one home arranged to have neighbor women and relatives come for a day to paint the barn's window sashes.

Gardening, except perhaps for the initial spading in the

spring, is the sole responsibility of the wife. The Amish housewife usually has a large variety of edibles, with as many as
twenty-two kinds of vegetables. She makes sure that there are
plenty of cucumbers and red beets, because they are part of
the standard lunch at Sunday services. Typical Amish gardens
abound with flowers. One garden had twenty-four varieties.
Order and cleanliness tend to be distinctive features of Amish
gardening. Orchards are a part of the typical Amish landscape,
and spraying, if done at all, is the man's job. More often than
not fruits are purchased from commercial sources, because expensive equipment for spraying is considered too costly for
a small orchard.

Food processing consumes a large part of the wife's time.
In summer she preserves fruits and vegetables and in winter,
various kinds of meats. One housewife estimated that she had
a thousand quarts of canned goods in the cellar at the end
of the summer. The frozen-food locker establishment in a
nearby village is also used for preserving meats, fruits, and
vegetables. Meat curing is done by the husband, often at the
suggestion and according to the plans of the wife.

With regard to the woman's role in religious services the
teaching of the Apostle Paul is literally obeyed: "Let the
woman learn in silence with all subjection." In leadership activities, the woman is not "to usurp authority over the man."
At baptismal service, boys are baptized before girls. Women
never serve as church officials, but women as well as men
participate in the *Rat* (counsel) of the church.

Voting in state and national elections, which was more widespread among the Amish in the past than at present, is done
by men but rarely by the women.

The Amish woman's role is well defined, circumscribed by
duties involving home and family. The man, as husband and
father, is expected to assume the leadership role.

## Personal Relationships

Personal relationships between husband and wife are quiet
and sober, with no apparent demonstration of affection. The

relationship is strikingly different from the way sentiments are indicated and affection expressed in American society. Patterns of conversation vary among Amish mates, but terms of endearment, or gestures which would indicate any overt expression of affection, are conspicuously absent.

The husband may address his wife by her given name, or by no name at all. He may merely begin talking to her if he wants her attention. In speaking about his wife to others he may use "she," or "my wife," but rarely her given name. The mother of the family in like manner may refer to him simply as "my husband" or "he."

Irritation between mates is expressed in a variety of ways, but is conditioned by informally approved means of expressing dissatisfaction. As a rule institutional patterns outweigh personal considerations. Little irritation is observable among the Amish. Displeasure or disapproval is expressed by the tone of voice, by gesture, or by direct statement. The husband may express disapproval by complete silence at the dinner table and the wife is left to guess what is wrong. The usual conversation may lag for several days before it is completely restored to a normal level. Harsh and boisterous talk between mates occurs infrequently and then is known to be manifest only by more or less maladjusted partners.

The bond between husband and wife tends to be one of respect rather than personal attraction based on romantic love. The role of the parents is defined in terms of traditional familial patterns, and this relationship is to some degree controlled by kinship ties. The husband and wife are not individuals connected only by personal sentiments, but they are members of a group who must maintain the standards and dignity of that group. This tendency toward the consanguineal system compares favorably to the findings of Thomas and Znaniecki in their discussion of the Polish peasant family in which they say, ". . . the marriage norm is not love, but 'respect.' . . ." They explain further the meaning of this respect: "The norm of respect from wife to husband includes obedience, fidelity, care for the husband's comfort and health;

from husband to wife, good treatment, fidelity, not letting the wife do hired work if it is not indispensable. In general, neither husband nor wife ought to do anything which could lower the social standing of the other, since this would lead to a lowering of the social standing of the other's family. Affection is not explicitly included in the norm of respect, but is desirable. As to sexual love, it is a purely personal matter, is not and ought not to be socialized in any form; the family purposely ignores it, and the slightest indecency or indiscreetness with regard to sexual relations in marriage is viewed with disgust and is morally condemned." [3]

The Polish pattern of marital relationships compares very favorably with the Amish. The Amish are in addition very conscious of the biblical pattern: "Wives, submit yourselves unto your own husband, as unto the Lord . . . So ought men to love their wives as their own bodies . . . and the wife see that she reverence her husband." [4]

## Children and Growing Up

Amish children appear innocent and unspoiled by the things of this world. The birth of a child brings joy to the family and community, for there will be another dishwasher or wood chopper, and another church member. Thus children are wanted. At no time in the Amish system are they unwelcome, for they are regarded as "An heritage of the Lord."

The first two years of life are undoubtedly the happiest. Baby obtains what he wants. He is given permissive care with great amounts of love from mother, father, brothers, sisters, aunts, uncles, grandfathers, grandmothers, and cousins.

After about the second year, restrictions and exacting disciplines are continuously imposed upon the child until well into adolescence. He must be taught to respect the authority of his parents and to respond properly to their exactness. The

[3] William I. Thomas and Florian Znaniecki, *The Polish Peasant in Europe and America* (Knopf, 1927), Vol. I, 90.
[4] Ephesians 5:22, 28, 33.

child is considered sinless since he does not know the difference between right and wrong. It is the duty of parents to teach him this difference, so that he will realize his moral inadequacy and choose the "right way" of the Amish religion.

The Amish home is an effective socializing agent, directed at making the child a mature person in the Amish way of life. Early in life the child learns that Amish are "different" from other people. Thus, he must learn to understand not only how to play the role at home and in the Amish system, but also how to conduct himself in relation to the norms of his "English" neighbors.

He cannot have clothes and toys just like the "English" people have. He soon learns to imitate his parents, to take pride in the "difference," and appears no longer to ask "why" until adolescence.

The Amish boy or girl is raised so carefully within the Amish family and community that he never feels secure outside it. The faces of many Amish boys and girls reflect pure intent, a sincere, honest, cordial, and well-bred disposition. The extraordinary love and discipline they get prepares them well for Amish womanhood and manhood.

Each family is expected to transmit to the child a reading knowledge of German. This is done traditionally on Sunday, alternating with the preaching service. The family members gather about the sitting-room table, and each having a German Testament, take their turn spelling, enunciating the alphabet, and reading. In some families, this program is carried on daily in connection with the family worship. Even preschool children, ages four and five, take their turn by repeating words or syllables as they are pronounced by the family head.

Amish children do not receive regular allowances from their parents. A young person who works a day or half day for a neighbor is often permitted to keep the earnings, but is expected not to spend them. When parents take their children to town they may be given a small sum for buying candy. Early in life parents may provide a bank in which to save pennies. The necessity of taking good care of one's clothing and other personal items is strongly emphasized to the child.

Teaching the child to work and to accept responsibility is considered of utmost importance. The child begins to assist his parents at the age of four and is given limited responsibility at the age of six. The boy learns to feed the chickens, gather eggs, feed the calf, and drive the horses. The girl is trained to perform small jobs for her mother and to learn early the art of cooking and housekeeping. Some parents give a pig, sheep, or calf to the child with the stipulation that he tend the animal and take care of it. In this way the child is motivated to take an interest in the farm.

The role of the child and the work performed by each is well illustrated in a family of six children, five boys and one girl. Five are old enough to perform certain tasks. Their ages are: 22, 17, 15, (girl) 12, 8, and 3. The two oldest boys, ages 22 and 17, and the father, carry on the farming operations and field work. The 15-year-old boy, who is still in puberty, and though regarded capable of doing a full day's work, performs the lighter tasks about the barn. The girl, aged 12, and a boy 8 attend public school, and the youngest, a three-year-old, is in the age of curiosity.

The girl enjoys helping her mother with the household duties, especially setting the table and preparing meals. She and her younger brother help their mother with the garden. When the time comes to do the chores, each has his specific assignment, but their duties also overlap. The four oldest children and the father milk 15 cows regularly. The oldest son feeds and beds the horses, hogs, and calves. The second feeds the laying hens, and the third tends the pullets on range and carries wood for his mother. The girl milks three cows, feeds the rabbits, and gathers the eggs. The eight-year-old boy has no regular work assignment but assists his mother or one of the older members of the family. The two older sons frequently help on washday with the heavier tasks such as carrying water. The third son has a decided dislike for house work.

In the Amish family, sons who reach the age of 21 are paid monthly wages if they are unmarried and continue to work at home. A young man may hire out for the summer, but this practice has almost completely disappeared among the Amish who farm with tractors. Farmers who need assistance frequently request help from a neighbor or a relative for a few days. Single girls occasionally work as maids in local villages but more frequently assist in another Amish home. A *Maut* (maid) among the Amish enjoys the same privileges as other members of the family.

The solidarity of the family and its ability to act as a unit in an emergency is illustrated by the co-operation at occasions when the livestock breaks out. Charles P. Loomis, who worked at an Amish place as a farm hand, describes such an incident. As they were seated at the supper table: "Mattie got up to get some milk and saw that the cows were getting through the gate. She screamed and the whole family dashed to the door. Mother hurriedly put the baby into the carriage. We ran after the 22 cows. The big family encircled them, one girl having run over a mile on plowed ground. We got them back in. They had not been out this spring and were wild. Mother said she has read in books about stampedes in the west. Chris and I put them back in their stanchions after supper. He fed them grain first, but still we had a job. He said, 'They're out of practice. When they get to going to the meadow each day they will do better.' " [5]

From the discussion this far, it will be seen that the relations among family members have many economic functions concerned with production. In this respect the Amish family is like the rural-farm type in America, but unlike the urban family.

Masculine dominance is evident in brother-sister relationships. The father and boys sit down first at the table while the mother and girls bring on the food. At a family ice-cream supper the boys went to the cellar to refill the big dish with ice cream, and, upon returning, they helped themselves first before passing the dish.

Strict obedience to parents is a profound teaching stressed

[5] Charles P. Loomis, "Farm Hand's Diary" (unpublished, 1940).

over and over by Amish parents and by the preachers, a principle based upon several passages in the Bible. An Amish lad who runs away from home, or even an adult who leaves the Amish church, is held guilty of disobedience to his parents.

Amish children manifest resentments as do all children, by pouting, or by negative responses. But when these manifestations are overt, "smackings" are sure to follow either with the palm of the hand, a switch, a razor strop, or a buggy whip. Temper tantrums, making faces, name calling, and sauciness among youngsters are extremely rare, as the child learns early that his reward for such rebellion is a sound threshing.

Disputes between boys are perhaps as frequent in Amish as in non-Amish families. The manner of expressing dissatisfaction is mostly verbal, especially among youngsters, but broken noses do occur. Profanity is not permitted, and if discovered by the parents, is usually promptly treated with punishment. Resentment toward a brother or sister is expressed rather mildly in the presence of older persons. In the presence of parents, a quarrel may be expressed to a chum by silence, hesitancy, or by completely ignoring the situation.

The subject of sex in Amish life is regarded as a purely personal matter. Adults purposely ignore any mention of the subject, especially in the presence of children. Very little sex instruction is given to the ordinary Amish child. In spite of this suppression the child acquires gradually, piece by piece, an elementary knowledge of the process of biological reproduction. Perhaps not until he arrives at the age of marriage does he have a fair knowledge of the subject.

The Amish child most certainly does ask questions about the sexual behavior of animals on the farm. To satisfy his curiosity, the child more often than not talks such matters over with associates of his own age. The jokes of young men show that sexual interests are developed before marriage and long before courtship. Any remark about sex in private conversation between a boy and girl of courting age is inopportune, but an indecent joke is not uncommon among a group of men.

## Mate-Finding

The young Amishman's choice of a wife has several limitations conditioned by his value system. He must obtain a partner from his own Amish faith, but not necessarily from his own community. Because of minimum contact with Amish young people of other communities and states, marriage in the large settlements has been limited largely to the immediate community. The choice of a mate is also governed by core values. First-cousin marriages are taboo while second-cousin marriages are discouraged but infrequently do occur.

The rule that marriage must be endogenous with respect to group affiliation has certain exceptions. It is always permissible to marry into a more orthodox affiliation if the nonmember joins the more conservative group. Young people intermarry freely among Amish districts and settlements which maintain fellowship with one another. It is impossible without serious consequences to leave a church and join a more progressive one through marriage. This act would bring *Meidung* upon oneself in a strict group.

The occasion which provides best contact for young people is the Sunday-evening singing. The singing is usually held at the same house where the preaching was held. The youth from several districts usually combine for the singing. This occasion provides interaction among young people on a much broader base than in the single district.

On Sunday evening after the chores are done, the young folks make preparations for the singing. The young man puts on his very best attire, brushes his hat and suit, and makes sure that his horse and buggy are clean and neat in appearance. He may take his sister or his sister's friend to the singing, but seldom his own girl friend. If he does take his own girl, he will arrange to pick her up about dusk at the end of a lane or at a crossroad. In Lancaster County, Pennsylvania, the young people meet in villages to pair off, but this is not customary in other settlements.

A singing is not regarded as a devotional meeting. Young people gather around a long table, boys on one side and girls on the other. The singing is conducted entirely by the unmarried. Only the fast tunes are used. Girls as well as boys announce hymns and lead the singing. Between selections there is time for conversation. After the singing, which usually dismisses formally about ten o'clock, an hour or more is spent in joking and visiting. Those boys who do not have a date usually arrange for a *Mädel* (girl) at this time.

Although there are other occasions when young folks get together, such as husking bees, weddings, and frolics, the singing is the regular medium for boy-girl association. Both the boy and the girl look upon each other as possible mates. Social activity is naturally arranged with marriage in view. A boy or girl may "quit" whenever they please, but limited selection also limits variation. The usual age for courtship, called *rumspringa* (running around), begins for the boy at sixteen, and for the girl at fourteen to sixteen. Secrecy pervades the entire period of courtship and is seldom relaxed regardless of its length. If a boy is charged with having a girl friend he will certainly be very slow to admit it. Courting that cannot be successfully disguised becomes a subject for teasing by all members of the family.

In one home a girl's handbag was found by the children in the farm hand's buggy. It had been forgotten and left there by the boy's girl friend, and it became the subject of much laughter and joking. The maid in this home said, "That's as bad as I. Once, I left a tablecloth in his [meaning her escort's] buggy."

Among themselves, young people seldom refer to their boy or girl friends by first name. The pronoun "he" or "she" is used instead. The terms "beau" and "*Kal*" (fellow) are used in general conversation. The term "dating" is used, but has no dialect equivalent.

Besides taking his girl home after the singing on Sunday evening, the young man who has a "steady" girl will see her fortnightly on Saturday evening. When Saturday evening comes, he dresses in his best; he makes little ado about his departure and attempts to leave the impression that he is going to town on business.

Before entering the home of his girl he makes sure that the "old folks" are in bed. Standard equipment for every young Amishman of courting age is a good flashlight. With his light focused on her window, the girl has the signal that her boy friend has arrived; she quietly goes downstairs to let him in. The couple may be together until the early morning hours in the home on such occasions.

Courting normally takes place in the kitchen or sitting room. The Amish feel that it is none of the "outsider's" business how their courting is conducted. The clatter of horses' hoofs on hard-surface roads is evidence of lovers returning home in the early hours of the morning.

The old way of spending the time together was for a boy and girl to lie on the bed without undressing. The Amish have no uniform word in their speech for this practice, which to them, in earlier times was very ordinary. *Bei-schlof* (or with sleep) is a usage in one area. In English this behavior pattern is known as bundling, but the modern American society does not approve of this practice. It is little wonder that Amish persons in the most "nativistic" settlements, who are sometimes asked whether they bundle, do not know the meaning of "bundling." There seems to be a tendency for this form of courting to disappear among the Amish as their communities change, but it still prevails in some districts. Unfortunately the subject has been exploited by pamphleteers and story writers. The practice has been sharply condemned by some Amish ordained men and defended by others as something almost sacred.[6] Already in the nineteenth century new settlements had been started by those families who wanted to get away from the practice. Those communities that have assimilated most to the American society have felt the depre-

---

[6] Reported in *Eine schädliche Ubung* (n.p., 1929). Other tracts are: D. J. Stutzman, *A Call to Repentance* (Millersburg, Ohio, n.d.), and *Our Youths, A Collection of Letters Pertaining to the Conditions Among our Youths, The Amish Mennonites* (Lynnhaven, Va., n.d.).

ciating attitude of outsiders and tend thus to oppose the practice of bundling. Those which have retained their traditional culture most consistently have been least opposed. The practice has disappeared without argument in other areas with the influx of modern home conveniences (living-room suites, etc.), and with a wider range of social contact with the outside world.

Premarital relations are disapproved of and condemned by the church. Transgressors are expelled from the church and shunned for a period of several weeks or until reinstatement, which requires a statement of confession before the church assembly. Violation of the rule of chastity is hardly regarded worse than other faults—at least the moral stigma does not remain with the individual as it often does in the great society. Finding a mate takes place in the confines of the little community, rather than outside it. Conflict and casualties resulting from mismating are absorbed by the culture. Conflicts appear less obvious than in the great society. The wedding is a climactic experience for family and community and the families of both bride and bridegroom take an active part in helping the newlyweds to establish a home.

It is an important task of the family to provide a dowry. Homemade objects and crafts play an important part in the family. Furthermore, it is understood that each person invited to a wedding brings a gift for the new couple. These tokens of friendship, which are usually displayed on the bed in an upstairs bedroom, consist of dishes, kerosene lamps, bedspreads, blankets, tablecloths, towels, clocks, handkerchiefs, and small farm tools.

The parents of the bride and bridegroom also provide furniture, livestock, and sometimes basic equipment when the couple moves into their home. For instance, one bridegroom, an only son, had the farm deeded over to him together with the farm machinery and livestock. The bride received from her parents a cow, tables, chairs, a new stove, dishes, bedding, and many other items. The dowry of the bride was in this case not unusual. All mothers by tradition make a few quilts and comforters for each child. These are usually made years in advance so they will be ready when needed. One housewife made three quilts and two comforters for each child; she had seven boys and three girls.

## The Mature Years

Respect for the aged, already obvious among youth, is even more pronounced with regard to mature Amish people. The individual never outgrows the command to obey his parents. The command is binding not until parents die, but even after they are gone. All age groups in both sexes revere parents, grandparents, and great-grandparents. The duty to obey one's parents is one of the main themes in Amish preaching. Perhaps the verse most often repeated on this point is one of the Ten Commandments: "Honor thy father and thy mother, that thy days may be long upon the land which the Lord thy God giveth thee." [7]

Not only is there respect for the aged, but authority is vested in the old people. This arrangement naturally lends itself to increased control of life by the aged. Preservation of the religious ideals and mores is thereby insured, and the younger people who are inclined to introduce change can be held in check.

A strong consciousness of kinship is peculiarly favorable to gerontocracy, or social control by the older members of society. As in the ideal type of the little community, this control is informal rather than formal or obvious, but nevertheless, "closer to us than breathing, nearer than hands or feet." [8] The part which old people have "in drawing forth and molding the character and life-policy of every younger person in the kinship group makes the necessity for direct control much less frequent in isolated culture than in more accessible communities." [9] The relatively integrated community is associated with effective rules imposed by the aged, be they parents or

[7] Exodus 20:12; also Ephesians 6:1 and Colossians 3:20.
[8] Howard Becker and Harry Elmer Barnes, *Social Thought from Lore to Science* (Dover, 1961), 11.
[9] *Ibid.*

church leaders. Thus deference to age pervades not only familial relationships, but also the religious leadership of the group. Furthermore, the counsel of the older bishop or minister carries more authority than that of younger ones.

The Amish farm typically contains two dwellings, one of which is the *Grossdaadi Haus* that houses the grandparents. At retirement the older couple moves into this house and a married son or daughter falls heir to the farm responsibility. The grandparents may retain some type of control of the farm until the couple demonstrates its ability to manage the farm. The grandparents have not only a separate household unit, but a horse and buggy of their own. Instead of dual houses, many farm dwellings are large enough to accommodate two separate household operations. When there are no grandparents to occupy these quarters, they are sometimes rented to other Amish people, or occupied by the hired man and his wife.

Some of the Amish who retire in or near a small village will erect a small barn beside their dwelling so that they can feed and maintain a horse. Those families living in town do not take their turn for the preaching service, as facilities are not adequate to accommodate 80 to 120 people and from 25 to 30 horses. Instead, they may ask another family to take the service while supplying food and costs.

By the time they are 60, most Amish have accumulated enough wealth for a satisfactory retirement. Traditionally, no Amish accepts old age assistance or public assistance of any kind. Neither do Amish take any life insurance. Needy older persons are aided by relatives. Should close relatives be incompetent or unwilling, the church will come to their assistance.

The retirement of father and mother from active life on the farm stabilizes the social organization of the entire Amish community. While the young man is free to make his own decisions, the very presence of the parents on the farm influences the life of the younger generation. The young couple is not obligated to carry out the wishes of the parents, yet an advisory relationship stimulates not only economic stability but also religious integrity. The Labrador Eskimos, for example, regarded the words of their aged as final, believing that the old contain the wisdom of the ancestors. The Iroquois Indians reverenced the aged, in spite of the fact that the old were often helpless. The Kwakiutl made their old men masters of ceremonies at public gatherings. The Dahomeans respected both aged men and women because of their close affinity to the ancestral dead.[10]

The Amish consider their practice as merely a continuation of the old Hebrew attitude. For them, the Hebrew system provides a rational explanation. "The hoary head is a crown of glory . . . the beauty of the old men is the hoary head. A wise son heareth his father's instruction. Hearken unto thy father that begat thee, and despise not thy mother when she is old. Thou shalt rise up before the hoary head, and honor the face of the old man. . . . Honor thy father and thy mother, . . . and he that smiteth his father, or his mother, shall be surely put to death. I said days shall speak and a multitude of years shall teach wisdom."[11]

One cross-cultural study of the aged in seventy-one widely different societies concludes that: ". . . when conditions called for respect to the aged they got it; when these conditions changed, they might lose it."[12] The respect for the aged in Amish life seems to be connected with the permanence of residence, and a conservative attitude stemming from a religious concept. Respect for the aged is thus consistent with the social and cultural behavior patterns in the little Amish community.

### Recreation and Leisure

Recreation and leisure are informal and also related to work; they are not entered into as pursuits in themselves. Spending

[10] Leo W. Simmons, *The Role of the Aged in Primitive Society* (Yale University Press, 1945), 51–61.

[11] The quotations are from Proverbs 16:3; 20:39; 13:1; 23:22; Leviticus 19:32; Exodus 20:12; 21:15; and Job 32:7.

[12] Simmons, *op. cit.*, 50.

money for recreation is taboo. Nonetheless, there are certain games which Amish children and young people play. Clapping hands is a common form of indoor play among adolescent girls and is frequently played at informal family visits. They call it "botching." There are several ways of playing the game. Two people, seated on chairs and facing each other, clap the palms of their hands together alternately, then alternately strike each others lap until there is a decided loud clap. The feet may be used to keep proper timing. If the couple is efficient, a vigorous contest will ensue to see who can go the fastest. These clappings are sometimes played to the tune of "Darling Nelly Gray" or "Pop Goes the Weasel." For children, homemade rather than store-bought toys are allowed.

Visiting the relatives, the older members of the community, and the sick, and attending weddings in the fall occupy much of the leisure-time of the Amish members. Easter and Pentecost, observed not only on Sunday but on Monday as well, provide long weekend occasions for visiting. In large settlements where distances are as long as forty miles, a family may start early on a Sunday morning and attend church in a neighboring district. They will drive still further in the afternoon, stop for Sunday-evening supper with a family, and continue their journey after supper until they reach their destination. On Monday they may start for the trek homeward, visiting three or more families on the way.

Weekly auction sales and household auctions are a common form of pastime for many family members. For some boys and men, hunting is a favorite sport in season. Softball is rarely played on Sunday. Young people of courtship age play ball on special weekday holidays such as Ascension Day or Easter Monday. Hiking is a common pastime among boys.

The use of tobacco can be classed as another form of pastime. Its use varies from one area to another and with *Ordnung*. Many districts have officially discouraged its use and will excommunicate a persistent smoker, but conservative groups have tended to have little or no scruples against its use. Among Lancaster County Amish who themselves raise tobacco as a cash crop, single and married men, including preachers, use it. There is no effort on the part of the young people to conceal smoking in those districts where it is permitted. Where forbidden, it is often done secretly. Older men appear to have more "right" to chew or smoke than young men. The use of cigarettes is largely taboo, while pipe and cigar smoking is the accepted practice. Modern lighters are used by some. Older informants among the very orthodox Amish say that as far back as they can remember the people have used tobacco.[13] It was formerly common for women to smoke a pipe and a few of them still do, but this is not done openly.

The scope of reading material in the Amish home varies considerably, depending on the leadership of the home as well as the particular church group. Devotional readings such as children's Bible storybooks, in addition to English and German Bibles, the *Martyrs Mirror*, prayer books, and perhaps the writings of Menno Simons, may be found in homes. Some homes also subscribe to Mennonite periodicals, but most of the Old Order do not. The *Herold der Wahrheit*, officially sponsored by the Old Order Amish and the Conservative Amish Mennonite bodies, does not have wide acceptance. Many subscribe to a village paper and a few to daily papers. Farm magazines are common. Most homes receive *The Budget*, the standard weekly newspaper of the Amish. In addition to news items, this paper sometimes carries opinions and discussions on current items of concern to the Amish.

## Ceremony and Existence

Ceremony in Amish life is largely a function of the congregation or district rather than the household. According to older Amish informants, the only religious rite observed as a family group in bygone days was silent prayer before and

[13] Further observations are given in the following: John Umble, "Amish Mennonites of Union County," *M.Q.R.* (April, 1933); "Tobacco," *Mennonite Encyclopedia*, Vol. IV, 732; and J. W. Fretz, "The Growth and Use of Tobacco Among Mennonites," *Proceedings of the Seventh Annual Conference on Mennonite Cultural Problems* (1949), 87–100.

after meals. Bedtime prayers were repeated silently in bed. This is the traditional pattern still practiced by the most orthodox clans. Some families kneel together before retiring while the father reads a prayer from the prayer book. Rarely is there a spontaneous audible prayer, except in those families which have been more exposed to influences of fundamentalistic sects.

The Amish have retained some of the ceremonial practices of the Reformation, such as the use of prayer formularies and prayer books, silent prayer, and Luther's German translation of the Bible, while the Mennonites, who have borrowed much from American Protestantism, have completely dropped the use of printed prayers.

At meal time each member at the table repeats silently his own prayer. Children, upon reaching the age of puberty or earlier, are taught to say their own prayers. These prayers are memorized, in German of course, and they may consist of the Lord's Prayer or a prayer of about the same length taken from a prayer book. The following are examples of Amish table prayers with translations supplied.

### Gebet Vor Dem Essen

O Herr Gott, himmlischer Vater, Segne uns und Diese Deine Gaben, die wir von Deiner milden Güte Zu uns nehmen werden. Speise und tränke auch unsere Seelen zum ewigen Leben, und mach uns theilhaftig Deines himmlischen Tisches durch Jesus Christum. Amen. Unser Vater, etc.

### Prayer Before Meal

O Lord God, heavenly Father, bless us and these thy gifts, which we shall accept from thy tender goodness. Give us food and drink also for our souls unto life eternal, and make us partakers of thy heavenly table through Jesus Christ. Amen. Our Father, etc. [Lord's Prayer is repeated].

### Gebet Nach Dem Essen

O Herr, wir sagen Dir Lob und Dank für Deine heilige Speis und Trank, für Deine vielfaltige grosse Gnaden und Gutheiten; Herr, der Du labest und regierest, ein wahrer Gott bis in Ewigkeit. Amen. Unser Vater, etc.

PRAYER AFTER MEAL
O Lord, we give praise and thanks for your sacred food and drink, for your manifold great grace and goodness; Thou who livest and reignest, a true God till eternity. Amen. Our Father, etc. [The Lord's Prayer].

In the Amish home, the "place at the table" becomes symbolic of belonging. When this place is vacated by death, by marriage, by sickness, or by father having gone to town, or by the discipline of the ban, it becomes a subject of deep awareness and concern. The seating is traditionally arranged with father at the end of the table, the boys to his right from youngest to the oldest. Mother is seated just to the left or right of father with the girls on her side of the table. The diagram below shows the arrangement of a typical family, accommodating father, mother, and the children, with ages, before the marriage of any of the children.

The family table becomes the scene for the evaluation of

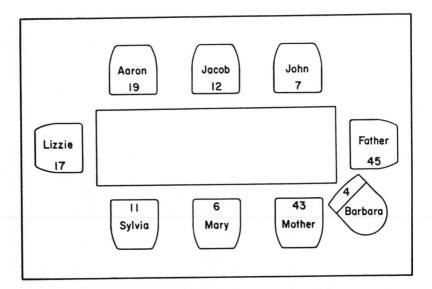

*Figure 11.* Diagram of Seating Arrangement at the Family Table.

behavior, for expressing personal likes and dislikes before the group, and for decision-making. Conversation is not encouraged for its own sake. Conversation at breakfast is typically about the work that needs to be done, how and who should do it, and division of work for the day. The mother may indicate that certain decisions need to be made relative to preparing the brooder house for the chicks, or about the apples that need to be picked. The father may delegate this responsibility to one of the sons, to be done after school or when there is time. The absence of the school-age children at noon makes possible a more intimate conversation. A progress report on the work accomplished thus far is often the topic of conversation. Father and mother may evaluate the products of a salesman who called during the morning hours. In the evening the entire family is gathered about the table. Silence during this meal is often interrupted with an occasional belch, a question from a child, or the bark of a dog.

The Amish family eats well and generally has an abundance of foods. The standard breakfast in Mifflin County includes eggs, fried cornmeal mush, liverwurst, cooked cereal, and often fried potatoes. There is no meal without bread, butter, and apple butter. The usual diet is rich in fats and carbohydrates, consisting of potatoes, gravy, fried foods, and pastries.

Food in variety as well as in quantity is not lacking on Amish tables when relatives, friends, or threshing crews are entertained. The following menu was served to relatives for Sunday dinner, arranged in the approximate order in which the foods were eaten: bread and butter, grape jelly, apple butter, mashed potatoes, gravy, fried ham, macaroni, baked beans, coffee, cole slaw, pickles, pickled melon, sliced tomatoes, cracker pudding, peaches, angel food cake, English walnut pie, and half-moon pies.

Young couples who have just begun housekeeping frequently find it difficult to compete with the older, established families in serving meals. Their resources demand that they be stringent in spending. As an example, the following menu was served to a threshing crew: bread and butter, jam, mashed potatoes, scalloped corn, fried hamburger, cold ham, cabbage slaw, cheese, cracker pudding, cherries, and raspberry pie.

Some wives are considered better cooks than others. A wife may gain prestige by having more variety on the table than other women. Generally speaking, every Amish woman takes pride in her cooking, and Amish cooking in contrast to "English" cooking is considered superior. Amish women at Belleville, Pennsylvania, were asked to contribute a substantial number of recipes to the cookbook published by the Ladies' Aid Society of the Presbyterian Church at Belleville.[14] One Amish lady remarked about a relative who "married English": "I just bet he gets awful hungry for some good Amish cooking."

The outdoor bake oven is still being used in some Amish homes. It is preferred for drying fruits and vegetables and also for baking great quantities of pies and bread for the preaching service. Furthermore, field corn is dried and browned in the oven before it is ground into cornmeal. Amish cooks prefer winter wheat for making pies and pastries and spring wheat for baking bread. Ground cereals—cornmeal, wheat hearts, and whole wheat flour—are used extensively. These products are frequently processed and sold locally by the village mill or store.

The Amish home is the center of life and place of belonging for all the family members. Home is a place of security. It is a center for decision-making with respect to work, play, and exposure to the wider community and to the outside world.

[14] *Kishacoquillas Valley Cook Book* (Belleville, Pa., 1950), 216. The well-known *Mennonite Community Cookbook* (Winston, 1950), compiled by Mary Emma Showalter, also includes many recipes contributed by Amish women. *Favorite Amish Family Recipes* was compiled by an Old Order Amish couple, Joseph N. and Sylvia Peachey, of Belleville, Pa., and published by Pathway Publishing Corporation, Aylmer, Ontario, in 1965. A short documentary film, "Bread Baking in a Rural Household" (16mm. silent; 13 minutes), produced in 1965 by The Pennsylvania State University, shows the traditional method of dissolving the yeast and baking bread in a wood-fired oven.

# CHAPTER 8

# THE LIFE CEREMONIES

THE THREE MAJOR RITES of passage, or *Les rites de passage* as conceived by Arnold van Gennep, center around birth, death, and marriage. The general purpose of the rites of passage is to mollify changes of state, which Gennep says ". . . are not accomplished without troubling social and individual life, and it is the purpose of a certain number of rites of passage to check their noxious effects." [1] Death, for example, marks a state of change for the individual which is acknowledged by propitiation ceremonies. Ordination to office in many societies is associated with ceremonies that admit the ordained to exercise authority with divine approval. The ceremony of marriage admits the individual to the privileges of sex experience, procreation, and family responsibility. The ceremony gives social sanction to the new social status of the individuals involved. We shall examine the nature of the ceremony, the significance of the absence or presence of such rites of passage in Amish life, the relation of life ceremony to community experience, and the effect of the "real and awesome" dimension of ceremony on the individual.

## Birth

In many small societies ceremony associated with birth is extensive and complex, but in Amish society such activity is nonexistent. Some folk beliefs about pregnancy and birth can be found, but there are neither sacred nor kinship ceremonies

[1] Arnold van Gennep, "On the Rites of Passage," in *Theories of Society*, Talcott Parsons *et al.*, eds. (Free Press of Glencoe, 1961), Vol. II, 950.

centering around the birth of an Amish child. The addition of children in the society is not "troubling" in any way, and their coming is not an economic burden, but is normal and congruous with the charter of family expectation. With the exception of the first child, birth normally takes place in the home in the supporting presence of the father. Children are wanted, and they are well cared for in Amish society. Birth is regarded as fortunate rather than unfortunate. No social ceremony is needed to "check any noxious effects," because there are none.

Secular ritual such as baby showers, with their consumptive function, have no place in the unassimilated Amish family. Infants are dressed functionally, as are adults, and they are not lauded with fancy or expensive clothing or equipment.

The social-psychological factors of a high fertility rate in Amish society are similar to those among the Hutterites, for whom a generally high level of reproduction has been found.[2] The charter places a positive value on having children and birth control is regarded as sinful. The economy permits the family to support a large household, and only a small proportion of the adult population remains unmarried. The Amish have no taboos against good medical care. There is no divorce, and very little separation of husband from wife during the period of fertility. There are instances of surgical interference with reproduction for reasons of health, but such instances have little impact on the total population growth.

As long as the Amish family is so effective in socializing the child for adult life, there is scarcely any need for ceremonial connection to the religious community. The Amish are adult baptizers; therefore, there is no need for infant baptism, and parents are held accountable for the training of their children. The custom of assigning godparents to newly born children is nonexistent in the society. It is only after the child has been raised to "a way of life" that he is brought into a formal relation to the religious community through baptism. Baptism is of

<hr>

[2] Joseph W. Eaton and Albert J. Mayer, *Man's Capacity to Reproduce* (The Free Press, 1954), 55. Family size is discussed in Chapter 3.

course a very "real and awesome" experience and admits one to a new state. It logically belongs here in the discussion of the life ceremonies, but because of its importance I have treated it earlier as part of the Amish charter.

## Marriage

A wedding in Amish life is an elaborate affair, for the whole community has a stake in marriage. For the community it means a new home, another place to have preaching when the couple is located on the farm, and another family to raise children in the Amish way. Marriage also means that the young couple is ready to part with their juvenile and sometimes wild behavior and to settle down to keeping the faith in a mature way. For the couple itself marriage is a rite of passage marking the passing from youth into the age of adult responsibility.

Amish courtship is secretive, and the community at large is not to know about an intended wedding until the couple is "published" in church, usually two Sundays before the wedding. Signs of an approaching wedding, however, provide occasion for joking and teasing. Since there is nothing among the Amish that corresponds to the engagement, other signs of preparation become indicative of a potential marriage. An overabundance of celery in the garden of a home containing a potential bride is said to be one such sign, since large quantities are used at weddings. Another cue may be efforts on the part of the father of the potential bridegroom to obtain an extra farm, or to remodel a vacant dwelling on one of his own farms.

Weddings are traditionally held in November and December, since this is a time when the work year allows community-wide participation. The great amount of preparation requires that weddings be held during the week, usually on a Thursday, or on Tuesday if there are conflicting dates with other marriages. Second marriages or those involving older persons may be held anytime during the year and often do not involve such elaborate preparations.

Shortly before a young man wishes to be married he approaches the deacon or a minister of his choosing and makes known his desire. The official then becomes the *Schtecklei-mann* or go-between. His task is to go secretly, usually after dark, to the home of the bridegroom's fiancée and verify her wishes for marriage and to obtain the consent of her parents. Of course the girl and her parents have by this time already given informal consent, so that the duty of the intermediary is little more than a formality.

The deacon reports his findings to the bishop who announces or "publishes" the intent of the couple at the next preaching service. The bridegroom-to-be, who is always present at this service, leaves immediately after the important announcement, just before the last hymn is sung. He hitches his horse and is off to the home of his fiancée, where she is awaiting the news that they have been "published."

After being "published" the bridegroom lives at the bride's home until the wedding day. They are busy during this time with the innumerable preparations that must be made. Walnuts and hickory nuts need to be cracked, floors scrubbed, furniture moved, silverware polished, and dishes borrowed.

The bridegroom's first assignment is to invite personally all of the wedding guests. He sets out in his buggy early Monday morning to invite two hundred or more friends, relatives, and neighbors agreed upon informally by the parents of the couple. No wedding invitations are mailed. Invitations include entire families, or certain members of the family, such as the husband and wife only. Children are specifically mentioned if they are invited. Some are invited only for the evening. Honorary invitations are extended to uncles, aunts, and neighbors to serve as cooks. Both men and their wives serve in this capacity. The parents of the bridal party decide who shall be invited to the wedding and who shall have special honors in serving the meal.

Wedding customs vary from one ceremonial and ecological community to another, especially in menu, physical arrangements, and whether games are played. The following are observations made by the writer at a wedding in central Pennsylvania.

Large-scale preparations began on the day before the wedding. The cooks, married couples numbering thirty persons in all, began to arrive at the bride's home at seven o'clock in the morning. Custom requires that the bridegroom cut off the heads of the fowl. Men picked the chickens, ducks, and turkeys. The women washed and dressed them. The women prepared the dressing, stuffed the fowl, washed dishes, baked quantities of pies, peeled two bushels of potatoes, and cracked nuts. The men cleaned celery, supplied plenty of hot water from large kettles, emptied garbage, and constructed temporary tables for the main rooms in the house. These tables, made of wide pine boards and trestles, were placed around three sides of the living room. Two tables were in the kitchen and one in the bedroom, making the equivalent of about six tables with a total seating capacity of one hundred. The dressed, stuffed fowl were placed in the large outside bake oven on the evening before the wedding.

The wedding day itself was a great occasion not only for the bride and bridegroom, but for the kinship community and guests, especially the young people. Before daylight on the day of the wedding the bride and bridegroom and their two attending couples went to a neighbor's place a mile from the bride's home where the preaching and ceremony were to take place. A usual four-hour preaching service was held for the event, lasting from nine in the morning to one o'clock in the afternoon. This service was open to the public, but was attended chiefly by those who were invited to the wedding.

As wedding guests arrived for the service the bridal party was already sitting in the front row. When the house was filled, the ministers proceeded to the council room and the bride and groom followed. Here they were given private instructions concerning the duties of marriage, while the assembly below sang wedding hymns (*Ausbund*, selections 97, 69, 131). Upon returning to the assembly the bridal party (holding hands) took their special seats near the ministers' row, the three young men facing their partners. Their clothes were new, but typical of their regular Sunday garb. The main sermon delivered by the bishop focused on marriages in the Old

Testament: the story of Adam and Eve, the wickedness of mankind after the flood in that "they took them wives of all which they chose," the uprightness of Noah's household in not intermarrying with unbelievers, the story of Isaac and Rebecca, and the adulterous plight of Solomon. The sermon was concluded with a rehearsal of the story of Tobias (from the Apocrypha) and how he got his wife. Two passages of Scripture were read with little comment.[3]

Near the hour of twelve noon and at the end of his long sermon, the bishop asked the couple to come forward if it was still their desire to be united in matrimony. The ceremony was completed without the aid of a book or written notes. It consisted of a few questions and responses and concluded with the bishop placing his hands on the clasped hands of the couple as he pronounced a blessing upon them. The vows appeared to be similar to those of other Protestant groups, but no special prayer was offered. The ceremony, in translation, is given below.

### MARRIAGE VOW [4]

You have now heard the ordinance of Christian wedlock presented. Are you now willing to enter wedlock together as God in the beginning ordained and commanded? (Yes)

Do you stand in the confidence (*Hoffnung*) that this, our sister, is ordained of God to be your wedded wife? (Yes)

Do you stand in the confidence that this, our brother, is ordained of God to be your wedded husband? (Yes)

Do you also promise your wedded wife, before the Lord and his church, that you will nevermore depart from her, but will care for her and cherish her, if bodily sickness comes to her, or in any circumstance where a Christian husband is responsible to care for, until the dear God will again separate you from each other? (Yes)

---

[3] I Corinthians 7; and Ephesians 5:22–33.
[4] This is a translation from a nineteenth-century source (*M.Q.R.*, April, 1959), 142. The form used by the well-known Bishop Eli J. Bontreger appears in *Handbuch für Prediger*, L. A. Miller, ed., 1950.

Do you also promise your wedded husband, before the Lord and his church, etc. (Yes)

The couple then clasped their right hands together and the bishop continued: "So then I may say with Raguel (Tobit 7:15), the God of Abraham, the God of Isaac, and the God of Jacob be with you and help you together and fulfill his blessing abundantly upon you, through Jesus Christ. Amen." The bishop pronounced them husband and wife.

At the end of the ceremony several close relatives, cooks for the wedding, left the service. The bridal party remained a full half hour for *Zeugnis* and the usual closing prayer, the benediction, and a hymn. When the service was ended, they were the first to leave the assembly. They walked briskly to the yard gate in couples where they were met by three hostlers each with a buggy ready to go. Each hostler remained in his buggy and sat on the lap of the couple as he drove them to the bride's home for the wedding dinner.

At the bride's home the couples alighted from their buggies and walked quickly to an upstairs room. Their mood was most serious, and there was no shouting or handshake of congratulations offered by the onlookers.

The tables were loaded with food, ready for the large crowd which began to gather about the house and barn. The cooks had already eaten, so that they would be ready for the afternoon's work of serving tables. Two couples were assigned to serve each table.

Guests were seated under the supervision of the bride's father, who ranked all but the young people of courting age according to kinship. The bridal party sat at the *Eck* (corner table) located at that part of the living room most easily seen by everyone. The bridegroom sat to the right of the bride with attendants on either side. The unmarried girls, cousins and friends, filled the back of the bridal table around three sides of the room. The young men sat facing the girls on the opposite side. Then the married women took seats in similar fashion around the wall at tables in the kitchen and bedroom,

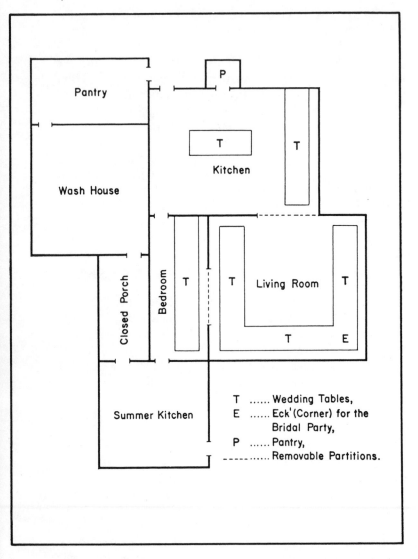

*Figure 12.* Diagram of an Amish House Showing Arrangement of Tables for a Wedding.

while the men sat on the opposite side facing the women. Opposite the bride and bridegroom sat the *Schnützler* (carver) who would carve the roast for the *Eck* and see to it that the bridal party was well served.

When the places at the tables were filled the bishop gave the signal for silent prayer: *Wann der Disch voll iss, welle mir bede.* (If the tables are full, let us pray.) All bowed their heads in silent prayer. For the wedding dinner there was roast duck and chicken, dressing, mashed potatoes, gravy, cold ham, cole slaw, raw and cooked celery, peaches, prunes, pickles, bread and butter, jams, cherry pie, tea, cookies, and several kinds of cake. The meal was a jolly occasion with plenty of opportunity for visiting. All were expected to eat well. Some brought tablets and mints to aid digestion.

The *Eck* contained no flowers, but fancy dishes, cakes, and delicacies were abundant. No less than six beautifully decorated cakes (baked by friends) and numerous dishes of candy were on display. One large bowl of fruit was in the center of it all. An antique wine flask and matching goblets (containing cider) were used by the bridal party.

When the first group had finished their meal the dishes were quickly removed, washed in portable laundry tubs, and replaced for a second sitting. The bridal party did not leave the table. When most of the people were through eating, a hymn was announced by one of the singers. All heartily joined in singing, except the bride and bridegroom, who by custom do not sing at their own wedding as it is considered a bad omen. Each guest brought his own songbook, the small *Lieder Sammlungen.* There was a considerable volume of singing until about five o'clock in the afternoon when many older people went home. Some slow tunes were used, but most of the hymns were sung to the fast tunes. Women, who ordinarily assume no leadership in religious services, announced hymns and led the singing the same as men.

It is the custom at the wedding supper for the young people to sit in couples, thus each boy was forced to take a girl to the table whether he wanted to or not. The older boys who had "steady" girls had no difficulty in pairing off, but young boys with little or no experience in courtship showed great timidity in finding a partner. Those who refused to find partners were seized and brought to the door forcibly. Once in line, all resistance ceased and each couple went to the table holding hands, following the example of the bridal party. The supper consisted of roast beef, roast chicken, noodles, beef gravy, chicken gravy, mashed potatoes, cole slaw, prunes, fruit salad, potato chips, cookies, pies, cakes, and for the bridal group and cooks there were, in addition, baked oysters and ice cream.

Hymns were sung during the supper hour, which continued until ten o'clock. The bride and bridegroom during this time sent plates of extra delicacies—cakes, pie, and candies—from the *Eck* to their special friends seated in various parts of the house. The final selection sung after the evening meal was *Guter Geselle* (good friend), a semireligious song which is always sung last at Amish weddings. This selection cannot be found in any of the Amish songbooks. It is largely sung from memory, although it has been printed in leaflet form. The first verse reads:

> Guter Geselle, was sagest du mir?
> O guter Geselle ich sage dir,
> Sage dir was eins ist.
> Eins ist der Gott allein,
> Der da lebet und der da schwebet,
> Und der den wahren Glauben führet
> Im Himmel und auf Erden.

> (Translation)
> Good friend, what do you say?
> O good friend I tell you—
> I tell you what one thing is;
> One is God alone,
> He who lives and He who soars,
> And He who leads the true Faith
> In Heaven and on Earth.

After supper the young folks again went to the barn where they played games until midnight. At this point most of the married people returned to their homes, but the two dozen or more cooks had to stay to wash dishes and care for the remaining food.

The bride and bridegroom spent the night at the bride's home. No one molested them, nor were any pranks played for their benefit. The bridegroom was not thrown over the fence, which allegedly is the custom among Lancaster County Amish. There was no immediate honeymoon, but what might be its equivalent is the practice of visiting uncles, aunts, and perhaps some cousins for a few weeks following the wedding. The couple had scarcely appeared together in broad daylight before. The bride, who in this instance came from a more traditional group, had not yet become familiar with her husband's family. In contrast, the bridegroom had become somewhat acquainted with her family during his courting days. Amish newlyweds occasionally go on an extended tour of two weeks or more to other Amish communities. After the wedding or after their return from this visiting trip, they may go to their former homes for a few months until separate living arrangements can be prepared in early spring. This is a characteristic feature of the consanguinal system carried over to the present day.

The parents of both were neither present at the ceremony, nor were they given special recognition at the celebration. They were constantly supervising and managing the kitchen and entertaining, seeing that the supply of food was adequate, and that the serving was progressing according to schedule. Their role was chiefly that of servant and overseer of the occasion. They ate with the cooks and took a subordinate role.

The bride and bridegroom were highly esteemed as they sat in the *Eck*. The occasion was geared for their full enjoyment. However, when they mixed in the crowd separately, between meals, for instance, they were seemingly ignored or treated as ordinary individuals. There was no expression of best wishes. This seems to have been taken for granted. The wedding gifts displayed on the bride's bed consisted chiefly of kitchenware and farm tools.

Barn games are commonly played at weddings and husking bees in some of the most conservative groups, and in the larger settlements they have "gotten out of hand" so that there are weekly hoedowns. Yoder [5] mentions five games played at Rosanna's wedding: "Bingo" (not the conventional game but the singing and marching game), "Skip to Ma [My] Lou," "There Goes Topsy Through the Window," "O-Hi-O," and "Six Handed Reel." These and also the following games have on occasions been used: "Little Red Wagon Painted Blue," "Granger," "Charlie Loves to Court the Girls," "We Will Shoot the Buffalo," "The Needle's Eye," and "Six Steps Forward-I-do-I-do." These games, also known as party games, involve holding hands and swinging partners.

Many families and church leaders are opposed to barn games, not because they are wrong in themselves, but because they have led to excesses, and often attract non-members with musical instruments. The opposition is based upon the conviction that it is unnecessary, hilarious conduct and does not conform to the Christian standard of good behavior. The practice flourishes chiefly among some of the most conservative groups. These party games are characteristic not only of the Amish, but of other Pennsylvania Dutch people.

Marriage in Amish life, in summary, is not simply a romantic affair. The preoccupation with personal likes and dislikes so common in Protestant Christianity, where even the sermon content and sometimes the ceremony are dictated by the couple, are conspicuously different in Amish life. The dress of the bride and bridegroom are made in traditional styles. Marriage is bonded by the community. The expectations allow no room for divorce and separation is almost unknown. The ceremony is elaborate because much is expected in the way of community conformity and responsibility. In marriage all institutions of the community obtain reinforcement.

[5] Joseph W. Yoder, *Rosanna of the Amish* (1940), 160.

## Death

Death in the Amish home, as in society at large, is a sober occasion. In some respects, however, it is taken as a matter of course, as the Amish person lives his life in the shadow of death and in conscious submission to the forces of nature.

The Amish community is very conscious of sickness, and if someone is seriously ill, a sense of religious duty compels members of the church and community to visit the home of the sick, though it may be only a five or ten minute call.

One evening I visited the home of a sick member who was expected to pass away shortly. The children of the sick father were all present. The women, dressed in black, were washing dishes and seemed busy with work. Evening callers entered the door without knocking, whereupon they were invited to enter the sitting room.

The visitors, consisting of neighbors, friends, and relatives, extended the usual handshake with all others in the sitting room and quietly found seats. Only a word or two was exchanged with the wife of the sick man when she came out of his room. She, as spokesman concerning the latest condition of her husband, conversed with one of the women seated in the circle of visitors. All others, particularly men, were quiet and resigned. An air of seriousness prevailed during long periods of silence.

News of a death spreads throughout the Amish community very rapidly. Such notice along with other important community events is written on the village blackboard or conveyed by the milk-truck driver.

When death overtakes a family member, few decisions need to be made for which tradition has not provided. Neighbors and non-relatives relieve the bereaved family of all work responsibility. The family is not confronted with the numerous decisions faced by the typical American family at such a time. Community responsibility relieves the Amish family of the tension and stress relating to decisions of the kind of coffin, place of burial, and financial worries associated with death.

Four young men take over the farm chores and an older married couple takes on the responsibility of managing the household. They secure as many other helpers as they need for cleaning, food preparation, and burial arrangements. The closest kin spend their time in quiet meditation and in conversation in the living room around the bier where guests are received. Still other friends come to the home to sit up all night while the closest of kin retire. The Amish still observe the old custom of the wake by sitting up all night around the deceased, and young people gather at the home to sing on at least one evening. Generally, funerals are held on the third day following death.

By tradition the dead are dressed in white. For a man this includes a white shirt, trousers, and socks. A woman is clothed in a white dress, cape, and organdy cap. The cape and apron are frequently those which were worn by the deceased on her wedding day. Those groups who do not embalm, wash and dress the body and place it in the coffin themselves.

Amish coffins are made by an Amish carpenter or by an undertaker catering to their specifications. Formerly they were made of walnut wood, but probably due to the scarcity of this lumber, pine is now ordinarily used. A coffin consists of a plain-varnished wood box with no side handles. The coffin is not entirely uniform in all Amish settlements and varies with patterns of change. The inside is lined with white cloth for some groups, but there is no lining used among the more traditional. Some groups prefer to have the lid all in one piece. For viewing the body, the lid is slid back about two feet. Other groups have a two-piece lid, and the upper part of the lid is fastened with hinges and is opened for viewing. In both types the lid is fastened with wooden screws.

Upon the death of a member, a measurement of the length of the body is taken to the village undertaker.[6] With this in-

[6] Funeral customs vary from one community to another as has been observed by students of Amish life. On the death of a member in Iowa a measurement of the deceased was taken to the coffinmaker in the form of a stick cut the right length. Melvin Gingerich "Custom Built Coffins," *The Palimpsest* (December, 1943), 384.

formation he is able to supply a coffin and the "rough box," a wooden vault with no bottom. Most Amish groups have the body embalmed, though others of a very strict order do not. The undertaker never sees the body of the deceased person in the latter case. In some communities the body is never taken away from the home until the day of the funeral. The undertaker executes the burial permits.

From four to six pallbearers, depending on the need, are selected by the family. Their duty is to dig the grave, assist with the seating arrangement at the funeral, open and close the coffin for viewing at the funeral, arrange for transportation, and cover the body with earth at the grave.

The funeral and burial are strictly "plain." There is no modern lowering device, artificial grass, carpet, or tent at the grave, nor are there flowers. The expenses of an Amish funeral would hardly exceed fifty dollars (the cost of a coffin and embalming). For those groups who do not embalm the cost would be about half that amount. Simple obituaries, if requested by the local newspaper staff, are sometimes published in the village newspaper.

The following is an account of the funeral of an Amish patriarch that was held at nine o'clock in the morning on a February day at his old homestead.

On our arrival, the barnyard was already full of black carriages. People gathered slowly and silently into the large white house, first removing their overshoes on the long porch. Inside there were three comparatively large rooms. The wall partitions had been removed so that the speaker could be seen from any part of the three rooms. Benches were arranged parallel with the length of each room. About 300 people were present. The living room held 62 persons, including the 14 ministers (many of them guests) seated on a row of chairs down the center of the room. The large kitchen seated probably 80 persons and the third room held about 50 persons including children. Of the remaining people, some were upstairs, others were standing in the summer kitchen, and more were outdoors.

The third room was ordinarily the master bedroom, but had

been used as the living quarters of the deceased grandfather. It was in this room that the body of the deceased was resting —in a coffin which had been placed on a bench situated against the farthermost wall. Relatives were sitting facing the coffin, those of nearest kin being nearest to it. They had their backs toward the speaker.

The house gradually filled. The head usher, a friend of the family but not a close relative, with hat on his head, seated incoming people and reserved special space for relatives. When every bit of available bench space was full, as well as chairs crowded in at odd corners, the audience waited in silence for the appointed hour.

After the clocks in all three rooms struck nine o'clock the minister at the end of the long row removed his hat. At once all the other men present removed their hats in perfect uniformity. The first minister took his position at the double doorway facing the audience in the kitchen and living room. His message, similar to an ordinary introductory sermon at a regular worship service, was full of biblical admonition, largely from the Old Testament. This gathering, he reminded his hearers, was of a very special kind. God had spoken to the church through the death of a brother.

He made reference to the life and character of the deceased, but these remarks were incidental to the sermon. The minister continued, "The departed brother was especially minded to attend worship services the last few years of his life, in spite of his physical handicaps. Those who ministered to his needs have nothing to regret because they have done their work well. His chair is empty, his bed is empty, his voice will not be heard anymore. He was needed in our presence, but God needs such men too. We would not wish him back, but we should rather prepare to follow after him. He was a human being and had weakness too, but his deeds will now speak louder than when he lived."

After thirty minutes the first speaker sat down. He was followed by a second minister, a guest in the community, who delivered the principal address. He too reminded his hearers that a loud call from heaven had come to the congregation, and that the Scripture warns every member to be ready to meet death. "We do not know when 'our time' will come, but the important thing is to be ready," the minister warned. "Death is the result of Adam's sin. Young people, when you are old enough to think about joining the church, don't put it off." Such direct admonitions to the young, linked with intense emotional experience, provide motivation for conformity to the traditional values.

Two passages were read, one near the beginning and one near the close of the address. The portions were from John 5 and Revelation 20. The sermon was far from a eulogy. The emphasis was personal and direct, to the audience. It was an appeal to all to live righteously, inasmuch as a day of reckoning will come for all people. The minister said he did not wish to make the sermon too long because the weather was unpleasant for the horses standing outside in the rain. After speaking for forty-five minutes he read a long prayer as the congregation kneeled. At the conclusion of the prayer the audience rose to their feet, and the benediction was pronounced.

At that point the audience was seated, and the brief obituary was read in German by the minister who preached the first sermon. In behalf of the family he also thanked all those who had shown kindness during the sickness and death of the departed one and invited all who could to return to the home for dinner after the burial. The assisting minister read a hymn. There was no singing.

The minister in charge announced that the boys could retire to the barn. The reason was apparent, as rearrangement was necessary to provide for the viewing of the body. Except for the ministers, the living room was entirely vacated. Next, the coffin was moved to a convenient viewing place inside the main entrance. Everyone present formed a line and took one last look at the body of the departed brother. Sorrow and tears were evident but little audible weeping. The nearest relatives stood back of the coffin during the viewing and followed it as it was moved from the house to the grave.

Meanwhile friends and helpers had prepared the hearse for

transporting the body to the graveyard. The hearse consisted of a one-horse springwagon with the seat pushed forward. Because of the rainy weather, a canvas was placed over the coffin to keep it dry. The horses of the mourners were hitched to their carriages by the many helpers. Relatives of the deceased entered their buggies and formed a long line to follow the body to the *Graabhof* (graveyard). The procession traveled very slowly, seldom faster than the ordinary walk of the horses.

Upon arrival at the graveyard the horses were tied to the hitching posts. The coffin, supported by two stout, rounded, hickory poles, was immediately carried to the open grave and placed over it. Relatives and friends gathered near. Long felt straps were placed around each end of the coffin. The pallbearers lifted the coffin with the straps and a bystander quickly removed the supporting crosspieces. The coffin was then slowly lowered into the grave where it rested. The long straps were slowly removed. One man stood in the grave on the frame that surrounded the casket, placing short boards over the casket as they were handed to him. With shovels the four pallbearers began to fill the grave. Soil and gravel hit the rough box with loud thumps. When the grave was half filled the shovellers halted as the minister read a hymn. As is the custom, all the men held their hats to one side of their head. They filled the grave and mounded the soil. Family members turned from the scene, slowly got on their buggies, and returned to the home of the deceased one.

In summary, death and its associated ceremonies are conditioned by the beliefs and attitudes of the Amish community. In death the deepest emotions of community are engendered, which are true sentiments of *Gemeinsamkeitsgefuehle*. The act of dying, which is the most private act that any person can perform, is transformed into a community event. While death may shake the emotional foundations of the individual it does not threaten the moral foundations of the society. Community organization is not adversely affected by the death of individual members. The reasons for death are understood within the context of the meaning of life.

The custom of having a meal following the burial is one which helps the mourners resume their normal role and responsibilities. Here the bereaved experience belongingness and togetherness, not only *Gemeinsamkeitsgefuehle*, but also *sinnhafte Verstaendlichkeit* and ethnic affinity and *Verwandtschaftsgefuehle*.[7] Conversational and interaction patterns are restored to their normal function. The family is quickly reintegrated into the community, in sharp contrast to the typical American family, where even close neighbors have not known of an intimate death, and where sympathies are expressed over long periods of time in more remote and anonymous contacts.

Burials frequently were made on the farm, and this is still the case in some communities. In Illinois the Amish bury their dead in rows in the order of their death without regard to kinship connections. The later practice has been to have a community cemetery, and in some places the Amish bury their dead with regard to family connections both in their own cemeteries and in community cemeteries where non-Amish people are buried.

When people cling to life and enjoy it to the full, death is considered the greatest menace, and emotional crisis is the severest. The Amish, who profess not to be conformed to this world, turn to the promise of life beyond death. The belief in the divine order of all things including immortality is a source of comfort to the mourning family and community. The ceremonial emphasis is merely a substantiation of the will of God.

[7] Max Weber, in *Theories of Society,* 307.

# Part III

# CHANGE AND STRESS

CHAPTER 9

# SCHOOLING: VALUE SYSTEMS
# IN CONFLICT

AMISH SOCIETY has been presented thus far as a functioning whole. The problems confronting Amish society and the impact of change on the community will be discussed in the next few chapters. Chosen for special consideration are: schooling, motivations for leaving the culture, the marginal person, group deviations, the problems of population density, and pathology.

A serious problem confronting Amish society from the viewpoint of the Amish themselves is the threat of absorption into mass society through the values promoted in the public school system. Since school in any society is an institution for drilling children in cultural orientations, the traditional Amish values often do clash with those of the modern American public school.[1] Although the school conflict is relatively recent, tension between the Amish and the state is not new historically. As early American immigrants and Christian ascetics, they came to this country to obtain religious freedom. As a separatist Anabaptist sect, they have experienced many tensions with the outer culture. They are keenly aware of the monolithic power of government.

Government officials generally interpret the conflict over schooling in legal terms, the local populace frequently takes the view that the Amish are stubborn and economically ex-

[1] For values promoted in the American high school as seen by an anthropologist see Jules Henry, *Culture Against Man* (Random House, 1963), Chapters 7 and 8; also A. B. Hollinghead, *Elmtown's Youth* (Wiley, 1949) and J. S. Coleman, *The Adolescent Society* (Free Press, 1961).

ploitive of their children, while the Amish interpret the conflict in religious and moral terms.

As Anabaptists, the Amish have always held that the task of training children belongs to the church-community and not to the state. Although the Amish, along with other groups of Pennsylvania Germans,[2] were apprehensive of compulsory public education at various times during the nineteenth century, it was not until well into the twentieth century that most Amish communities developed widespread objections to the public schools. When public schools and compulsory education were first enacted in the various states, the Amish frequently served as board members. When attendance was required beyond the fourth grade and to the age of sixteen, there were a few instances where Amish parents were summoned to court. But reluctantly and gradually the Amish complied with attendance requirements through the eighth grade. What has really brought the conflict into the open has been school consolidation and compulsory attendance after the children have completed the elementary grades.

The objections to education beyond the elementary grades and to the high school in particular are well-grounded in the social structure of Amish society. High school comes at a time in the life of the Amish child when isolation is most important for the development of personality within the culture. During this period he is learning to understand his own individuality within the boundaries of his society.[3] As an adolescent he is learning for the first time to relate to a group of peers beyond his family. As with most adolescents, he is testing his powers against his parents and the rules of the community. It is important for the church that his group of peers include only other Amish persons. If the child should acquire competence in the English culture at this stage, he will very likely be lost

[2] Clyde S. Stine, "The Pennsylvania Germans and the School," in *The Pennsylvania Germans*. Ralph Wood, ed. (Princeton University Press, 1942).

[3] The Amish ideal with respect to unpretentious and agrarian-oriented education was discussed previously (pp. 143–45). Observations on the high school years in this chapter are based on G. E. Huntington, "Dove at the Window" (Ph.D. dissertation, Yale University, 1956), with permission.

to the Amish church. A period in which the parents are loosening their direct control, and the community has not yet assumed much control, is too critical to expose the child to outside influences.

The American high school would break down this needed period of isolation by taking the youth away from the family farm and by teaching him to identify with non-Amish associates. This is what the Amish mean when they say that the high school is "a detriment to both farm and religious life." The public high school also teaches ideas that are foreign to the Amish culture and not appreciated by the community. The "way of life" of the high school is feared perhaps even more than the curriculum itself. If the child is removed from the community for most of the working hours of the day there is virtually no chance that he will learn to enjoy the Amish way of life. The incentive to comprehend his individuality, to master the required attitudes and skills necessary to enjoy life as an Amish person, are achieved during adolescence within the context of family, kinfolk, and church-community.

Amish parents, like most parents in American society, recognize the critical teen period. The Amish family needs the help of its teen-age children more than the typical American family, and the child feels the family's need of him. To know that the family needs his physical powers and to know that he is an economic asset to the welfare of the family are important to the individual. Quitting school after the elementary grades for greater identification with family and for the rewards of participation in adult society is normative. The typical Amish boy or girl who learns to enjoy his family and his way of life has little regret when leaving school. Rather than rely on authority as a means of controlling the child, the parents now exercise control by showing the adolescent clearly how much the family needs him. The young person who works on the farm can understand and feel the contribution he is making to his family.

These are some of the informal and "real" reasons for objection to higher education. The formal or "ideal" objections are based on religious precepts. "The wisdom of the world is foolishness with God" (I Cor. 3:19) is frequently quoted. The world is educated, the Amishman would point out, but is plainly corrupt. Education has produced scientists who have invented bombs to destroy the world and through education the world has been degraded. A "high" education is believed to militate against humility, obedience to Christ, and to submission to the will of God. The Amish make no attempt to prevent outsiders from educating their own children, but they themselves do not want to be contaminated by the harmful effects of higher education.

## The Little Country School

The one-room rural elementary school served the Amish community well in a number of ways. As long as it was a public school, it stood midway between the Amish community and the "world." Its influence was tolerable, depending upon the degree of influence the Amish were able to bring to the situation. As long as it was small, rural, and near the community, a reasonable influence could be maintained over its worldly character.

Many Amish parents took an interest in the local school despite claims by school officials to the contrary. Many attended PTA meetings, raised money for school equipment, donated labor to the school, and attended cleanup frolics and school picnics. They helped elect school board officers and influenced the choice of teachers, and Amish fathers frequently served as board members. The school building and its facilities were generally acceptable to the Amish even though they included some things forbidden in Amish homes. The interior had electricity, central heating, and frequently a phonograph, piano, or radio which was tolerated as necessary to the curriculum of the public school. The country school often had no indoor plumbing and modest play equipment. The school was the child's first experience with the world, and through it he discovered by personal experience the difference between his world and the other world. The teacher dressed differently and spoke a different language. With the help of an older brother or sister the Amish child acquired competence in both cultures.

Amish parents often say that their children need some contact with English children. It was in the traditional country school with other children that the Amish child received "a little contact" to make being Amish more desirable and more secure. In the country school the Amish child was treated as a member of a group rather than as a unique personality. The songs learned were largely religious; they were copied into notebooks and sung in unison as is done in Amish tradition. The state curriculum was carefully followed and there was little variation or room for individual initiative. The Amish children achieved basic skills in reading, writing, and arithmetic, and the school was acceptable even though a considerable portion of the program was neither meaningful nor related to the Amish way of life.

Amish parents have always feared a strong, progressive public school, for they know that its aim is making the child self-sufficient and competent, and perhaps moral without being Christian. They fear what is being taught to their children when they are far away from home by teachers whom they do not know. They resent the school's taking too much time away from the family, from the community, and from the discipline of farm work. Learning, or reading, for sheer enjoyment and pleasure is foreign to Amish tradition and not encouraged by most parents. In spite of any adverse influence the little one-room school had on the Amish child, it helped to make of the child a good Amish person. It provided enough contact with outsiders to enable the child to participate minimally in two worlds, and just enough indoctrination into the outer culture to make the child feel secure in his own family and community.

With large-scale consolidation and collectivization of school facilities, all this changed. Although the Amish founded a private school in Delaware as early as 1925, it was not until after 1937 that they began to operate many private schools. In most districts the Amish prevailed upon the school boards to keep the one-room schools open, but most were gradually closed.

In the process of consolidation, the public school officials often regarded the strongly populated Amish areas as a "problem" in attaining their goals of reorganization. Never did they view consolidation as a disruption of Amish life and their education. Most states with Amish populations have attempted to compel the Amish to meet the minimum standards required by law.

## The Pennsylvania Plan

Pennsylvania was the first state to attempt enforcement of the attendance law. The law required children to attend school until their seventeenth birthday, but children engaged in farm work were permitted to apply for a permit, which excused them when they reached the age of fifteen. However, many had repeated the eighth grade and were still not old enough to apply for a farm permit. The conflict erupted when schools were no longer willing to tolerate the practice of allowing the Amish children to repeat grade eight. School officials tried withholding the farm permits. When the parents did not send their children to the consolidated high school, the parents were summoned to court and fined. They refused to pay the fines on grounds that this would admit to being guilty. They were then sent to the county jail. Anonymous friends and businessmen frequently paid the fines to release the parents from prison. Some were arrested as many as ten times. The Amish fathers and mothers took the position that compulsory attendance beyond the elementary grades interferes with the exercise of their religious liberty and that the values taught in the public school are contrary to their religion. Attorneys and friends of the Amish who took the case to the courts found no legal solution.[4] After many confrontations and embarrassments, Governor George Leader in 1955 arranged a reinterpretation of the school code to legitimize a compromise plan, the Amish vocational school.[5] Amish lay leaders took the in-

[4] Commonwealth v. Beiler, 79 A.2d 134 (Pennsylvania, 1955).
[5] Policy for Operation of Home and Farm Projects in Church-Organized Day Schools. Department of Public Instruction, Commonwealth of Pennsylvania, October 5, 1955.

itiative in developing the vocational schools for those pupils who are not of legal age to obtain a farm permit. Under this plan the pupils perform farm and household duties under parental guidance, keep a daily journal of their activities, and meet in classes several hours per week. The schools are required to teach certain subjects, and to file attendance reports, but teachers are not required to be certified. In 1967 Pennsylvania had 25 Amish vocational schools and Ohio had 28.

A few school districts have provided country schools for pupils in the more heavily populated Amish areas, thus forestalling the establishment of private schools by the Amish. The boards of these schools seek teachers sympathetic to the Amish way of life and, in keeping with respect for cultural diversity, see that religious values of the pupils and parents are not offended. A few schools following such a policy have achieved remarkable results. The arrangement provides for state certified teachers, more modern curricula and facilities than are possible in the private Amish schools, and for enlightenment that is fitted to the culture.

## The Iowa Showdown

While the conflict in the various states has taken different forms, the controversy in Iowa during the mid-1960's illustrates the stresses and intensity of feelings behind the scenes as a school "problem" comes to a head. In a small Amish settlement centering in Buchanan County, school authorities forced their way into an Amish private school in order to compel the children to board a bus to take them to the consolidated town school. The press got wind of impending events and recorded the scene as frightened youngsters ran for cover in nearby cornfields and sobbing mothers and fathers were arrested for noncompliance with an Iowa school law.

This little Iowa community became the subject of worldwide publicity. School officials were deluged with insults and adverse reactions from people who sympathized with the Amish. The eruption was the culmination of long-standing intercommunity tensions broader than the "Amish problem."

Tensions had been building up for some years prior to the widely publicized crisis. Unwittingly, the Amish had served as pawns in a local school election involving intense feelings of hostility.

The Amish settlement of six church districts was founded in 1914 by families from Johnson County, Iowa, who tended toward more than average conservatism in their practices. They were joined by families from Kansas and many other states. Two Amish parochial schools were established. As time passed they tried to comply with the state's growing requirements for certified teachers, but the Amish said that when they sought and found qualified teachers the school authorities refused to certify them, or offered the teacher more pay in town. The two Amish schools ended up being taught, as in Pennsylvania and Ohio, by Amish girls who were selected for their teaching aptitude but had only an elementary education.

The root of the problem in Iowa was deeper than mere certification.[6] Two of the local school districts, Hazelton and Olwein, were in the process of merging. Many people in the Hazelton district opposed the merger and, remembering the years of rivalry between the two towns, opposed the takeover by the city of Olwein. The people in Hazelton fought the merger and refused to put the matter before the voters. Finally, through a few residents who desired the alliance, Olwein school officials pushed the legal petitions to require a referendum. The Hazelton-Olwein reorganization was particularly bitter. Old friends stopped talking, vicious rumors spread, and secret meetings were held. The Amish wanted to be attached to the adjoining Fairbank Township area, where one-room schools were still maintained, and in keeping with the required procedures petitioned a meeting of the various county officials who were responsible for drawing the boundaries of the new districts. The Olwein officials helped to arrange the rejection of

[6] Donald A. Erickson, "Showdown at an Amish Schoolhouse," Background Paper No. 3, Freedom and Control in Education, National Invitational Conference on State Regulation of Non-public Schools, March 28–29, 1967. Publication of the entire proceedings is planned by Donald A. Erickson, Center for Continuing Education, University of Chicago.

the Amish petition and, in so doing, hoped to gain the extra tax income from farm children in the district who attend non-public schools. The superintendent of the Olwein district, who was described as brilliant and an expert in virtually every aspect of school affairs, was worried about getting the required votes in both districts. The Amish might sabotage his efforts by casting their ballots against the referendum. In consultation with the state officials, the Olwein superintendent arranged for a "deal" with the Amish: if they would vote in favor of re-organization, the Amish could keep their one-room schools just as was done in nearby counties. The task of persuading the Amish was not easy, for their schools were in the opposing Hazelton district. But on the promise of the superintendent, "I expect to be superintendent for many years to come, and I will always recommend that the board honor our agreement," they consented.

The voting in Olwein was overwhelmingly in favor of merging and in the Hazelton district the measure passed by a narrow margin. The people of Hazelton's district became furious when they discovered that the Amish voted favorably but could easily have defeated the referendum by voting against it. Residents to this day insist that the Amish swung the election and forced Hazeltonians to come under the Olwein board. Those who wanted the referendum to pass brought carloads of Amish to town to cast their ballots, and numerous local people saw what was happening. Old grievances were revived and bitter prejudices were activated which formed the groundwork for intense pressures against the Amish. Local residents were prepared to see that the Amish obeyed every "inch" of the new school code.

The Amish, who had cited religious principle as the basis of their action, now were accused by Hazeltonians of "using religion as an excuse for everything they want to do." Locally the Amish were branded as hypocrites, as people motivated by economic greed, wanting only to keep their school costs down and to exploit child labor in the fields.

Meanwhile the Olwein school officials arranged for help from the state level. The two state inspectors who visited the

Amish schools were "shocked" by the outdoor privies and the austerity of the facilities and found them "impossible." This action allowed the Olwein school board to "get off the hook," and from this point on, the Olwein school board took the position that it was helpless to aid the Amish unless they agreed to the state's requirements. Meanwhile the Amish returned to running their schools with their own staff of uncertified teachers. The time was right for the local officials to take revenge.

The Amish were summoned before the justice of the peace. The parents were found guilty of violating the law by staffing their schools with uncertified teachers. Nightly for several weeks fourteen Amishmen showed up Monday to Friday, to be fined twenty dollars plus four dollars costs each day. Each parent refused to pay on religious grounds. They were warned that their farms would be sold to pay the levies if they did not pay. The amounts levied soon reached into the thousands of dollars, and at this rate it would not have taken long to ruin the Amish financially. It was at this point that the Olwein school bus came on November 19, 1965, with its truant officer and staff, to take some forty Amish pupils from their private school, against the wishes of the Amish, to the consolidated school. The plan, according to the school officials, was to load the children into the buses in spite of Amish resistance. After a few days, it was thought, compliance would be achieved and the trouble would be over. Against the advice of the Iowa Attorney General, the showdown proceeded and was greeted with widespread national repercussions.

Governor Harold E. Hughes ordered a truce of three weeks to permit exploration of alternate solutions. There were to be no more attempts to take the Amish children to Hazelton, and prosecution of parents was to cease. County officials seized Amish corn and real estate to collect the unpaid fines, but most sales were forestalled because the fines were paid by anonymous donors. The Governor visited the home of Dan Bontreger, chairman of the Amish school board, and one of the Amish schools, then talked to the students at Olwein's junior high school, and met with the school board for two hours. A longer cooling-off period of two years was provided when a private foundation gave $15,000 to pay the salary of certified teachers in the two one-room schools for two years.

The Iowa case, called attention to a number of educational, administrative, and legal problems involved in running non-public schools. This prompted Donald A. Erickson, of the University of Chicago, to call a two-day National Invitational Conference on State Regulation of Non-public Schools on "Freedom and Control in Education." Attending were members of state departments of education, members of the law profession, representatives of religious denominations operating private schools, and a few anthropologists. A group of concerned citizens organized the National Committee for Amish Religious Freedom, chaired by a Lutheran pastor, Rev. William C. Lindholm, to take to the United States Supreme Court a Kansas Supreme Court decision against Amishman Leroy Garber.[7] A number of religious leaders, politicians, and educators wrote articles in national magazines advising moderation. Governor Hughes of Iowa said: "I am more willing to bend laws and logic than human beings. I will always believe that Iowa and America are big enough in space and spirit to provide a kindly place for all good people, regardless of race, or creed."

Franklin H. Littell, Reformation historian, and president of Iowa Wesleyan College, said: "These people are exemplary American citizens of long duration. This is a test case to see whether we believe in religious liberty when it is for others and not ourselves. Certainly we are sick of soul if we cannot put up with 23,339 frugal, law-abiding 'peculiar people.' "

"The Amish people's approach to education," said Donald Erickson, "is one of the most effective yet devised, with little unemployment, crime, and juvenile delinquency. In time, given

[7] The Garber case is described in a brochure "Do We Believe in Religious Liberty—for the Amish?" edited by Rev. Wm. C. Lindholm, East Tawas, Michigan (1967). See Jurisdictional Statement, Leroy Garber v. The State of Kansas, in the Supreme Court of the United States, October Term, 1967. No. 393; also Brief and Appendix, *Amicus Curiae*, by Leo Pfeffer. In a 4–3 decision the court declined to hear the case. The reaction of Amishman David Wagler was: "The trouble with a lawsuit is that if you lose you lose, and if you win, you lose too (in good will)."

some liberty, the unequivalent schools may even teach us something. The public school approach has worked well for many, but it has been an obvious failure outside the cultural main."

In 1967, after a great deal of effort, the Iowa legislature amended its school code to permit a religious group to apply for exemption from compliance with the educational standards law. Proof of achievement in certain basic skills was made conditional. In the same year Maryland amended its school law, so that the Amish were classified as a bona fide church organization and therefore not required to obtain approval of the Superintendent of Schools to continue to operate schools in that state.[8] In Indiana the State Superintendent of Public Instruction encouraged the Amish to organize their own schools and develop standards in keeping with their prerogative as a religious denomination. The courts tended to take the position that unless it could be shown that the Amish were endangering the state or becoming welfare charges, the arrests were unjustified. If it was not illegal to be an Amishman, was it illegal for a parent to send his children to a school where Amishmen are trained?

## The Human Relations Problem

There is a common element running through each of the controversies in the various states, regardless of the details. All of the disputes involve sincere Amish parents who refuse on religious grounds to obey state laws when their children's education is at stake, and sincere public school officials who feel obliged, on legal grounds, to enforce the school laws the Amish refuse to obey. Several contributing factors, pointed out here, add to the perspective of the human relations problem.

1. The Iowa Amish community was small in comparison to

[8] The Iowa Legislature amended Code 299.2 in 1967. For Maryland see S.B. 470. While Ohio has not modified any of its laws to meet Amish objections, that state issued a report: *Amish Sectarian Education*, Research Report No. 44. Ohio Legislative Service Commission, 1960. A more recent treatment of Amish schools in that state is contained in Frederick S. Buchanan (1967). See biblio.

the larger Amish settlements in Pennsylvania, Ohio, and Indiana, and the Amish population here was much more in the minority than other larger Amish settlements. This settlement was not buffered by Mennonite or other ethnic groups of Pennsylvania German descent whose empathy for the Amish comes as second nature. There were few informal liaison relationships between the Amish and the "English."

2. The Amish people are seldom fully informed about school reorganization plans and rely on the personal integrity of local officials. Accustomed as they are to renting and loaning money to one another without legal formalities, they enter into informal agreements with persons whose goodwill they respect. Somewhat naïvely, when they thought they were doing the Iowa school officials a favor by voting for reorganization, they were in fact undermining the confidence of their closest neighbor farmers.

3. Pressure from local residents to make the Amish conform to the school laws is often reinforced by long-standing antagonisms. Local Iowa officials reportedly said: "We are going to assimilate these people, whether they want to be assimilated or not." When pressed about the ethics or constitutionality of such an approach, they replied that they couldn't see any problem.

4. There is an absence of clear-cut legal procedures in enforcing the laws. There often appear new as well as contradictory regulations between the officials of the school district and the state departments of education. When negotiations break down on the local level the state has intervened. The major means of enforcing school laws is to prosecute parents under the provisions of the compulsory attendance laws. Few states empower their officials to close substandard schools, and those who have attempted to close Amish schools have usually evoked the disapproval of the public.

5. Administrators have shown little inclination to use the anthropological approach to understand a culture that is different from their own. There is frequently lack of rapport between the Amish and the school authorities in local communities. Many state department of education staffs have made little

effort to understand the Amish. Contacts are primarily in the context of legal language and terminology. Some continue to repeat many of the derogatory and untrue stories about the Amish, which imply deep suspicion and mistrust of them.

6. Over the past fifty years, it may be observed that in those regions where encouragement and informal relations were maximized there have been very different results from those in areas where laws were strictly enforced. Officials have not learned, in many cases, the difference between those issues on which the Amishman will "bend" and those on which he will not compromise. The secular orientation of schoolmen is probably a barrier to understanding the Amish.[9]

7. Educational administrators know that the Amish fear the loss of their tradition, but for the Amish parent it is not simply the fear of the children becoming "English," but of losing ties with them for eternity. In explaining this principle to the State Board of Education in Ohio, Henry Hershberger quoted from the Bible and then, shaking his head, said, "I don't think I can make you understand." [10] Some Amish fear that their children will be literally taken from them and turned over to the world, as happened to Anabaptists in earlier times. Not to be able to teach and hold their children in the Amish way of life has a twofold threat: (a) parents are held accountable for rearing their children in the fear of God; to fail in that is to leave a blemish on the church, and (b) to lose one's children to the world is to lose hope of their salvation and of spending eternity with them in heaven.

### The Professionalization of Amish Schools

Unknown to most of the school officials, one of the most important consequences of the Amish–public school controversy has been the institutionalization of Amish educational efforts. Not only have the Amish built and staffed their own elementary and vocational schools, but they have gradually

[9] An observation made by Buchanan, *op. cit.*
[10] *Ibid.*

organized on local, state, and national levels to cope with the task of educating their children.[11] School board members are elected to raise funds, acquire equipment and books, and to hire and regularly pay for teachers. Persons who are ordained to an office in the church are not required to serve as school board members and rarely do. Teachers are selected on the basis of their natural ability with children. They learn to teach by helping the more experienced teachers over longer periods of observation. A new teacher is often helped by an experienced teacher during the first week of school. Most teachers are unmarried girls; however, some are Amishmen who are engaged in light or part-time farming. A magazine for Amish teachers, *The Blackboard Bulletin*, published since 1957 and presently with a circulation of over 2,500, stimulates both parents and teachers to the importance of training in schools. The Pathway Publishing Corporation of Aylmer, Ontario, a private nonprofit corporation founded by a few Amishmen, built a publishing house in 1966. Although book selling and publishing religious literature are its main enterprise, it also has published books for school use.[12] Amish teachers meet annually to share their aims and purposes. Nearly two hundred elementary Amish schools are now in operation, and the number is growing each year. There were over 50 Amish vocational schools in 1967, attended by 385 ninth and tenth grade pupils.

Although Amish parents are not unanimously happy with the accomplishment of their schools, they are generally satisfied with a compromise plan that permits them to keep the one-room rural school, with their own teachers. Parents are not unanimous about the goals they want their schools to accomplish. Some want "a little more contact" with English-speaking

[11] Minimum standards for schools have been adopted by the Ohio Amish (Henry J. Hershberger, Rt. 2, Apple Creek, Ohio) as well as by the Pennsylvania Amish (Aaron E. Beiler, Rt. 1, Gap, Pa.) and in 1967 by a state-wide Amish committee in Indiana; see Wells (1967).

[12] E.g., *The Challenge of the Child*. Pathway Publishing Corp., Aylmer, Ontario. Other book titles issued by Pathway are: *Worth Dying For* (1964), *The Mighty Whirlwind* (1966), and *Who Shall Educate Our Children?* (1965). See also biblio.: Uria Byler (1963), Jonas Nisley (1965), and Noah Zook (1963). Manuals for teachers are now in preparation.

people, where their children have a better chance to learn English. Not all are agreed that their own teachers should teach religion in the schools. All want their children to be emotionally and intellectually equipped to live on the family farm. The achievement level of the Amish pupils is presently under study.[13] Although intelligence test scores given to Amish children frequently show norms that are generally below national norms, and slightly above those of rural children, exercises of a non-verbal nature show that the Amish pupils are strongly motivated toward the expectations and roles of the adults in their society. Amish pupils have a positive attitude toward physical work and have a wide range of ability in manual skills in performing household and farm activity. The Amish children need a different type of schooling from that given to most American middle-class children if they are to develop the skills needed by their culture and to internalize the values of an agrarian-directed religious community.

[13] John A. Hostetler, Educational Achievement and Life Styles in a Traditional Society (The Old Order Amish). Research project in process.

# CHAPTER 10

# INDIVIDUAL ADAPTATIONS
# TO CHANGE

## Social and Cultural Change

No SOCIETY IS EXEMPT from change. Societies differ in the rate of change. To understand changes is to understand the ongoing problems of survival. Social change "is the process by which the existing order of a society, that is, its social, spiritual, and material civilization is transformed from one type into another." [1] Stress occurs when the individual is no longer sure of himself or of the values which he has traditionally held. Stress becomes apparent when social problems arise that threaten core values. When it is recognized that people act in a way they are not "supposed" to act, then stress is present.

Social and cultural change involve whole processes within a society: material resources and consumption of goods, spatial and territorial settlement, laws and social institutions, beliefs and knowledge, and the system of training the young. Such changes are characteristic of all societies; "it goes on everywhere and at all times." Changes may arise from forces within the society that may be designated as independent developments, or from changes due to contact with a different or "outside" culture, a process called diffusion.

Any number of studies on the Amish have pointed out the isolation features of this small society. To understand how people can isolate themselves in the modern world is presumably worth knowing, but the aspects of human behavior we know little about are the conditions under which social change occurs in the little community, the effect of innovation on

[1] Bronislaw Malinoski, *The Dynamics of Culture Change* (Yale University Press, 1961), 1.

personality, and the management of change in the small society. Is it reasonable to assume that the Amish communities will lose their identity in the next quarter or half century? Will the direction of change be the same as for other religions in America, which Will Herberg has described as "an other-directed gospel of adjustment, sociability, and comfort, designed to give one a sense of belonging, of being at home, in the society and universe"? [2]

The subject of change in Amish society is a complex one. It is complex because the social sciences have not yet succeeded in understanding social change in terms and concepts that can be made simple. Furthermore, human behavior cannot be explained in simple terms. In understanding change in the small, stable, and homogeneous society, we can learn some principles about change in the great society.

One way to understand social change is to observe how the Amish social system [3] becomes dependent on the outside world. We have earlier noted ways in which the Amish society is not independent, but is in fact a part society. Its continued existence depends upon maintaining unchanged certain forms, such as the prohibition of automobiles and electricity; yet its survival depends upon some contact with the outside world.

Change through diffusion, or the acceptance of outside ways, such as new tools and technology, can take place in a slow manner without causing any social "upsets" in the community. On the other hand, extensive borrowing of culture often precedes violent changes in the social life of a people. There are two ways to view the changes in the social life: the first is the individual as he breaks with his own culture, and the second is the formation of subgroups within a society which initiates changes. The present chapter deals with the individual.

## Conformity and Rebellion

Individuals within a culture-bearing society make different adjustments to their culture. Not all of the rules of a society

[2] Will Herberg, *Protestant, Catholic, Jew* (Anchor Books, 1960), 261.
[3] Charles P. Loomis, *Social Systems* (Van Nostrand, 1960), 240–48.

Table 7

A Typology of Modes of Individual Adaption

| Modes of Adaption | Cultural Goals | Institutional Means | Future Orientation |
|---|---|---|---|
| I. Conformity | acceptance | acceptance | fixation |
| II. Innovation | acceptance | rejection | renewal |
| III. Ritualism | rejection | acceptance | resignation |
| IV. Retreatism | rejection | rejection | irrelevant |
| V. Rebellion | rejection | rejection | substitution |

SOURCE: Robert K. Merton, *Social Theory and Social Structure* (The Free Press, 1957), 140. The scheme has been modified by the addition of column four, "Future Orientation." Used by permission of author and publisher.

are understood by all individuals in the same way. Nor are all values taught with equal intensity to all the members of a society. Individuals respond differently to expected behavior patterns, so that there are various types of behavior within any given society. In observing change among the Amish we want to know how individuals deviate from the traditional norms and what the consequences of such behavior are. Robert K. Merton [4] has outlined five types of individual adaption to a traditional culture. This scheme has been found useful for understanding individual adjustment and is presented in Table 7, with modifications.

In a stable Amish community we may expect that conformity (type I) is the most common adjustment. Individuals generally conform to culture goals through institutionalized (or routine, approved) means, the purpose of which is to maintain the *status quo*. In a society where many people are not conforming to the goals or where the institutional means are not being accepted, there is instability and change. To the extent that the conforming members in a society have their basic needs satisfied from birth to death, the pattern of life is stable and life is an orderly reality. The Merton scheme must of course be viewed with reference to a given society. The Amish society taken as a whole is not conforming to the great

[4] Robert K. Merton, *Social Theory and Social Structure* (1957), 150.

society around it. But members within the Amish society are generally conforming to Amish norms. The individual conforms to this model expectancy. "In Amish society," said a former Amish girl after graduation from college, "one is always conscious of keeping as many rules as one can, and each person tends to feel an obligation to see that other members of his family also keep these rules." But not all persons conform to the expectant behavior and it is these people with whom we are concerned in this chapter.

Innovation (type II) is a form of behavior in which the individual accepts the goals of the society but uses means other than the traditional ones to achieve the goals. Farming and making enough money to buy additional farms for his sons are legitimate goals for an Amish farmer, but were the Amish farmer to buy a rubber-tired tractor so that he could achieve this goal through non-institutional means, he would violate the norms. The effect on social change would be important. When such adaptive behavior occurs in a society the innovator utilizes the traditional goals, but not the means, in order to improve the society. There are two types of innovators—those who get by, and those who are expelled.

Ritualism (type III) "involves the abandoning or scaling down of the lofty cultural goals . . . to the point where one's aspirations can be satisfied." Although the individual rejects the obligations to get ahead in his society, at the same time he abides compulsively by the institutional norms. Persons who cannot enhance their status by achieving the goals of (Amish) society alleviate their anxieties and fears by lowering the level of aspiration. In Amish society strong sanctions for deviation produce few innovators (type II), but this would tend to increase the inclination toward ritualism. Of course, individuals may shift from one type of adaption to another. The person who tries to be an innovator but does not succeed may become an ardent conformist. He may lower his aspirations and become a "bureaucratic virtuoso," [5] steeped in all the meticulous rules and symbols of conformity. The ritualistic status role in

[5] *Ibid.*, 152.

Amish society is that of deacon, a position held for life. There is generally no prospect that the person in this position will ever become a bishop and usually not a minister. His status therefore makes him responsible for maintaining the ceremonial rites and for getting others to conform to the rules.

Retreatism (type IV) is a type of adjustment in which the individual rejects both the cultural goals and the institutional means. He is indifferent to the values of the society, and while he conforms to the society, he is apathetic toward its goals. The individual is capable of achieving the goals, but the contradiction between approved means versus disapproved means becomes so great for him that he gives up the competitive struggle. "Defeatism, quietism, and resignation are manifest in escape mechanisms which ultimately lead him to 'escape' from the requirements of the society." [6] Though the individual may still hold to the supreme goal of the society, he is unwilling to use the legitimate means because of internalized blocks. The conflict is resolved by retreatism and escape. He becomes a non-productive liability in his society. It is unlikely that the Amish society could tolerate many individuals of this type. But so long as the norms are not violated, they would be retained in the society. To retreat from the goals because they are not worth striving for, yet to keep the rules because there are no alternatives, presents the Amish society with a peculiar type of adaptation. The Amish have no tramps or vagrants in their society, but upon close observation it is possible to find individual adjustments that are of the non-productive, liability type.

Rebellion (type V) is a type of deviation which leads persons outside of the society to envision new goals by complete alienation from the parent social structure. Rebellious behavior is manifest frequently in "diffuse feelings of hate, envy, and hostility; or in a sense of being powerless to express these feelings actively against the person or social stratum evoking them." [7] The rebellious type differs from retreatism in that it

[6] *Ibid.*, 156.
[7] *Ibid.*, 156.

regards the institutional system as a barrier to satisfactory achievement of the goals. Organized movements of rebellion must provide new myths which locate the large-scale frustrations and at the same time provide an alternative social structure. The new myth becomes the charter for action, as was the case with the Amish rebellion from the Swiss Brethren. The Amish person today who engages in this type of adaption might reject the Amish hair style and form of dress as a goal or a means to salvation and adopt modified ideals by changing his affiliation to the nearest religious kin-group, the Mennonites. In this case he would not need to create new myths, but simply adjust to an existing group outside the Amish society. This, as we shall see, is the most common form of adjustment of those individuals who rebel against the Amish society.

The desire to leave one way of life for another presumes that the individual has some knowledge of the outside world. A knowledge of alternatives must be possible. When individuals in the Amish community find meaningful and satisfying experiences outside of the Amish bounds, their relationship to the traditional community is altered. This is normal with the lessening of isolation. The Amish no longer have the advantages of natural or geographic isolation; the influences of mass communication, travel, marketing, and technology are exerted on them. The barriers of language, dress, and ignorance no longer function as effectively as they once did.

Under what conditions do we find the desire for life outside the Amish society? Does the Amishman who leaves his culture become secular or does he retain a primarily religious orientation to life? Several general hypotheses may be stated at the outset. Persons who deviate from the Amish norms experience (1) ideological conflict with Amish doctrine, (2) interpersonal frictions within the society, and (3) personal frustrations and need-fulfillment, or all of these. Further, we may expect to find a higher rate of rebellion among the children of families who are "marginal" to the culture than among "conformist" families. In other words, if either the mother or the father show nonconformist tendencies, or if one of the parents have had difficulties with the discipline, we could expect to find a tendency toward rebellion to the Amish way of life among the children. Similarly, we may expect to find a greater deviation in those districts experiencing disintegration as evidenced by sudden changes, by chronic "church trouble," by division, and by instability of leadership. Families who live on the fringe of the Amish settlement would appear to experience great social stress unless they conform to the ways of the great society.

The data which we have are based upon depth interviews of persons who have defected from the Amish way of life. All were between the ages of eighteen and thirty-two. These life documents are productive of insight into stress and change. All of the cases below are illustrative of Merton's type-IV rebellion. Defection here means, of course, conformity to the great society, which the Amish constantly resist. We shall consider the conditions that led to deviation as well as the break from the Amish church. All names are purposely fictitious.

## The Desire for Learning

The desire for formal education is one of the factors associated with individual deviation. The first case is that of an ex-Amish person whom we shall call Sam. Sam recalls his early interest in schooling, leading up to his decision to enter college. "I always loved school from the day I started. My parents didn't start me until I was seven so I wouldn't have to go to high school. They thought I couldn't learn very well and I wanted to show them I could. When my mother was young she taught school. She wanted to go on to school, but never had a chance. I sort of caught this desire from my mother." In school Sam could succeed, but at home he was less certain of success. He said, "It made me mad when my father kept me home for a day's work. Sometimes when I was to stay at home, I would switch into my school clothes at the last minute and get on the bus."

Sam was adept in making friends at school and during his

last grades in school, he said, "I hated that I came from such a backward family." The animosity for his backwardness grew as he learned to know his classmates and especially a certain non-Amish girl. "We were always the top two in the class. I could beat her in arithmetic but she always beat me in reading. It was always tit for tat between us. We were always together in those early years. I always hated that I was an Amishman. My older brother was a 'good' boy and listened to daddy but was always getting into trouble. Sunday after Sunday I would go to church, and all we would do after church was sit out on the buggies and tell filthy stories. I was the cockiest guy I guess, as I was more or less the leader of our group of boys. My, how I used to get whippings from my father. I hear other people brag how they thank the Lord for their whippings, but mine just did not make sense."

With the completion of grade school Sam wanted to go to high school but could not. "I felt there was nothing to do but stay home and work for dad till I was twenty-one. My life was terribly lean during those years." Sam was baptized in the Amish church. After he reached legal age he was drafted into wartime conscientious-objector service. Here he was exposed to a wider association of friends, most of them Mennonite. Following his release from service he entered a Mennonite college. Although for some years he attempted to retain his Amish affiliation, eventually he became a member of the Mennonite Church.

Another case is that of Rebecca who turned from her Amish background at age eighteen without having been baptized. "I read a great many books and anything I could get my hands on. I tried to persuade my father to let me go to high school. But he would not. After grade school I was Amish another six years and this was a very difficult time in my life. My dissatisfaction began to show in physical ways. I had no energy, I was anaemic. Nothing interested me. I didn't fit in with the Amish young people and I sort of despised them for their lack of learning. I made attempts to be popular among the Amish and dated a few times, but I didn't like it very much. I was pretty lonely, and it was a very miserable time for me. I was the oldest of eight, and mother kept on having children and this tied me down and I was constantly resenting this. I was always running away to read, and I hid books. When mother was not watching I would read everything I could.

"When I was eighteen, I thought mother had reached the age when she could have no more children. Finally, I thought I could begin to see daylight, have a little more time to myself, and to keep the house neat without working so hard. Then I learned that mother was pregnant again, and this was the last straw. I simply could not face this. I went to the basement and just cried. I told father I had had enough, I was leaving. While I packed my suitcase, mother became very upset. Father knew that mother needed my help. So we worked out a compromise. Father said if I would stay until the baby was born, the next year I could go to Bible school. Two of my father's brothers had gone away for a six-week term of school. This was enough for me; then I could get away and go where there was a library and read."

Rebecca went to college and left the Amish way of life. Later her brothers and sisters followed her example, and after several more years the whole family left the Old Order Amish faith and joined a Mennonite group. It is not uncommon for one or two of the children to break with the tradition with the result that the parents do so later.

A third case whom we shall designate as Chris, says, "I wanted to go to high school so badly that I remember crying about it, trying to persuade my parents. They gave us achievement tests after grade eight and I found out I was the highest in the county. I competed from grade one through grade eight very closely with a girl who went on and became valedictorian. In the accumulative tests which included all eight grades I had all A plusses except I had one A, and she had all A plusses except two. My principal talked to my father several times and told him I had possibilities. I was only fourteen, so my father made me repeat the eighth grade the next year. After getting all A plusses in grade eight I barely got A's the second time. I was very athletic though, and even though I was not going on to high school the principal let me go all out for athletics. All the time the kids and neighbors [non-Amish] wanted me to go on to high school. In my second year in the eighth grade, I quit when April came because it was time to start plowing. I went home and remember how terrible I felt."

With all his chums now in high school, the lad returned to the principal and explained his painful experience. The school principal gave him ninth grade books, and Chris promised that he would study them and appear for the semester tests. He said, "I hardly touched the books but I took the first semester test and got all A's and B's. But I finally gave up and returned the books. But I knew I would never stay Amish because the principal convinced me the Amish should not keep their children home from school. He told me I had brains. He told me I could be more than a farmer.

"Most of the next two years I spent at home brooding. I was insecure within myself. I wouldn't work at home very much. When I had to work for another Amish farmer for no wages I felt my leg was being pulled. I did a lot of local-diner-and-gas-station-hanging-out with my friends, and though I dressed Amish I fitted in somehow." A few years later Chris achieved financial independence by working as a hotel waiter in a very distant state.

These three life documents illustrate how linkage is achieved with outside social systems. The three persons individually found attachment and meaning in human groups outside Amish bounds. These satisfactions led to inevitable conflict with traditional values and animosity toward parents. In each case the father became the object of opposition. These individuals found their meaningful outside associations in the public school where many faiths were represented. In many instances even public-school contacts are extremely limited as most of the school population is Amish. The Amish have begun action in other settlements to modify the influence of the public school by erecting private schools, owned and staffed by the Amish themselves. Association with non-Amish children in the school environment is then impossible.

## Conversion and Innovation

The need for personal fulfillment in religious experience is vocalized by many who defect from the Amish way. This type of mobility occurs among those who completed public school with no thought or desire to be anything but Amish. But today they find themselves outside of the Amish society. How have these individuals been influenced?

In the case of Mike, we have a boy who was raised strictly in the Old Order Amish tradition. He was personally conscientious and practiced his religion zealously, but when he was drafted into service as a conscientious objector he came in contact with and under the influence of non-Amish religion for the first time. Though his own account of what happened is lengthy, it is explicit and illustrates the frustrations and the influence of outsiders on a person who was isolated all his life from other Christian groups. Dissension in his home district was already apparent at the time he was drafted, for "Church trouble was going on at the time. My wife and I would visit on her side, the more liberal one, and then in my district. We would listen to them see-sawing all the time.

"Then I got my notice to go to camp. My mother was very much concerned and when I left she about cried her eyes out. She was afraid I would slip and not stay with the Old Order. So I made up my mind to be true and to be a good example of the Old Order. But when I marched up to get on the train, two Pentecostal boys played 'God be with you till we meet again.' Inside the train the other boys started to sing. This was something I was not accustomed to, and it gave me a spurt. I felt strange. I sat down beside a sober-looking boy and I thought I'll cheer him up.

"Across from me were two Christian boys. One of them reached over and asked my name. He asked my background,

church, locality, and said we might as well get acquainted. I
noticed that these two boys were friendly, and they always
had cheerful friends and talked spiritually. This impressed me
and I was attracted to them. Then I met a Negro boy who was
a Christian. He began talking to me, telling me how surprised
he was that so many C.O. boys smoke. This was a surprise to
me because this is what I had always done. Then he said he
doubts whether many of the boys had had a conversion experience. This struck me, and I expect he noticed it on me.

"That night the Mennonite preacher who accompanied us
began to conduct a devotional period right on the train. He
went right ahead even if there were soldiers walking through
the coaches. I thought, that's just the way it should be. Then
I thought to myself, would our Amish preachers have done
this? I thought, no. Would my preachers have held a service,
or would they have kept quiet and kind of hid their religion?
When we arrived, the minister said, now we are going to have
a prayer meeting to thank the Lord for taking care of us. This
was a new experience for me. Everybody knelt down and nobody had a prayer book in their hand. It was just spontaneous,
and when one was done the other would pour out his praises.
I was there on my knees, all ears, and I could hear this colored
boy pour out his heart to God. After the meeting I thought,
well that's just the way it should be.

"On Sunday I sat in my first Sunday-school class. They
gave me a book but I could not discuss any spiritual depth.
Here the boys were discussing the lesson and really enjoying
it. Then on Sunday night the minister said we are going to
have a testimony meeting. The boys got up, one after another,
with faces aglow, giving Scripture verses and testimony. Each
boy said how he was saved, but I thought, no, we do not know
whether we are saved until we get over yonder. I got uneasy.
Was I supposed to be on guard for false doctrine in this group?
I pondered this after the service, yet these boys had a joy I did
not have. After church one of the boys nudged me and asked
me to go for a walk.

"We got to talking about the meeting that night. I told my

friend that I enjoyed the enthusiasm of the boys but that what they said was farfetched. They said they were saved, but they are still living here. My friend said we can know that, but I tried to change the subject. I sensed that the boys were on one side of the fence and I on the other. I did not want to lose them as friends. One night they asked me to take charge of prayer meeting for the next time. I agreed because I did not want to disgrace the Old Order church. That day I started memorizing a prayer, but when the time came it did not go very well but I got through.

"One night a Pentecostal boy and I went for a walk down town and we passed the poolroom. He asked if I played pool and I said yes. He said he wouldn't. I said, it's just a game and lots of fun. Then we began discussing movies. He said he would not attend any. I said, why not? Once I saw how a submarine worked in a movie. He said, do you know who is putting on that show? He said they were just a bunch of adulterers and fornicators who are living after the dictates of the flesh; then we pay to see it and expect to get some good out of it. This made me think. Another thing I noticed was the difference in speech. In my home community we used to tell a lot of filthy stories, but these boys in camp just wouldn't tell stories like we did back home. I noticed that their standards in this regard were above mine, but I had the outward appearance. This bothered me.

"In my heart I felt the spirit starting to convict me. When I worked in the timber I had a few close calls. What if I would be killed, I thought. What is the value of my being in camp if I would die as a hypocrite? I could see that the other boys were saved and now they were giving their life back to God. I had long hair and plain clothes, and I had always been taught that their clothes were worldly. I was as confused as I could get. Then I came home for Christmas.

"I thought, maybe the Old Order preachers did preach salvation by faith, and that perhaps I was too indifferent that I never caught on. So when I went home I listened carefully to them. They used the same Scripture verses, but explained it differently and just seemed to explain away the meaning. I had decided not to drink when I got home. It worked all right for a few places, but then I got to my brother-in-law's place and he brought up a pitcher of cider and started laughing when I refused. 'So you want to be good, do you,' he said. That was too much for me so I took a little, but then there was no stopping. Then I felt miserable.

"I talked to my dad about how different the Christian boys were in camp. I told him that the victory of the boys lies in the point that they believe they are saved, that Christ died for them and now they have a desire to live better. I could see it. Dad said, well, he heard a story one time. A man told how sure he was that he was saved; he was as sure as taking the next forkful of meat. But at the point of putting it in his mouth, it fell from the fork and the dog swallowed it. So dad gave me little help. I was uneasy, miserable, and wretched.

"I spoke to my youngest brother, telling him how the boys were so clean and pure, how it seemed to come from the fact that they have assurance, or they say they have. He said, well, when you read the stories in the Bible it seems to imply that. Yet my brother didn't seem to have this experience, nor did my parents.

I dreaded to go back to the boys at camp. I knew that if I got to camp conviction would get deeper within me. Then I returned to camp, and I never felt more wretched. I was caught between what the boys were in camp and what the preachers said at home. I kept my misery camouflaged as much as I could. I tried to be cheerful. It was the same at camp. These boys had something. They met every night for worship and always gave a testimony. What they talked about meant so much to them. Everybody at prayer meeting would give a testimony but me. Those who were not Christian would not attend the service. I attended because I did not want to let down the Old Order Amish church, to have it look as though we were not a spiritual people. But I was as miserable as I could get. I went to bed that night and turned to the wall, and I was just beat. The boys told me what they thought, but the preachers at home told me what they thought. The gap was as wide as you could make it.

"When a missionary preached about the foolish virgins, I just knew I was one of them. I knew I should raise my hand and ask for prayer but I was too proud. I couldn't face it. If I went home this way, I would be thrown out of church, I would have to part company with my wife. I felt I was going to be a nervous wreck."

It was not long until Mike reached a crisis which relieved the contradictory expectations. He became a Christian, experiencing conversion like the other boys, according to his own words. This opened the way for him to meet the expectations of the other boys in camp, but still left problems that had to be solved when he reached home, his wife, and family. From the time that Mike resolved to defend his Old Order faith and to be loyal to his mother, we can see the development of conflicting expectations. The camp experience was the first he had had with other Christian boys of his own age. In his own peer group, it was customary to smoke, drink, and attend movies. His own religious training gave him no familiarity with audible praying, testimony, or with the taboos of fundamentalist religion. Later in life, after his return to his community, he faced the ridicule of his kin, and then changed his religious affiliation and was ultimately given a responsible position.

Another case is that of Paul, who soon after baptism got into difficulty with the *Ordnung*. His parents were meticulous conformists, and an older brother once ran away from home but then became an ardent member.

He says, "When I joined the church I was a little unsettled. I didn't expect to stay, but I did it to please my folks. I didn't have the nerve not to join. But after I was baptized I thought maybe I would stay after all." One Sunday soon after his baptism the bishop announced that all members were to stay away from the forthcoming community-wide revival meetings. "This made me curious," he said. "I wanted to hear an English sermon.

"So, on Sunday evening I was loose, that is I didn't have to take my sisters to the singing. One of my buddies and I went to the tent meeting in his buggy. We tied the horse at the nearest farm house and walked over to the tent. We first decided to stand outside and listen. But my buddy said we should go inside and see how it looks and take a back seat. An usher got hold of us and took us up farther than we wanted to go, and I heard my first English sermon. The sermon put me under conviction. I felt I was not at peace with God and then I couldn't sleep well.

"By Tuesday my parents found out that I was at the meeting. Then the preachers got after me, and I decided to make a confession in church. But I still could not forget the sermon I heard. The next thing that made me think was when my brother was suddenly killed. This was an awful shock to me. The day after that I took out my cigarettes, broke them in two and threw them in the field. I decided to live for the Lord. Another thing that made me think was the scrapping between our parents. My brother who died often talked about that. Once he told them: 'The scolding may be worse than what you are scolding about.' That saying of his left an impression on me. I started thinking that the confession I made in church I should not have made."

About this time, Paul went to visit two of his former but now excommunicated friends. From them he received nourishment for his Amish discontent, and here also he discussed "assurance of salvation." After church one Sunday the preachers "cornered" him and his parents. He was asked, "Do you have some of this strange belief that is going around?" Paul promised to "do better" but "it didn't really last long." At the singings he began to discuss the Bible with his chums. "When they were suspicious, they offered me a smoke. When I refused, they asked me to repeat a story I told once. I told them I quit telling dirty stories because I didn't believe it was right. From then on it was just picking at this and that."

Paul was excommunicated and shunned for having a *fremder Glawwe* (strange belief), a term covering non-sanctioned religious beliefs, such as favoring the doctrine of "assurance of salvation" and other fundamentalist teaching. Persons who suddenly discontinue smoking, telling the usual Amish jokes, or argue about doctrine, come under suspicion for having a "strange belief."

Cultural insulation in the case of Paul was overcome by his curiosity. The English sermon that was forbidden provided a meaningful reference point and made a lasting impression. The dislike for severe arguments between parents was repelling. The death of a brother, taken as a supernatural act, turned him against the traditional norms and provided additional incentive for him to live by the English sermon he had heard. In the meantime he also had achieved financial independence by working for a non-Amish person on a construction gang. Another factor was, "The girl I liked turned me down, and that settled it."

## Directions of Change

These life-history cases are sufficient to illustrate some important factors in the change process. First, Amish young persons of school age have associations with outsiders that become meaningful in later life. To grow up and become a conforming Amish person requires that a boy or girl who likes school must learn to be indifferent toward it. If the experience of learning in the public school develops beyond the expectations of the parents, the adolescent is headed for serious personal conflict. Persons who nourish these conflicts, who are unable to substitute the school experience for approved Amish goals, vocalize their concerns to persons who come to their assistance. Meaningful reference groups are then discovered in the outside social systems.

Secondly, we observe that deviation is associated with religious experience. The Amish society is a religious society, and defection from it takes the form of religious rather than secular symbolism. An Amishman would not be likely to become an atheist, and, in finding reference groups outside his society, he chooses religious groups. In spite of the strong prejudice against Mennonite teaching, this barrier is overcome, and a Mennonite group is usually more acceptable to the deviating person than is a Protestant or Catholic group. Thus it is easier to go from one religiously oriented primary group to another than it is to join a religious group where there are probably no relatives and one that has very different beliefs from Anabaptist groups. There is a tendency to go to the one symbolically the closest rather than to one that is more distant.

Thirdly, persons who have been raised and conditioned to life in a small, informal, multibonded society, cannot be lured to the outside world by a single reward, or by a unibonded association. To turn against the moral training of early life, against kin, and against the symbolism learned in the formative years requires a cultural and religious shock. This suggests that revival, guilt, and conversion play prominent parts in the experience of the deviating Amish young person. The desire for new types of farm machinery and for the conveniences of home appliances on the part of enterprising young Amish couples is associated with change of religious values.

The loss of members is very limited in some Amish districts and considerable in others. Groups who are most conservative appear to lose fewer members than those who are partially assimilated or have established close contact with the Mennonite groups. The *streng Meidung* groups lose fewer members than those who practice the mild form of shunning. In a mobility study of one Amish church in Pennsylvania, it was found that 30 per cent of the offspring did not join the church of their parents. Of all those who did not join the church of their parents, about 70 per cent joined a Mennonite church and less than 10 per cent joined other Protestant denominations.[8] In a study of religious mobility in the Mennonite Church, it was found that 24 per cent of the converts came from Amish churches, while it lost only 3 per cent of its members to the Amish.[9]

[8] John A. Hostetler, *The Amish Family in Mifflin County,* 210.
[9] John A. Hostetler, *The Sociology of Mennonite Evangelism* (Herald Press, 1954), 257.

The entire configuration of a dozen or more Mennonite and Amish groups appear to form a conservative-liberal continuum.[10] We may think of them as units on a ladder of assimilation. A person may move from a conservative to a more liberal group without losing his Mennonite identity. The many splits are evidence of divergent practice, but in basic doctrine there is little fundamental difference. It has been observed that the membership-gains in the more liberalized groups are not the result of evangelistic activity, but a reflection of the secularization processes. The many divisions have probably served as agents to preserve the general conservatism of the sectarian society.

The traditional ways of building up anxieties against the outside world, or certain segments within it, are no longer convincing to the defectors. In other words an education or an automobile are no longer considered dangerous by them. A. I. Hallowell [11] has observed that certain anxieties are usually inculcated in individuals as part of their socialization experience in order to motivate them in the direction of approved behavior. They are taught that certain types of deviation bring painful or dangerous results. The traditional way of reducing these threats and of relieving the psychic pain in Amish society are correspondingly no longer meaningful to the defectors. They are organizing their life around goals on the outside of the tightly integrated Amish system of values.

[10] This tendency is illustrated at some length by Karl H. Baehr, "Secularization Among the Mennonites" (B.D. dissertation, University of Chicago, 1942).

[11] "Social Psychological Aspects of Acculturation," in Ralph Linton (ed.), *The Science of Man in the World Crisis* (Columbia University Press, 1945), 194.

CHAPTER 11

# THE MARGINAL AMISH PERSON

PERSONS WHO ATTEMPT to simultaneously accept selected values from two diverse cultures become marginal persons. A marginal person "is one whom fate has condemned to live in two societies and in two, not merely different but antagonistic, cultures."[1] Amish persons who have repudiated their culture to pursue education or aggressive religion often cannot take their family and their kin with them. Not infrequently they attempt to accept the new value without breaking with the little community; they must make peace with two societies and conform to certain expectations of both. The marginal Amishman is an inevitable product of the process of acculturation, a process in which a subordinate culture is modified to conform to the culture of the dominant society.

The adjustment of the marginal individual takes the form of his own conception of himself. The marginal man, as a personality type, is well known to us in the American scene. Out of the conflict of races and cultures new societies and cultures come into existence. The larger the proportion of marginal men within a society, the more we may expect to find the roles of the cosmopolitan and the stranger.[2]

There are several conditions closely associated with marginality that we shall consider. One is the rise of cultural contradictions and role stress; another is the role of change agents in aiding deviating persons; still another is the life adjustment

[1] E. V. Stonequist, *The Marginal Man* (1937), from the Introduction by Robert E. Park.
[2] The Amishman generally becomes a sacred stranger in a secular society. See Howard Becker and Harry Elmer Barnes, *Social Thought from Lore to Science* (Dover Publications, 1961), Vol. I, 39–42, 145.

of the marginal Amish person. The more contradictions there are within a small society, the more favorable are the conditions for the rise of marginal persons. Where the needs of the person are well provided from birth to death and the answers to life questions satisfy, we would expect to find few marginal persons. On the other hand, where the socialization processes do not provide the basic answers, we may predict that there will be a larger proportion of marginal persons.

## Detecting the Deviant

How does deviation come to the attention of people within a society? Some types of deviant behavior are highly visible and create much more comment and action than others. In the American society there are many acts of crime or deviation which are not even likely to be reported to the police. In Amish society, not only deviation, but attitudes which would lead to deviation, are quickly detected. The slightest deviation is visible not only to the ministers on Sunday, but to members of the family or neighbors on any day of the week. One young man was "up for baptism" who said, "I had some chrome rings on my harness and I did not have a large enough brim on my hat quick enough, so they excluded me." As in the sacred society described by Becker, "the sudden intrusion of new thoughts and disturbing examples breaks down the entrenched tyranny of the single sacred code." [3]

Deviation varies with status roles in Amish society. Permissive behavior of certain types are normally expected of the single rather than the married. Youth is the normal time for deviation in the otherwise stable group. Before marriage deviation tends to take the "wild" or "worldly" kind of thrust. Cutting the hair too short, or wearing clothes that are too gay, or driving an automobile are all ways in which the deviation occurs. Smoking may or may not be a sign of deviation depending upon the local *Ordnung*. Where smoking is normally practiced, to quit smoking may be taken as a sign of sympathiz-

[3] Becker and Barnes, *op. cit.*, 13.

ing with the Mennonites. Since most young people who leave the Amish group become Amish Mennonite or Mennonite, signs of being like them are avoided as much as possible. An elderly visitor from Ohio who stayed overnight at a friend's house in Pennsylvania smoked only after he learned the attitude of his host. The visitor explained that he quit chewing tobacco, that he wanted to quit smoking but did not because "some feel that when a person quits, it is a sign he is thinking of going to a 'higher' church." For the sake of keeping good relations with his fellow members, and to avoid the possibility of being misunderstood, he chose to conform. A young man said, "My chums got suspicious and were afraid I had 'a strange belief' when I refused to smoke."

Persons who conform to the outward symbols but change their beliefs are detected in a different manner. The young persons who reject the hoedowns, the bundling, and the rowdy behavior [4] of their own age group, and who meet secretly for prayer and Bible study, come under suspicion. A mother told her seventeen-year-old son as he was leaving home for a secret Bible study group: "We know that it can't be the Lord's will for the young folks to come together to study the Bible like that." On another occasion a young man talked to a feed salesman: "I told him I was a Christian. The preachers found it out and condemned me. On Sunday, the minister said in his sermon that it is very, very wrong to say that you are a Christian. They think that to say you are a Christian means the same as saying you are saved. When the preacher openly reprimands me, the other young people believe him. Most of them think I am wrong."

Ridicule may arise if the deviating person takes a firm stand. "It takes a group to be with in order to stand," said one informant. "The gang would purposely say things in my hearing to irritate me. When they knew I didn't believe in smoking they would say, 'give me a cigarette.' One evening when they were dancing up in the barn they came to me and said:

[4] Readers should bear in mind that this chapter deals with marginal persons and not the typical youth.

'Why aren't you dancing? You used to. You were a big dancer.' " When a non-smoker was invited to a birthday party for one of his friends, he overheard the boys saying, " 'If Fred comes, he better keep his mouth shut or he goes out the door.' That is what they think of me. They often say, 'there go the goodies.' It shouldn't bother a fellow, but it does."

More patience is exercised with young offenders than with married or older persons. Young people are permitted a certain amount of liberty during the "running-around" period, and parents pretend to be ignorant of some of the deviant behavior of the young. But with baptism, and much more with marriage, the young people must take on the serious duty of keeping the *Ordnung.*

In large Amish settlements the practice of not only owning drivers' licenses but also automobiles has become a form of institutionalized deviation. Unbaptized boys cannot be punished by the church for this. The parents are the ones who must deal with such innovators. Some parents on discovering that their son has an automobile have been known to smash in the windows and demolish the exterior with an axe. Where strenuous objection is anticipated the boy may leave the vehicle in a nearby village, parked at a used car lot or at a filling station. Other parents have not objected to the unbaptized son having a vehicle, and in some cases they have given the boy financial assistance.

Some of the boys who own autos have difficulty concealing their identity when they drive around in the neighborhood. But several devices are used to further concealment. One Sunday evening, at a village intersection, the writer observed a used black car coming to a halt at a red-light intersection. While waiting for the green light, I could see signs that the driver was a deviating Amish boy. His face was hidden by a sun visor on the windshield of the automobile and by a large "English" cowboy-style straw hat on his head. While waiting for the light to turn green, an Amish buggy with a family passed directly in front of him. The father looked very intensely at the person behind the wheel, then turned to his wife

and smiled. Both smiled as they drove away from the intersection. When people begin to smile at their own inconsisten-
cies, there is sure to be more change ahead.

Boys who have been baptized and get caught owning or
driving an automobile must make a confession in church. They
cannot be reinstated unless they sell the vehicle. The ease of
access to automobiles and the threat which this represents to
the community have given rise to special rules made by the
church, for both members and their children. On Sunday one
may ride with an outsider in his car, but one may not ride
with a relative who has a car, such as an unbaptized boy who
may have an automobile. This is a safeguard against the dangers of immediate travel facilities.

## Contradictions and Role Stress

In Amish society there are contradictions which become
apparent as change proceeds. These vary in their intensity and
importance to the individual, and they differ widely within
the Amish society. When contradictions develop which no
longer "make sense" to reason, the new generation will develop unfavorable attitudes toward their native society. What
are these contradictions in Amish society? "To go into a bar
is very, very worldly, but to drink back of the barn is all
right," was contradictory to one person. The prohibition of
telephones in homes but the use of them in the store, or at the
neighbor's place, or to use the pay telephone becomes a contradiction. To permit a tractor for belt power but not for field
work is still another. But to conforming members of the small
ethnocentric society these do not appear contradictory. We
must therefore examine contradictions from the standpoint of
the participating member as well as their effect on his personality.

A young man who described his childhood days as happy
ones and his home as devoutly Christian, said, "I was not happy
with the few social activities of the young people, so I went
to fairs and farm shows to satisfy my social longing. Without
my parents knowing it, I attended the theater; about the same

time I took my first drink. This led to card playing and gambling. I pretended to be a Christian when I was home, then I would go away and seek the pleasure of the world to satisfy my own desires. Thus, I lived deceiving my parents and the church." This young man respected his parents, but could not adjust to the restricted life of the young people. His deviation was not antagonistic but after two years of "double-faced life," he abruptly ran away from home. He recognized the contradictions but found no solution, as he put it, but "to break the heart of my parents."

There are, of course, contradictions in all societies, but they vary in intensity and in number.[5] The more contradictions there are the more we may expect to find symptoms of role stress, anxiety, and confusion. The mere existence of complexity and confusion in values within a culture may be conducive to stress. Change, in and of itself, constitutes a threat in Amish society. New problems requiring adaptations not provided for by traditional solutions set in motion many anxiety drives. Threats to traditional Amish values and patterns constitute important stress factors. The status position of young people in Amish society is particularly vulnerable to stress dimensions. Persons caught in contradictory expectations are troubled by what is right. An Amish boy who reflected on his adolescent years said: "You suffer terribly in those years." Another said, "I became insecure from many little things. We lived in a district where three buttons were allowed on the shirt, and when I worked for an uncle who wore four, I felt he was a sinner." Statements from others indicate considerable role stress: "I started thinking that I should not have made the confession I made in church." "I kept my misery camouflaged as much as I could." "There was nothing to do but live it out with dad until I was twenty-one." "My sisters and others got me convinced that I should stay Amish. I kept changing my viewpoints. I was converted first one way, then another, and

[5] Read Bain, for example speaks of "Our Schizoid Culture," *Sociology and Social Research* (January–February, 1935), 266; and Lawrence K. Frank refers to the American culture as being "sick, mentally disordered and in need of treatment." (*Society as the Patient*, Rutgers University Press, 1949, 1.)

I kept changing my mind." Stress arises not only between family heads and the ministers and between families, but also within families, as evidenced by the following statement: "Dad wanted to change churches but mother didn't. We remained, but Dad was getting more of what he wanted because he was able to farm with more modern equipment."

Young persons who can achieve independence away from home frequently manage to reduce the stress factor. One young man said, "I spent my summers at home working and my winters in Florida as a hotel waiter. I made so much money that I would go home and work free of charge for my father because I kind of felt that I owed my father a little something. Since I never behaved for him, I worked for him free of charge." An Amish person in a Mennonite college said, "I felt like I was a man without a country. I didn't fit in at home too well, and I didn't fit in at school."

Persons required to live in a culture where they recognize contradictions find it most difficult to rationalize such practices. In a district where tractors with rubber-equipped wheels were allowed, members soon found additional uses for the tractor. Not only were they used for field work, but with platforms on the rear they could be used for hauling produce to the local village. With a fifth gear they were used for running errands from one farm to another. Draft horses were soon entirely displaced and each family kept one or two horses for driving the buggy, which was used on Sunday for going to preaching. One father who felt the incongruity of two forms of transportation said, "It will not be long until some change will have to be made. When the youngsters grow up they will not understand why horses must be used on Sunday, but tractors can be used on weekdays." Cultural contradictions not apparent to the aged members of the society are frequently recognized by the younger generation.

## Change and Acculturation Agents

A change agent in Amish society is an Amish person who assists the marginal person in establishing favorable attitudes toward change. An Amish father who takes no action against his son for buying an automobile becomes an innovator. When a boy who went to a revival meeting was "found out" his sister "raised cain," but an older brother took the position that "there are worse places to go." Persons within the society who merely refrain from taking negative sanctions are in a favorable position for introducing change, especially if they are from high-status families. Amish parents who are good farm managers and farm owners, generally ardent conformists, and who take a moderate view of enforcing the *Ordnung* in the case of a son or daughter, become effective as agents in permitting an attitude of discussion. The son or daughter becomes a change agent through personal influence within the group. Change agents conform to Merton's innovator type discussed earlier. They accept the goals of their culture but use other than approved or institutionalized means.

Those persons outside the Amish society, who because of their position or occupation can assist a deviating Amish boy or girl, are "acculturation agents." They help to bridge the gap between the in-group and the out-group. These individuals include school principals or teachers, missionaries, pastors of nearby Mennonite and other Protestant churches, older brothers or sisters and uncles who have left the Amish way, and occasionally neighbors. Amish youth who obtain drivers' licenses, for example, must have some kind of assistance from the outside. Prior to taking the test they will have learned how to drive a car from a friend in the Church Amish (Beachy or automobile) group, or in some cases from an employer. Those who wish to complete high-school examinations in order to qualify for entrance to college receive assistance from a school principal, a college, or from a friend who is also taking the examination.

There is some exploitation by outsiders due to the ignorance of Amish youth, as in automobile transactions, but characteristically the outsider wants to see the Amish youth become competent in the outside ways of life. The acculturation agents are the middlemen who work between the small and the great society. Many automobile salesmen, salesmen of musical instruments, insurance salesmen, and issuers of drivers' licenses, do business secretly with young Amish people so that the parents and the public do not discover the activities and special procedures. When Amish youth are arrested or convicted, their names are often withheld from the newspapers if they request it. There are instances when the postman will hold certain mail until he sees the recipient personally, so that parents will not be aware that the item reaches a family member. This is frequently the case for insurance policies, driver's license applications, and other materials received by registered mail.

Young Amishmen who have been stopped for speeding, or for charges having to do with the condition of a car, such as faulty mufflers, are said to have been released because a police officer "favored" or "pitied" them. A few are reputed to have passed drivers' examinations with a little manipulation or bribery, and some examining officers have the reputation among Amish youth for passing them easily on driver examinations. Persons under the legal age may on occasion be issued licenses, as may trustworthy Amish youth who have not had adequate driver training. Sometimes a hint that a county ham or a homemade pie would help to make the transaction complete is acted upon.

There are service stations which permit Amish boys to park their automobiles. A used-car salesman allows boys to keep their cars on his lot when they are not driving them. This is done with the understanding that they buy the car from him and allow the firm to service it. A number of service stations receive much Amish patronage on weekends.

Increasing numbers of Amish youth patronize bars and liquor stores, minors included, because they are trusted and favored by many outsiders and usually have the reputation of causing little trouble. There appear to be few outsiders who co-operate with the elders and parents to keep young members "in line." Amish farmers in areas are industrious, thrifty, neighborly, and many outsiders desire to see Amish customs and qualities preserved and maintained in the county. Business and commercial interests, in particular, do not want to see the day when the Amish community will vanish.

For those who leave the group, making the initial break with the culture takes place in a number of ways and is of itself an adjustment to stress. Some run away from home without making a successful linkage with outside reference groups. A boy aged sixteen suddenly disappeared one Saturday afternoon. The first sign of his leaving was the discovery of his Amish hat a mile away from home. The father was alarmed but could do nothing but wait hopefully. The next day a neighbor received a phone call from a large city stating the exact place where the runaway boy could be picked up. The boy had discarded his Amish clothing, had got his hair cut, traveled to the big city, and then became despondent and gave up. Unknown to any of the family members the boy had entertained the notion of running away for many months. An unhappy encounter with his father was the occasion for the break.

Four Pennsylvania boys, two of whom were members, made their departure after midnight by walking and thumbing their way to Ohio. The first sign of their leaving was the discovery of long hair in an upstairs bedroom. Within two weeks all were back in their native community, though not all returned to their homes. Two of them joined the army and the other two soon married girls outside the Amish faith. A former Amish father who was asked by someone why boys sometimes run away said: "Who wouldn't? All the teaching they get is *Attnung* (*Ordnung* or regulations) and the command from their parents *Du bliebscht Deitsch* (you must stay Dutch)." Parents are too rigid in their demands and punishment, he felt. "My brother ran away from home last year and I can tell you why. Dad was awful rough with him. He gave us boys one licking after another. Even when I was eighteen he tried to lick me, but that's when I said, 'It's enough.' I didn't let him."

Slipping away from the Amish community with intent to return appears to be more common now than in former years. As outside pressures exert themselves on small neighborhoods and as young members have more and more knowledge about outside affairs, "having a fling" with the world and returning has become institutionalized. Thirty or forty years ago it was not uncommon for two or more Amish persons to go west and work their way with the harvest from Texas to North Dakota. They usually returned, and after marriage settled down as members in the Amish community.

The following is a contemporary case of a young fellow who made plans to go west.

After deliberate planning, Jake decided to leave home for the west coast. He went to the train station with a group of Amish girls to buy his ticket in advance of leaving. Each of the girls was giggling as the Amish girls are wont to do. The agent sold him a one-way ticket to California. The next day the young man was seen in his "English" dress with a crew haircut, flashy trousers, necktie, and jacket, all in poor taste as non-Amish standards go.

An outsider who knew the young man well met him in town and said, "I have seen you somewhere before. You remind me of an Amish boy named Jake."

"Well, I'm Jake."

"You are Jake? You don't look like him, you have a crew cut, and you don't look Amish."

"Well, I have my Amish clothes in that bag over there. I have two bags, one with my Amish clothes, and one for clothes I'm going to wear on this trip. I'm going west.

"I'll have a job out there. But that's not why I'm going. I just want to see the west. I have been to New York already, to Florida, too."

"Have you been baptized?" asked the outsider.

"Yes."

"Did you make the other trips after you were baptized?"

"No, before."

"So this is the first trip you're making after you are baptized?"

"Yes."

"What does your father say?"

"Well, he's liberal. Anyway, with fourteen kids on the farm, he doesn't miss one of us. There isn't too much work for us."

"Where did you get your money?"

"Hiring out."

Jake intended to stay in the west five or six months if he got a job, then return to his community.

"Suppose you find someone out west whom you want to marry?" he was asked.

"That isn't very likely."

"You know she wouldn't be very likely to come into the Amish church. In fact, it would be impossible, would it not?"

"No, I'm not going to worry about that, because I'm not fixing to get married."

"What if you get so interested in the outside world that you will want to stay? Don't you think you might want to stay?"

"No, I've been out before, and I always want to come back home, because you know, we have a way of life which is very nice and I like it. I like the farm, I like the family, and my people. I like New York for a couple of days, but I wouldn't want to live there. Florida was all right, but I don't like them women: they were all painted and so forth, artificial."

Jake showed considerable knowledge of the outside world and was conversant with it. He had already developed tastes and opinions about likes and dislikes within it. He knew about baseball, train strikes, international problems, and he had done some reading on the side which his father and church did not know about.

"Well, how are you going to take this trip without the bishop knowing about it?" asked his friend.

"Oh, the bishop don't know about it. Nobody is going to tell him."

"Nobody knows you're leaving?"

"Oh yes, my family knows, and a few other people."

"And the bishop won't know you are leaving?"

"Well, if he finds out, I'll have to make a confession. I have made one already because I drive a car."

"But suppose they put you under the *Meidung?*"

"No, they won't do that."

"How do you know? After all, this is the first trip you are taking since you were baptized."

"Well, if they do, I'll just go on another trip and come back again."

Jake seemed well poised, reasonably articulate, and his plans were well advanced. He planned to ride by coach all the way to the west coast. Jake reminded his friend that other Amish boys do the same. Many go to Florida during the winter months and hire out to hotels as bellboys. "There are lots of Amishmen all over the place that you don't know about," Jake told his friend. "It's the same with the girls."

In another case, quite unlike the above, two brothers purchased an automobile to see the world. "We traveled all over the United States and visited practically all the states. We just cut a high figure eight all over the United States. We were interested in traveling, and we told our parents, and then bought a car. We each had a half share and after returning I sold my share." The boys left in the spring and returned in the fall.

Another type of exodus was the boy who left as usual on Monday morning for work at a nearby Mennonite farm. "I did not want to leave this way, but I decided I would write my parents a letter after I was away so they wouldn't need to worry about me. I stayed away several weeks, then because I was not of legal age, I got a warning from the courthouse. I told my boss I did not think the warning meant anything because I was sure my father would not go to law. Then in a few days I got a phone call from my dad, and he asked if I am coming home. I told him I would come home to visit but I didn't feel too welcome. I said I could not stay home. So he said he would have to go to the courthouse. Then I knew he was not kidding. My boss went to the courthouse to find out what would happen. He found out they could only take me home, but they could make it bad for him as my employer. So I left his place and on the advice of a friend went to Florida. While down there I also got a warning from the courthouse, so I went to see them about it. They said Florida authorities could do nothing but the Pennsylvania authorities could come and get me, but it would cost them a lot of money and they probably would not. After they heard my story, they told me not to worry."

Another young man said, "I did not run away at night. After my father accused me of something I had not done, I just put on my old straw hat and walked down the road. I wanted to join the army but was too young. I worked for an English farmer not far away who hated the Amish. My father saw me in town one day and asked me why I don't come home. I said, 'I'm not coming home now nor will I ever come home.'" Meanwhile this young man joined a traveling medicine show which visited his home town. "They needed a boy to help. Of course, I was interested. I had read a lot about circuses so I joined the show. We traveled all over the state. I ran the popcorn machine, took the tent down, and cleaned up the papers and mess afterwards. The show did not get into any of the Amish communities. I would sell tickets at the door, and if the ropes needed tightening, I did that. On my birthday the recruiting officer got in touch with me. I left and joined the service."

The role of "change agents" or sympathizers within the Amish social system and of "acculturation agents" in outside social systems facilitates culture contact in many ways. These are a few selected incidents of life experiences. The nature of this contact consists not only of personally assisting the deviating person but also of transmitting ideas and knowledge from one culture to the other. The motivations for breaking with the culture as we have seen in this and in the last chapter are multiple. They tend to be associated with lack of personal fulfillment in the areas of education, middle-class American values, and religious expression. Acculturation agents tend to be of the kind which can give assistance or information in these areas.

## Meidung *and Mate Selection*

One of the obvious reasons for "taking a fling" is to travel and see the world before one settles down to married life.

After marriage Amish persons become less mobile. But another underlying reason for travel is to get out from under the *streng Meidung*. The threat of *Meidung* is given more than a little deliberation by some serious-thinking, single Amish persons. Marriage, among other things, means supporting the rule of the community. Some do not feel that they can conscientiously support strict shunning; travel to a settlement where the strict form of *Meidung* is not practiced has been one way to get out from under it.

The Pennsylvania Amish have been traditionalists in maintaining the strict *Meidung*, especially since the notorious case of Moses Hartz in the late nineteenth century.[6] From Pennsylvania the strict *Meidung* has been introduced to other settlements who are "in full fellowship" with the Pennsylvania group. To be in full fellowship means that preachers and especially bishops are in agreement with the *Ordnung* and may exchange visits and preach in each other's services. Other settlements who practice the strict *Meidung* include some districts in Ohio, Ontario, and Maryland. The midwestern Amish have not generally upheld the strict *Meidung*. It will be recalled that strict *Meidung* requires shunning between marriage partners as well as all who leave the Amish church to join any other affiliation, even Amish Mennonite or Mennonite. The Washington-Johnson settlement in Iowa will shun any excommunicated member but discontinues *Meidung* if the offender joins another nonresistant church. In Buchanan County, Iowa, where strict shunning is practiced, an excommunicated member continues to be shunned unless he returns to the Amish church. Some districts will discontinue shunning after two years.

This form of social control has great influence over mate selection. The controls are further complicated in that *Meidung* varies not only with geographic settlements but between different groups of Amish in the same settlement. Thus a man who marries a girl in a "strict *Meidung* church" is asking for trouble the rest of his life if the couple stays in their home community, since either he or his wife may have to be shunned

[6] See pp. 243-45.

the rest of their life by their in-laws. *Meidung* thus functions to produce the effects of a closed system of social class. The members must stay in the church into which they are born, must marry in the clan, and perform the occupations approved by the church.

One young man who realized the seriousness of the *Meidung* in his strict church went to Iowa to escape. He transferred his "church letter" to the Iowa Amish and was received in good standing. From the Iowa Amish he affiliated with the Mennonites in the same state. He is now out from under the shunning. In another instance, a former Amish member said: "The *Meidung* is a terrible thing. When there was a church split in my community, the *Meidung* was not practiced at first because there were too many people involved. But later when the strict church introduced *Meidung* against the others, it brought terrible trouble, especially among the young people. I know what I am talking about. I went with different girls, and their fathers always guarded against having the *Meidung* in their family. The fathers in the strict church would say, "I have nothing against _____ but we don't want the *Meidung* in our family." To have the *Meidung* in the family or among the relatives produces hardship, it strains the relations of the kinship group.

There are a number of marriages where the couple and their in-laws are torn between the loyalties of two groups. In one case the husband retained membership in a strict church while his wife belonged to the non-*Meidung* Amish group. Though they lived together as marriage partners, the husband did not join the church of his wife because it would mean being shunned by his parents and relatives. The wife, because of the strict shunning, refused to join the church of her husband. The marriage held together in spite of this cleavage and the children tended to belong to the church of the mother. But this marriage and family became a model for others in the community not to duplicate.

A Pennsylvania boy in a rather progressive Amish district wanted to marry a girl in the strict *Meidung* church. Both went to Iowa, but at different times. She left first and lived

in the Iowa community where she worked for some time as
a hired girl. The boy arrived later, but both learned that they
were not able to complete a marriage in Iowa without bringing on the sanctions of her church. From Iowa she went to
Indiana where she worked as a maid; while there she had her
church letter accepted in a district of Amish that had no strong
affiliation with the "strict *Meidung* people." The couple were
then able to marry without severe sanctions. In this way, the
in-laws were also happy, because a wedding could be arranged
in which both families could participate, and they would not
need to have the *Meidung* in the family.

### Marginal Occupations

Amish households generally rank each other by their success
as farmers and good managers. In farming first-rate importance
is given to a large family and to the family as a productive
team. There are always persons who by reason of health or
physical condition cannot make a success of farming, and
there are some who appear not to have the interest and the
skills for farming. Certain other farm-related occupations are
sanctioned, but such occupations are not given the same high
rank as farming.

Occupations which have traditionally been avoided are now
more widespread than before. Carpentry, masonry, cabinetmaking, processing plants, village factories (including garment
factories and trailer factories), especially in Ohio and Indiana,
have attracted hundreds of Amish laborers. Some engage in
this work to accumulate savings toward payments on a farm,
while others have no aspiration toward farming as long as factory employment is allowed. The extent to which one community of Amish has deviated from farming as the main occupation is seen in the accompanying table. The settlement around
Middlefield, Ohio, with 17 districts has 612 household heads.
Of those in active employment, only 47 per cent are engaged
in full-time farming. A high percentage are employed in factories, while some have combined farming with carpentry.
Others are employed as railroad workers and some are

Table 8

Occupation of Old Order Amish Family Heads,
Geauga County, Ohio, 1959

| Occupation | Per cent of Total |
|---|---|
| Farming (includes 30 retired) | 47 |
| Factory worker | 17 |
| Carpenter (full time) | 13 |
| Timber work, sawmilling | 7 |
| Carpenter and farmer | 4 |
| Shopwork (self-employed) | 2 |
| Butcher | 2 |
| Day laborer | 1 |
| Blacksmith | 1 |
| Railroad worker | 1 |
| Widows and single households | 4 |
| No information | 1 |
| Per cent | 100 |
| Number of Households | 612 |

SOURCE: *Ohio Amish Directory,* 1959. Includes seventeen districts in the Geauga County Area.

self-employed in small shops. Cross (1967: 49) observed that over one-fourth of the Amish in the Holmes County area were engaged in non-farming occupations. In the Nappanee, Indiana, community, Landing (1967: 118) found that nearly half the household heads were employed in small factories.

One of the professions making inroads into the Amish culture is teaching. When the Amish sent their children to the public school, they did not need to train their own people for this vocation. Now that schools have been consolidated, forcing the Amish to establish private schools, their own young people need formal training for this profession. The other alternative is to hire sympathetic non-Amish, or sometimes Mennonite teachers, but this has never been very satisfactory to the Amish. Mennonite teachers tend to teach religion to the Amish youngsters and for this reason the Amish parents take steps to guard against Mennonite teaching. The legitimation of the teacher role has caused the church to allow a few Amish youth to attend college for teacher training. But many

Amish persons teach who have never been to college and who would not qualify for state certificates. These persons, and especially those who have been to college, are engaged in marginal occupations. During the school term 1961–62 there were 102 private Amish schools in 12 states. Of the 122 teachers in these schools, 34 were men.

Another marginal profession is nursing and caring for the sick. A few Amish girls have become nurses. There are no Amish physicians, and this role appears not to be a likely one. An exceptional occupation is that of an Amish girl who is employed as a registered technician. She completed high school by correspondence and by loaning books from a local high school. She had always anticipated the vocation of nursing. Upon counseling with a director of nursing, she learned that a professional uniform would be required and no exception could be made. She knew that she could not remain loyal to the Amish church if she followed this vocation, so she began training for work as a technician. She commuted to a college and completed the courses for a registered technician. In this role she is not required to wear white shoes or white stockings and she may wear a white coat over her Amish uniform while on duty. The hospital officials have been very co-operative in helping the girl find security in her new vocation. Safeguards were taken not to give publicity which would jeopardize her relationship to the Amish church. When photos of her graduating class appeared in the papers, hers was omitted. Her Amish friends believe that if she keeps the *Ordnung*, she will be able to remain in good standing with her church.

These marginal vocations result in more intense contact with the outside world than does farming. The blacksmith in the following case appears to illustrate the outcome of frequent contact with outsiders.

Sam was a blacksmith in a small village. Outsiders liked to talk with him regularly over the anvil. He showed unusual articulation and grasp of the outside world. Upon returning to the shop one day, an English friend discovered that Sam was no longer around. Upon inquiring, he learned that Sam had bought a car, left the church, and changed jobs. The

English friend searched for his former Amish friend, and on finding him asked: "What gave?"

"Oh, I just got tired of taking orders. We can be saved on the outside too. The Amish church has no priority on salvation."

Sam found himself in a new world, a world that was perhaps much more insecure for his family. As a day laborer, he found himself going from one job to another. Although he was a hard worker and a strong man, he kept losing jobs. The negative sanctions imposed upon him by the Amish are believed to have contributed to job insecurity.

By comparing the new telephone directory with the old in areas heavily populated with Amish, it may be seen that many more typical Amish names appear each year. Small business and industry attracts some of the Amish fathers, usually on a part-time basis or as a hobby. There are many evidences of trading with outsiders, especially in the Lancaster County, Pennsylvania, community. Signs at the end of lanes announce goods for sale and among them are: potatoes, violets, lawn chairs, dry goods, saws sharpened, honey, lumber, brooms, home-baked bread, greenhouse plants, ice cream, and vegetables in season. One farm family sells ice cream to all who enter the farm lane; even though for a long time no sign at the lane indicated that anything was for sale, tourists to Lancaster County found their way to the farm by reading the "Amish tour guides." The farm is also a distribution center for rugs, quilts, china, and handcrafts. At any time of day and every day except Sunday visitors come and go from the farm.

A few of these part-time interests have led to full-scale production, altering the farm economy. An Amishman in Ontario has specialized in making self-feeders for threshing machines for many years. The firm manufactures a variety of farm implements. An enterprising Amishman in Pennsylvania invented a farm implement which developed a nation-wide market. The development of the business proceeded with a son-in-law who was a Mennonite, and in this way electric power could be utilized without sole Amish ownership. As the firm prospered, relations with the church became more strained and finally this man of excellent general reputation was excommunicated. In commenting about this person, a neighbor said: "The Amish began to be impatient with him because he was the kind of man who could see into things. In his factory he got along well, and the rest of the Amish just couldn't take it. He was not a man who was living for himself. He was a man who was able to do things, and he was willing to do things for other people. You just can't say of him that he wanted to make money for himself. He lived to be doing things for the sake of doing them. But they couldn't swallow this anymore and they kicked him out."

Sickness, incapacity, or chronic illness of a family head may lead to marginal occupations of certain types. Daniel, a man in his fifties, always loved farming. According to a neighbor, "He has been in many things." As a result of an accident in his youth, "he had surgery done on his head and has suffered many headaches since. He has taken many pills from different doctors which now affect his heart." Besides being a sales agent for seeds, which allows him to travel in many Amish settlements, he also has been engaged in dynamite blasting as custom work. In this business he served as supplier of dynamite for hardware stores in his region of the state. The dynamite was ordered by carload lots and stored on his farm. This occupation was perhaps more compatible with farming than many.

The question may be raised: why do Amish persons who are really marginal remain with the Amish community? One young Amishman after many years of trying to remain loyal to the Amish faith gave up. He said: "I would rather be a conservative Mennonite than a liberal Amishman." But many who are allowed to exercise a small degree of marginality, prefer to remain with their kin and community. The contradictions of their culture are still not so great that they hinder personal fulfillment. A marginal occupation may be tolerated by the community so long as it does not constitute a direct threat. However, where the person takes his marginal occupation seriously and wishes to excel as in nursing, teaching, or manufacturing, the stress would undoubtedly exceed toleration limits.

# CHAPTER 12

# GROUP CLEAVAGES
# AND SOCIAL CHANGE

No SOCIETY CAN PERPETUATE ITSELF without risking the hazards of change and ultimately of disintegration. Behavior patterns do not stay the same in any society. Men and women do not think precisely alike within any society. All do not have the same abilities or tendencies toward conformity. Some are conservative, while others are of the creative type and learn new ways of doing and thinking. Some aspire to goals and positions which do not interest others. In the past two chapters we observed how the individual loses his Amish identity by breaking with his culture when individual interests cannot be exercised within the Amish cultural pattern. Groups as well as individuals break the traditional patterns. We turn now to group processes in Amish culture and the way in which special-interest groups emerge.

## Variations in Culture

To the outsider the Amish society appears to be remarkably uniform; the person who never participates in it cannot know how much folkways and *Ordnung* differ from one community to another. But by comparing several communities we may observe that the symbols of Amish life differ markedly from one community to another. There are differences not only from one settlement to another but also among Amish clans in the same community. The carriages or buggies of the Amish, for example, have many variations. In Lancaster County the two-seated carriages have gray tops, and in Ohio and farther west they have black tops. But there are also communities in Pennsylvania with yellow tops and white tops. In Lancaster County the single-seated buggy has been interpreted by the outsider as a "bachelor" or courting carriage. But single-seated carriages are also driven by the married Amish for other than churchgoing activities. In midwestern communities, black tops appear on single-seated carriages. Here and in Ontario are also found settlements where no tops are allowed. Modifications on the traditional carriage that have occurred as innovations are permitted by the rules of each community. The presence or absence of dashboards, whipsockets, battery-operated lights, roll-up side and rear curtains, and brakes varies from one group to another. The harness used on the horses also varies and is subject to *Ordnung*. A horse collar rather than the breast strap is prescribed in most Amish settlements.

A non-material variation in culture is the singing at the Amish preaching services. While all singing is in German from a common book, the embellishments of the orally transmitted tunes differ, as well as the time it takes to sing a hymn. In all Amish districts the *Loblied*, with four stanzas of seven lines each, is sung as the second hymn of the service. In one very traditional clan it takes thirty minutes to sing this song while in another it is sung in eleven minutes. The slow-singing groups are invariably more traditional in their total culture than the faster-singing groups. Where tunes are sung more slowly, the dresses of the women will be longer, the hair of the men will be longer, and the hat brims will be wider. Where the tunes are sung faster more modern conveniences are accepted, and here also the use of tractors for field work is evident. Thus the pace of singing is symbolic of the degree of acculturation of the total culture. Faster-singing groups have little in common with the slow-singing groups in the same community. The slow-singing groups regard the fast-singing groups as too progressive or too "worldly." The diversity of singing comes into focus where Amish people from different states and settlements are suddenly thrown together. This has occurred in the winter months, for example, when Amish from various states live temporarily in Florida. The difficulty of singing a single tune together is frequently experienced, particularly if the song leader is of a different settlement from the majority of the congregation.

Buggy tops and singing are only two of many pattern differentiations. The cut of clothing, the shape of women's head coverings, the use of farm tractors, and travel beyond the local community are other variables. Some differences are clearly the result of cultural drift and fusion, while others are the result of cleavage between groups. There are many traditional differences in culture which are no cause for cleavage and are taken for granted. Thus, "other things being equal," the Lancaster County Amish who drive with gray carriage tops may be "in full fellowship" with an Ohio group that has black tops, or with an Ontario group that has no tops. But changes of a certain type are cause for group cleavage. The process of introducing new cultural elements may be viewed in three phases: (1) the acceptance of a change by a few members within the society, whom we designate as innovators, (2) the dissemination of change to other members within the society, and (3) the processes by which the changes are finally adjusted to the traditional culture matrix.[1]

The reasons for diversity in culture, and the motives of the innovators, are in most instances difficult to know. Curiosity, desire for advantage, and novelty are certainly among them. In Amish society the desire for higher education, the desire for automobiles, and the desire for the advantages of middle-class American values would appear to play a major role.

### Diversity in a Community

The community containing the largest number of cleavages in North America occurs in an area between two Pennsylvania mountains: Jacks and Stone Mountains, in the Kishacoquillas Valley in Mifflin County. Here there are five Amish groups and five additional Mennonite or Mennonite-related groups

[1] Ralph Linton, *Acculturation in Seven American Indian Tribes* (D. Appleton-Century Co., 1940), 470.

who occupy the same oval-shaped valley about thirty miles long. All originate in whole or in part from a single group of Amish who came to this region as early as 1791 from southeastern Pennsylvania. These rank themselves in the order of their assimilation into the prevailing American culture, or from "low" to "high" church. A low church is one that has retained the old traditions, while a high church is one that is more like "the world."

The cleavages [2] which gave rise to these groups are perpetuated largely through oral tradition. Here we are not interested in the historical account but in the boundary-maintaining symbols and mechanisms which prevent association.

The "Old School" Amish, also known locally as Nebraska Amish,[3] comprise groups I and II. Group I dates from 1881 and II from 1942. The name Nebraska derives from Bishop Yost B. Yoder of the state of Nebraska who was called upon to restore unity in the church in 1881. His efforts failed, and the faction with which he sided was dubbed "Nebraska Amish." The Old Schoolers, as they are called locally, wear their hair about shoulder length. They wear white shirts, brown denim trousers and coats, wide brim hats, no suspenders, and no belts. Trousers are held up by means of a laced crotch at the rear. The women wear a black kerchief tied on the head over the white covering, as bonnets are prohibited. Over this they wear the "scoop" or flat hat, made of straw, which resembles a European peasant hat worn two centuries ago. The wide brim is folded down at the sides by means of a string which is tied beneath the chin. Of all Amish women these wear the longest dresses, usually made of dark plain colors. In winter, women wear the *Mandel*, a long outer garment like

---

[2] The early cleavages of this community are discussed in part in an article by the writer in "The Life and Times of Samuel Yoder, 1824–1884," *M.Q.R.* (October, 1948). The nearby Union County division is covered by John S. Umble, *M.Q.R.* (April, 1933).

[3] See "The Amish in Gosper County, Nebraska," *Mennonite Historical Bulletin* (October, 1949), and Maurice A. Mook, "The Nebraska Amish in Pennsylvania," in *Mennonite Life* (January, 1962), and paintings in (July, 1961).

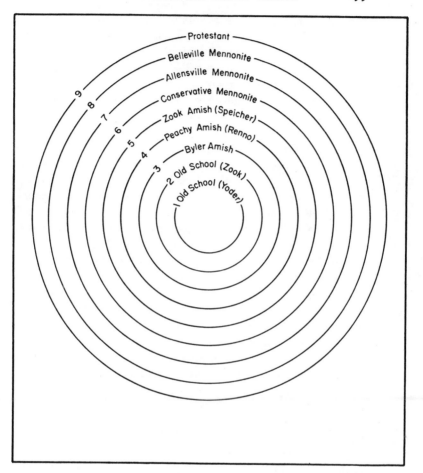

*Figure 13.* Diagram Showing Cognitive Orientation of Amish-Mennonite Groups from "Low" to "High" Church in Mifflin County, Pennsylvania.

an overcoat, and not shawls. Modern farm equipment is taboo. Until about 1940 these Amish people were threshing grain with horse power. Traction engines are taboo, but one- or two-cylinder engines are now used for belt power. Lawn mowers, screens at the windows or doors, curtains and carpets, are taboo. All buggies are two-seated with a white top. There are no single-seated or open buggies, though spring wagons or "market wagons" as they are called, with brown tops, are used. Seats have no springs, there are no coil springs, and there is no dashboard or whipsocket. Barns remain unpainted, and many houses also are not painted. A projecting roof at the gable ends of buildings is taboo.

Group II emerged as a faction from I about 1942, but to the outsider these groups appear identical. Each group has its own worship on the same Sunday, and each has two bishops to insure its independence from the other. The young people associate with each other and have a common singing. A difference of opinion arose between two ministers, according to one source, when a member moved onto a farm formerly owned by "English" people. The question was whether the new owner would need to saw off the projecting roof on the gable ends of his buildings. The group took sides on the question. A member in sympathy with the new owner built a doghouse with a projecting roof, which appears to have brought the division to a head.

The "Byler Church," group III, is sometimes called *die Alt Gemee* (the old church), and by a more descriptive phrase, the "Bean-soupers." The name comes from the practice of serving bean soup at lunch after preaching, but the same practice holds for groups I and II also. Generically this group traces its connection to the Samuel B. King division in 1849 and in its oral tradition regards itself as the oldest Amish group in the valley. One of the most distinguishing traits of culture is the use of yellow tops on the two-seated buggies. The men may wear shirts other than white, and blue is very predominant. Until recent years another distinguishing feature was no suspenders, but since they have begun to exchange ministers with group IV, the younger men wear a single suspender. The hair of the men is shorter than the above groups but still covers the ears. The women wear brown bonnets and black shawls but have traditionally also worn the *Mandel*. Tractors are used for belt power but not for field work. Single-seated buggies are used by this group, especially among the unmarried men. Spring wagons, one-horse buggies with one seat in the front and a long compartment in the rear, are used to haul bags of feed or other light loads. Buildings are generally painted and in good condition. Half-length curtains (lower half), window blinds, and screens are used, but no woven carpets so typical of many other Amish.

The Peachey group or "Renno" Amish, after Bishop John Renno (group IV), dates from 1863 when Abraham Peachey led it as a right-wing splinter group. A controversy over whether to baptize in the creek (advocated by Solomon Beiler) was a major cause of the division. Under Beiler's leadership two meetinghouses were also built in the valley, at Allensville and at Belleville.

The Renno Amish maintain "full fellowship" with their Lancaster brethren in practicing the *streng Meidung* and culturally conform to the same general standards, but with some exceptions. The men wear a single suspender and their hair covers the ears. The women wear dark, plain-colored dresses, black bonnets, white starched head coverings, and black shawls. The Sunday dress of unmarried girls above the age of puberty includes a white *Halsduch*, a white apron, and a black head covering. Families drive two-seated buggies to the preaching. Single boys drive a one-seated open buggy with dashboard, whipsocket, and battery lights. Spring wagons are also used for hauling materials from local villages. Farm buildings are painted and generally well kept. Barns typically are red and houses white, though there is no colored trimming on the buildings. Carpets, window blinds, and half-length curtains are common. Inside toilets and bath tubs are permitted, which represents a recent change.

The Zook church or "Speicher" group, after Bishop Jesse Speicher, but traditionally the "Zook" church, after Bishop John B. Zook, was a splinter from the Peachey Amish in 1911, mostly over the question of the *streng Meidung*.[4] When a seceding group in Lancaster County applied for ministerial

[4] Calvin G. Bachmann, *The Old Order Amish in Lancaster County, Pennsylvania* (Pennsylvania German Society, 1961), 281–88.

help in Mifflin County and John Zook came to their assistance, the division was initiated. Until 1954, when this group adopted the use of automobilies, they conformed generally to the typical Amish pattern of culture, but with two suspenders instead of one, shorter hair than the Renno group, and the use of sweaters and zipper jackets. The brims of men's hats were narrower; the dresses of the women longer. Tractors were used for farming for many years. Electricity was adopted by the group about 1948. The use of rubber-tired tractors preceded the adoption of the automobile. Carpets, linoleum, modern kitchen appliances, and wall mottoes are common. The adoption of the automobile has resulted in considerable social distance from the local Amish groups. It has brought indirectly many other changes, especially in occupation and in travel, and the group built a meetinghouse in 1962. The Speicher group exchanges ministers with "Beachy" Amish churches.

The Locust Grove or Conservative Mennonite church, group VI, was organized in 1898 under the leadership of Bishop Abram D. Zook by members of the Allensville and Belleville meetinghouse churches who felt that change was taking place too rapidly. The congregation is now part of the Conservative Mennonite Conference. The church is distinguished from others described so far in that it has a meetinghouse and Sunday school and generally conforms to Mennonite practices. Women's dresses are far more modern than the Amish ones, though sleeveless dresses and make-up are taboo. Print dresses, black stockings, cape dresses, white coverings embellished with strings, and an abbreviated black bonnet are characteristic of women's dress. The plain, collarless coat is encouraged for men, but there is no restriction on the length of their hair. There are no taboos on farming equipment and little proscription of occupation. Foreign missions, foreign relief, and benevolent giving are a part of the church program. The membership is made up almost entirely of former Amish families.

The Allensville and Belleville Mennonite groups, respectively, trace their origin to Amish congregations which established meetinghouses about 1868. Both congregations are affiliated with the Allegheny Mennonite Conference, a conference district of the Mennonite General Conference, the largest branch of Mennonites. Both churches are made up of families with Amish backgrounds. Differentiation between the two congregations are apparent in the dress and discipline of the members. Bonnets and cape dresses for the women, and plain coats for the men are not required or advocated by the Belleville congregation, otherwise called Maple Grove.

These ten groups of Amish and Amish Mennonites in one community represent the most divergent expression of Amish culture anywhere in North America. Ritual avoidance is maintained between orthodox groups. In secular activities, at sales, and in mutual-aid practices there is limited interaction. The "lowest" church has very little interaction even with other Amish that are "higher" and has tended to segregate itself at one end of the valley.

Two other distinctive groups have established themselves in this small valley since 1950 and now claim former adherents to the Amish faith. They are in some sense proselyting groups. The first is the Church of God in Christ Mennonite group now holding services in an abandoned school house. A young Amish member became "converted" to this denomination after leaving his home community. Upon his conversion, he became concerned about his "lost" Amish brethren and with assistance from Church of God ministers succeeded in attracting members of his former group to a new "sanctified way." Several families from the Renno church now make up this congregation, including a former young minister, a son of the bishop. The group adheres to the beard and *streng Meidung*, but has no taboos on farm machinery or automobiles. A strong doctrine of sanctification and "the second work of grace" make up the ideological content in addition to strict Biblicism. This group is also called "Holdeman Mennonites."

The other revivalist group that built a meetinghouse in Belleville in 1959 is the Brethren in Christ denomination. It gained adherents when members of the now mobile Speicher group attended Brethren in Christ revival meetings in and outside of Mifflin County. It too stresses a doctrine of sanctification combined with a devout interest in revival preaching, but does not require beards nor the *streng Meidung*. Both of the above groups remain small but very active in attracting members of the Amish to their ranks.

This highly stratified religious social system performs a number of sociological functions associated with maintenance of community boundaries. Except for the two proselyting groups last mentioned, each respects the customs and rights of the other. No effort is made to gain converts from one to the other. Each Amish group is highly endogenous and is so maintained by the threat of *Meidung*. This system of stratification permits the person to move gradually from a "lower" group to a more progressive one in a natural and slow manner. The abruptness of changing one's customs and beliefs to a radically different system is thus avoided. The greater the social distance between the clans, the less likely are the members to drop out and affiliate with the tribe nearest like it in *Ordnung*. Among the "lowest" two groups, there is very little tendency to join the "higher" groups. Defecting Amish young men, though very few, tend to make abrupt changes like joining the army. This tendency to accept no religious affiliation rather than a Mennonite congregation has been observed also in Iowa. Melvin Gingerich writes: "It was a great tragedy when one of their members joined another denomination, and the distrust of other church fellowships was often so great that even expelled members did not join other churches but remained away from all church contacts. . . ." [5]

The problem of land room is alleviated by the sizable number of persons who leave the stricter Amish groups and join a Mennonite congregation. In this way families become en-

[5] Melvin Gingerich, *The Mennonites In Iowa* (The State Historical Society of Iowa, Iowa City, Iowa, 1939), 173-74. Further insight into cleavages appears in the same source in Chapter XI, "Differences of Opinion."

gaged in occupations other than farming. The boundaries of each religious community are preserved by excommunication of the deviant person: he simply moves up the ladder to a "higher" church and in this way establishes adjustment without "contaminating" his own kin. Each ceremonial group thus retains its small size and conforms to the features of a homogeneous culture.

We have observed how differentiating groups emerge in the little Amish community. Cleavages form on the basis of unequal diffusion of culture. The attitudes of not only the leaders but also of the membership toward these and other innovations differ. In some settlements those who disagree with the rules have by common consent migrated to other settlements. An alternative to migration, as a method of settling differences, is the formation of splits or cleavages. When geographic distance no longer functions effectively, then social distance is achieved by symbolic differences and differentiation in *Ordnung*.

In Ohio, there are five different gradations or groups of Old Order Amish concentrated in the same community who have no fellowship or exchange of ministers among them. These are usually named after the bishop of each group. In Indiana and Iowa there are also such differences but perhaps less pronounced. In Lancaster County there has been little splitting into divergent groups except for the Weavertown Amish-Mennonite group. The bishops and ministers here have met more consistently over the years to iron out their differences, as they still do twice annually. Others, both bishops and lay members who disagree with the rules, have by common consent moved to other settlements. Migration in such instances prevents open cleavages.

## The Formation of Issues

To precipitate a division it is necessary for members to take opposing sides on a question. One or two examples will illustrate the nature and intensity of Amish cleavages. There is the notorious case of Moses Hartz, which has been called a *Hut-lerei*, a tangle of confusion. The incident occurred over half a century ago but is still vivid in the minds of older Amish people.

Moses Hartz was a prosperous Amish farmer, a preacher, and was regarded by many in his district as an unusually intelligent man and an able speaker. He often expressed affection for the Amish churches. Moses had a son, also named Moses, who took up the occupation of millwright. The son became an expert in selling and installing machinery in mills for a manufacturing company. To make a success of this occupation the son felt that he could not keep all the rules of the Amish church; for one thing, he wanted outside pockets on his coat, which the Amish forbade. So he "quietly went to the Mennonites."

The young Moses Hartz was excommunicated from the Amish church as is customary for transgressors, but without the full consent of the members. Although the decision to excommunicate him was not unanimous, the bishop pronounced him "out." Preacher Moses Hartz felt he could not shun his son just for joining the Mennonites. Because he refused to shun his son, he was "silenced" as a preacher. Years of contention and stress followed but no reconciliation seemed possible.

Finally, Preacher Moses Hartz and his wife made application to join the Amish-Mennonite church. This was a meetinghouse church made up of former Amish who were more progressive in their ways. The Amish Mennonites were hesitant about taking into their membership a silenced preacher from the Old Order church, but consented to taking Moses and his wife as lay members. The Old Order group then took action to shun the aged couple for joining the meetinghouse group. This provoked further discussion and contention in both churches. Some of the Amish Mennonites said it was wrong to receive members who were not in good standing in the Old Order. The decision of the Old Order church to shun the Hartzes had the effect of dividing the members in the Amish-Mennonite group. Of course, many of the people in the Old Order group were close relatives of those in the Mennonite group and kinship affinity was probably a factor.

An out-of-state committee was asked to investigate the entire affair and to make recommendations. After hearing the story from all sides, the committee recommended that Moses and Lena be given the choice of going back to the Old Order Amish group or making a confession upon their knees in the Amish-Mennonite church. The Amish-Mennonite group agreed to stand by the recommendations of the committee. The couple chose to make the confession.

With confession and full reconciliation to the Amish-Mennonite group, the trouble finally appeared to be settled. A delegation carried the news back to the Old Order Amish bishop. The bishop expressed pleasure with the decision. Moses and Lena had now been received into the Amish-Mennonite group from a state of excommunication or "Bond." They had acknowledged their faults. The way seemed clear to discontinue the practice of shunning them. At the next meeting of the Old Order Amish ministers the bishop reported the reconciliation of the Hartz couple to the Amish-Mennonite group. It was decided to drop the *Meidung*.

But one aged, influential bishop, David Beiler, had not been present at the above meeting of the ordained. At the next meeting of the Old Order ministers he used his influence to upset the decision and to renew the *Meidung* against Moses and Lena Hartz. To their deaths they were shunned. The incident culminated in a cleavage. About one hundred members withdrew from the Old Order to form a separate church. Years of contention and bitter feelings prevailed, bringing stress between families and relatives. One survivor of the Hartz incident said, "The old people rehearsed the doings until the people of my age grew sour on the avoidance principle." [6]

Cleavages are sometimes precipitated between settlements in

---

[6] C. Z. Mast, in a letter to the author (July 3, 1950), reports that "People would come from other states to contact my father Bishop John S. Mast about the proceedings. Father had the written account of his father John M. Mast (1829–1901)." Biographical material on Moses Hartz (1819–1916) and his son Moses (1864–1946) appears in *Moses Hartz Family History 1819–1965*, by Amos and Susan Hartz, Elverson, Pa., 1965.

different states or in those a great distance from each other. Sometimes an excommunicated member who moves from one state to another "to get away from it all" becomes the key figure of the division. Such a member in Ohio moved to an Amish settlement in Indiana. In Indiana he was received into the Amish church upon confession, or out of a state of "Bond." After several years the Indiana church wanted to have a "fellowship" status with the Ohio group. The Ohio bishop replied that this could be achieved only if so-and-so, the former erring Ohio member, were excommunicated from the Indiana church. The Indiana bishop excommunicated the member and announced that all who did not favor affiliating with the Ohio group could not take communion. The Indiana church was split when over half of the members decided to withstand the decision of the presiding bishop. Five of the bishop's brothers and two of his sisters were among the dissenters who called in another bishop to have communion.

In another instance, in 1884, a preacher in Indiana, Christian Wary, moved to the state of Iowa. "He intended to join the Old Order church and attended their services on his first Sunday in the community, but he was not asked to preach because he had a folding top buggy and a raincoat, two conveniences that were not tolerated by the Iowa group. When he was approached on the question, he replied that he was unwilling to give up anything that protected his health." [7] A group of seceding members in the community then asked him to be their minister. This group developed into the East Union Mennonite Church, near Kalona, Iowa.

### Assimilation Patterns in a Century

The main cleavages during the past one hundred years of Amish life in North America are shown in Table 9. The Amish settlements in America were small, scattered, and semi-isolated before 1850. As American industry, commerce, and agriculture grew, and communication and travel increased,

[7] Melvin Gingerich, op. cit., 137.

Table 9

Groups Emerging from Amish Background, 1862–1962

| Date | Name of Body or Emergent Group |
|------|--------------------------------|
| 1862 | *Verhandlung der Diener Versammlungen* (General Ministers' Conferences) |
| 1866 | "Egli Amish" or Defenseless Mennonite Church, later Evangelical Mennonite Church |
| 1872 | "The Stucky Mennonites" or Central Conference Mennonites (merged with the General Conference Mennonite Church) |
| 1888 | Indiana-Michigan Amish Mennonite Conference (merged with the Mennonite Church in 1917) |
| 1890 | Western Amish Mennonite Conference (merged with the Mennonite Church in 1920) |
| 1893 | Eastern Amish Mennonite Conference (merged with the Mennonite Church in 1927) |
| 1910 | Conservative Amish Mennonite Conference (affiliated with the Mennonite Church) |
| 1927 | Beachy Amish Mennonite Churches (unaffiliated) |

differences in culture and in ceremony began to be realized by the leaders. In order to reconcile differences in religious practices and to provide opportunity for regular consultation, an annual General Ministers' Conference was begun in 1862. The conferences were often held in a large barn, were open to the laity, and were attended by ministers from several states. Preachers brought their concerns and questions for clarification. Difficult questions were assigned to a committee that studied the problem thoroughly and brought recommendations to the assembly.

There was general unanimity on some of the answers to questions, but it soon became apparent that there was disagreement on a number of issues. During the Civil War there was general agreement that participation in war was not scriptural, that members could not engage in teamster service under military control, and that former members who had joined the army but who had been reinstated into the church could not receive pensions. Occupations which were closely allied with business were forbidden, such as managing a store, post office, or express office. Lightning rods, lotteries, photographs, insurance, and big meetinghouses were considered innovations and worldly.

An early American cleavage was the emergence of the "Egli Amish." Henry Egli, a bishop of the Amish group near Berne, Indiana, claimed to have experienced regeneration of heart and restoration from a prolonged illness. In his home church he preached the necessity of a vital religious experience and of experiential knowledge of conversion. He charged his church with formalism, lack of spiritual vitality, and looseness in maintaining the old customs, and began rebaptizing persons who had not experienced regeneration at the time of their first baptism. The Amish conference was unable to heal the breach which resulted in Egli's local church. The small congregation divided over the issue. The followers of Egli organized a separate church, but the contention spread to other Amish groups in Illinois, Missouri, Kansas, Nebraska, and Ohio. Egli visited these places and gained many supporters. The early emphasis on strictness in discipline, the banning of jewelry, tobacco, and alcohol, and the discipline of plain dress and the veiling for women was soon relaxed along with the switch from the German to the English language. After the death of its leader in 1890 the group developed interest in missionary work after the manner of Protestantism. Another division occurred in 1898 within the Egli Amish over the question of immersion and resulted in the formation of the Missionary Church Association. The Egli Amish adopted the name "Defenseless Mennonite."

A second cleavage occurred in 1872 with the development of the "Stuckey Mennonites." Joseph Stuckey, bishop of a church in Illinois, and a leading figure in the Amish conference, was more open-minded on some questions than other Amish bishops. Stuckey was well liked by his district but suddenly found himself under censure from the Amish Ministers'

Conference. A school teacher in his congregation wrote a poem in which he expressed the thought that all men will eventually be saved and none punished for their sins. This expression of universalism in Stuckey's church was rank heresy among the Amish. Several of the verses were read at the next Amish conference, and it was decided to expel members who did not believe in future punishment. Stuckey refused to excommunicate the man who had written the poem. His refusal was regarded as insubordination. After committee deliberations on the subject Stuckey was requested to make a public confession. This he also refused, and in 1872 he severed connections with the Amish conference. Stuckey's church stood behind his decision and there was no split in his group. Churches under his oversight prospered and in 1899 his group was organized as the Central Illinois Conference of Mennonites. The word "Amish" dropped into disuse. Stuckey died in 1902 and his following is now a part of the General Conference Mennonite Church, a progressive denomination.

Following two major divisions, and with a number of contentious questions unresolved, the Amish Ministers' Conference discontinued after 1878. The failure to reach common consensus on many issues, the inability to reconcile differences, and "many petty jealousies and lack of forbearance" [8] brought the sessions to an end.

After 1878 the course of Amish history took three general directions. First, there were churches who favored retaining the old traditions unchanged as much as possible and who became known as "Alt Amisch" or Old Order Amish. Before this the word "Amish" or "Amish Mennonite" was sufficient. A second cluster of churches affiliated with the more liberal groups such as the Egli and the Stuckey churches, which were both of Alsatian origin and had already parted company with the traditionally minded churches. A third group comprised the middle-of-the-road churches who favored moderate changes and who were not minded to go along with radical change nor with the traditional customs. These, under the

[8] C. Henry Smith, *The Mennonites in America* (Goshen, 1909), 251.

name "Amish Mennonite," later organized into three regional conferences and eventually merged with the Mennonite Church.

By 1910 there were a few more Amish churches that did not wish to adhere strictly to the Old Order. They wanted to engage in evangelism and have Sunday schools, so they organized the Conservative Amish Mennonite Conference. This conference attracted a number of local churches, and by 1961 had eighty churches and a membership of over 5,000. "Amish" was dropped from the conference name in 1954.

In 1927 another group, called Beachy Amish, emerged from the Old Order. The movement began at Grantsville, Maryland, and was named after Bishop Moses M. Beachy.[9] Beachy as a progressive leader experienced mild disagreement with other leaders of his district over the practice of having Sunday school and the use of electricity and the automobile. Then when Beachy refused to excommunicate and shun members of his congregation for joining the Conservative Amish Mennonite churches in the area, he drew sharp criticism from some of his conservative-minded members. A few of them withdrew to fellowship with the conforming Old Order Amish element. Not many years passed until other Amish districts followed Beachy's example. Those Amish churches today who want automobiles, electricity, meetinghouses, and field tractors, generally turn "Beachy," except that other names for local groups are also used. In Lancaster County the church with this *Ordnung* was for many years called the "John A. Stoltzfus Church" or the "Weavertown Amish." In Indiana the group was called the "Burkholder Amish." Although the present twenty or more churches of this affiliation are not organized into a formal conference, they function as a separately organized denomination in the exchange of ministers and in the support of relief and missionary work. They have retained the German language in their worship (with some exceptions),

[9] Alvin J. Beachy, *The Amish of Somerset County, Pennsylvania: A Study in the Rise and Development of the Beachy Amish Mennonite Churches* (Hartford Seminary Foundation, 1952).

the practice of unison singing, and the traditional Amish dress.

A potentially emerging group from the Old Order is the special-interest group surrounding the publication of a periodical called *Witnessing*. The conditions coagulating this group were varied. First there was the unusual incident of Russell Maniaci, a Detroit workingman, a Catholic. While in a state of uncertainty about the adequacy of his religion, he read a newspaper account of Amish in Kansas who sold their farms because oil was discovered on them and moved away. Maniaci concluded that "either these people were fools or their religion was real," and in hope that it was "real" he wrote to one of the Amish farmers asking how he could join their group. He was referred to an Amish family in his own state of Michigan. Here he met M. E. Bontrager of Centerville, and Maniaci says, "We were treated like millionaires." But the Amish had no precedent for taking in outsiders and Maniaci and his family were referred to a small Mennonite mission in the city of Detroit, which they joined. But realizing that it was the Amish who won him to Christ, Maniaci set to work to arouse the Amish to do missionary work. The Amish expression of the Christian life, he felt with deep sincerity, should be proclaimed wide and far. He began publishing a news sheet, *Amish Mission Endeavor*, and sent specially prepared letters to all Amish ordained persons in which he said: "My only interest is to see the Amish Church on fire for the Gospel. What about the debt that you as a leader owe to the unsaved? There are many young people in your church who are willing to launch out. . . . Will you lead them or will you cause them to join other churches?" Maniaci's efforts brought some results, and he succeeded in polarizing a "mission-minded" group from many states. The first of several Amish Mission Conferences was held at Kalona, Iowa, in 1950. Some Amish persons attended against the advice of their bishops. In some of these conferences a Mennonite missionary speaker was engaged. A Mission Interests Committee was organized, which began publishing the periodical *Witnessing* in 1953.

Maniaci was considered a dangerous innovator by the Amish

leaders. After all, he could not speak the language of the Amish and was regarded by them as an intruder. To offset this criticism from the Amish leaders, lay members held the annual missionary conferences in German. Maniaci concluded that "they did not like an outsider running their affairs." Nevertheless, with his pointed mimeographed messages, he had helped to form a special interest group within the Amish society and put these persons into communication with each other.

Meanwhile an Old Order Amish minister, David Miller of Oklahoma, traveled through several states preaching the Gospel in an evangelistic manner. He not only pleaded, preached, and prayed at the traditional Amish services in an unorthodox manner, but also preached to large crowds gathered on the lawns of Amish homes in the evening. He won the admiration of hundreds of Amish people by his new "biblical" messages stripped of the usual Amish singsong delivery and older terminology. His preaching was received with great satisfaction by those who had been "hoping and praying for release from sin and overbearing traditions," but it also brought stress and worry to those leaders who hailed his "new light" and free spirit as *eppes neues* (something new).

The work of Maniaci and evangelist Miller brought together a considerable body of sympathizers from among the Amish young people who had been holding secret prayer groups and from young men who had been in conscientious objector camps during World War II and were in sympathy with other forms of Christianity. Parents who no longer took the pains to teach their children the German language were also among their supporters, as were young people who did not like the traditional Amish singings.

Miller was eventually denied fellowship with the Old Order Amish churches, and his own congregation began a Sunday school and allowed automobiles. But during the brief time he was engaged in preaching directly to the Old Order in his travels, he made real progress as an innovator. His own church eventually affiliated with the Beachy group. But there are still other Old Order preachers and lay members vitally but secretly interested in the "missionary movement."

This backflash into the assimilation patterns of a century illustrates two of the three processes [10] of introducing new cultural elements: the acceptance of change by a small group of innovators and the dissemination of change to other members within the society. The formation of a special-interest group typically evolves into a cleavage. The first two emerging groups in the nineteenth century had a spirited leader who took with them a body of sympathizers. Among the three regional conferences of Amish Mennonites organized after 1882 there were no sharp cleavages, and assimilation into the larger Mennonite bodies occurred peacefully.[11] The Beachy splinter created a local cleavage which spread to other regions where the assimilation pattern was less contentious and of a more peaceful character. The development of the Mission Interests Committee was again of a diffuse character involving interested persons from many states, but it was sparked by an outsider. The typical road from traditional Amish to non-Amish begins with interest in evangelism and Bible study, and leads to Sunday schools, missionary work, and automobiles, and ends largely in Mennonitism. Such periodic schisms are sparked by innovators and acculturation agents, and today by improved means of communication.

[10] Ralph Linton, *op. cit.*, 470.
[11] H. S. Bender, "Amish Mennonites," *M.E.*, Vol. I, 97.

CHAPTER 13

# TENSION AND CRISIS
# IN THE COMMUNITY

DIVISIONS ARE EXTERNAL PATTERNS of adjustment, easily discernible, and observable. The internal patterns of adjustment within the community are more difficult to observe. As the population increases, interests and informal groups within the district and community also increase. When a settlement becomes so large that the Amish people scarcely know each other, then the conditions for retaining the interests and beliefs of the little community are very different. Controls which were effective in the small, primary community are no longer effective in a community where people do not know each other well. Much stress can develop under these conditions.

Under conditions of population increase, where land room is limited, where the Amish live in solid areas, and where they succeed in keeping their young people in the church, we may expect to find many interest groups developing. Social control becomes difficult and the society is forced to accept variant means of achieving it. One community which meets these conditions is the Lancaster County settlement. Although special interest groups emerge in all age brackets, we have chosen to discuss only one of them, the period of courtship and youth.

In Amish society youth is the accepted time for deviancy. In this chapter we are discussing the Amish youth who for a time rejects the values and norms of his society. It is not intended to be a rounded portrayal of all youth in the Amish community or of all communities. Deviancy tends to take two forms: running wild, or increased interest in Bible study and intellectual activity. In terms of persons leaving the group or of group cleavage, the latter poses the greater threat.

The number of Amish young people who defect between the ages of sixteen and twenty-three varies a great deal with each area. With marriage there is generally a settling down to the rules of the community and acceptance of its norms. Less defection occurs after marriage.

## Population Density and the Singing

The accepted occasion for association among Amish young people is the "singing" held on Sunday evening in the same home where preaching was held in the forenoon. The traditional singing takes the form of sitting around a long table with boys on one side and girls on the other. In small Amish settlements, of from three to six districts, the young people may have one singing. As settlements become larger, two or more singings may be held. In Lancaster County, where the area occupied by the Amish has been greatly expanded, no formal organization regulates the singing institution. The number of young people is greater than can be accommodated in a single home. There are so many that they cannot know each other face to face. The result has been the development of informal, special-interest groups. The quotations below are from Amish participants.

"When my parents were young," said one young man, "there was one gang, and it was possible to drive every place in a horse and buggy. Groffdale used to be the center of Amish activity, as the young people used to meet here to find out where the singing was; then shoot off to the singing. Now they meet in Intercourse which is more the center of the Amish, but still there are Amish who live thirty miles away from here. They can't communicate, and this constitutes a problem."

One evidence of differentiation is the development of names for the various groups. "There are three main groups: there are the Groffies, the Ammies, and then the Trailers. The Grof-

fies are the most liberal, then the Ammies, and then the Trailers." Each has a number of subgroups, and their names and
interests also change as the systems are articulated through time.
"Under the Groffies are the Hillbillies, Jamborees, and the
Goodie-Goodies. The Groffies get their name from the village
of Groffdale. The Hillbillies come from Strasbourg to Georgetown, which really has hills, large hills—it's no reflection on
their culture, but they fit it very well. The Jamborees are
called that because they act unruly and aren't exactly liked
by the larger groups. Then there are the Goodie-Goodies because they are Christians, but they belong strictly to the
Groffies, because they are kind of sympathetic toward cars.
They are missionary-minded."

"The Ammies, after the name Amish, were the most loyal
when I went to the singings. [Subgroup developments] under
the Ammies are the Lemons, Keffers, and the Shotguns. Even
in these little subgroups there are differences in appearance,
dress, and differences in taste. The Shotguns are about the
most liberal. There is not much association between Groff-
dales and Ammies, but from Shotguns to Hillbillies there is a
lot."

"Many groups split off from the Ammies. There were the
Mickies (flies), not quite as loyal. The girls would start singing, but after an hour or so the boys would sing a bit, then
leave. The Keffers (bugs) were such a mixed group, some
wild and some plain, that they gave them this name because
they were so different. It is the oddest group I have ever seen.
The Lemons were earlier called Trailers and were descended
from them. The Trailers broke up, and some went with the
Keffers, some with the Ammies. One small group wanted to
join the Ammies, but they got pushed back because they had
been Trailers. So they started a group of their own. Others
called them Lemons because they just seemed to sit around
and look at each other, and some thought they were kind of
sour."

The Trailers occupy the area in the southernmost part of
the settlement and represent the most orthodox element, which

has tended to concentrate there in recent years. There are also subgroups among "these people who dress very plainly and are a lot more conservative and a lot less socially adapted to to our society. 'Nine Points' is the name of the gang, and this village is the center of activity. Since the Quarryville road shoots in one direction, Kirkwood in another, and Georgetown in another, they are called the Trailers." It is also apparent that the name is descriptive of their social characteristics; as one boy put it, "they are trailing along behind." These subgroups change their character in a short time, so that they may not necessarily exist by the time this book is in print.

Patterns of differentiation occur among young people's groups in other large settlements as is evidenced by the practice of name calling. In Indiana young people's groups have generally followed the assimilation patterns of the three main differentiated adult groups, Clearspring, Barrens, and Clinton. "In Ohio the good ones and the bad ones went inside, and the others stayed outside." The person in Ohio who was on the borderline, not a goodie nor a "cut-up" was called a *Schwaddy*, literally meaning a piece of gristle. In Ohio and parts of Pennsylvania, a name used by some Amish to describe disparagingly the most long-haired Amish group was *Gnoddel-woller* (hairy waddles). Some of the young people distorted the name into "Noodle-roller." A half century or more ago in Iowa, the progressive district was called *die hochmüdiche Deer Grieker* (the proud Deer Creek people), while the district which was less inclined to change was referred to as *die schlappiche Laplander* (the careless Laps, or perhaps, patches).[1] Names like this are a reflection of pattern differentiation and potential cleavages.

"Every group has its leaders, the Ammies have theirs, and the Groffies theirs, and so on. Natural ability and having a way with the young people is one thing that makes a leader. The family the young person belongs to when he gets to be

---

[1] Sanford C. Yoder, *The Days of My Years* (Herald Press, 1959), 33. This book by a Mennonite bishop of Amish background contains a chapter on "Storm and Stress," which lends insight into stress factors.

sixteen is another factor determining leadership. You are partially branded when you are sixteen, depending on what your older brothers and sisters were like." The nicknaming of leaders reflects certain leadership characteristics.

The function of these differentiating groups is a most important consideration for sociology. In broad terms they permit the introduction of social change, provide personal satisfaction in small groups, and regulate the dating patterns. Differentiation permits change within the Amish social system without the assimilation of the entire group. "These kids get a lot of security because they have their own clans. The group is so large and so geographically spread that if they didn't have reference gangs the whole bunch would have to get cars."

Social distance between these groups varies considerably. "There are times when one gang has cut the harness of another to pieces. Or they have unhooked the horses of the others and let them run off. There have been vicious rumbles. The Groffies, as the most liberal, dress "worldly" with shorter hair; they go to movies, and the boys and many girls have drivers' licences. Many of them have cars, and many who don't belong to church take them home. There are boys who will wait till they are twenty-three years old to get baptized because they want to keep their cars until they get married. Getting married means getting rid of your car and joining the church."

"The Groffies never marry into the Trailers, and if one of them went with a girl among the Trailers, he would be laughed at. If she went with a Groffie she would be out. . . . There wasn't much singing among the wild ones, and they didn't call them singings anymore, but hoedowns. Some of them drank excessively, and they had big dances on the barn floor. The wild ones did not care about the regulation dress. If hat brims were to be three-and-one-half inches, they would make them shorter. If the church said they were to have no keepers on the harness, they would see many they could get on. Boys were supposed to wear their vests and plain suspenders. The wild ones would see how fancy they could make their suspenders. Some of these groups bundled, while others did not. Bundling was not outlawed, but some of the parents would allow it while others would not. This depended not on what the preachers said, but on what the parents said. In most cases it was the parents of the girl who had the say."

Differentiation determines patterns of smoking, entertainment, dating, and use of cars. "The wildest ones smoke cigarettes, while the others smoke cigars or Recruits. Recruits with filter tips are allowed. Anything black or brown is allowed, but not white cigarettes."

"The one group has a dance every Sunday night in the barn after the singing. They call it *Danze* [dancing] among themselves, in which they square dance. "Hoedowns are not hoedowns unless you have music and beer. Sunday afternoons they go to the ball park in Philadelphia, and in the evening they go to movies, and to the parks. They go to watch big league ball games too."

Use of musical instruments also varies within these groups. In the most traditional, the harmonica is the only instrument used. Ring games are played, like Skip to My Lou, Aunt Jemima, Same Old Tune in the Garden, and Captain Jinks. Other groups have record players, guitars, and banjoes. Sometimes they have the singing at one place, but split up into different groups to play."

"Outsiders are not welcome to these affairs. They do not want tourists or inquisitors who want to know more about the Amish—but people their own age from town, who come to play and have a good time, that is all right."

A group of Amish boys who sang and played their instruments developed moderate fame for their "Hillbilly Band." They sang and played together in public which made them popular among their Amish friends, because many Amish youth attended the public parks to hear hillbilly singing on Sundays. The applause and response were so great that they were asked to sing in many festivals. Eventually some in the group wanted to get married and it disbanded.

Age and marriage catch up to the Amish young person. One observant boy noted that "There is a wide gap between the old and young Amish people. There are few places where they are together informally. Even at the family dinner table there is a wide gap. When a boy reaches sixteen there seems to be little communication between him and his father. The boy walks the chalk line at home but not away from home."

Young people in some midwestern areas simply stop attending the Amish church. They find the German language too difficult to understand and find no meaningful association with the adult fellowship. Those who own a car before the age of baptism can live a very secluded, marginal life. Some find employment in a nearby town and come home weekends, and, unless they attend church elsewhere, often a Mennonite group, they make a direct transition from sacred to secular society. Some are believed to live the life of the beatnik. When transmission of values and teaching in the home is no longer operative, there appears to be little substitute in Amish society.

The goal of Amish culture, of the leaders and older people, is marriage. "They figure this way they will settle down and be obedient to the church. Marriage is definitely encouraged. So long as you are single you are just a little wild and wooly, and after marriage you must make a complete change. There is no way to get settled down without getting married. If you don't get married you are just considered a little odd. If a fellow is single, his vote or opinion in church is not considered much, no matter how old he is. It seems that when the wild ones settle down they become very loyal Amish members. They may become some of the most conservative Amish parents."

The presence of these differentiating groups leads to two obvious changes in the Amish culture. One is the toleration of drinking patterns and the other the toleration of a rather large number of boys who own and drive automobiles. The development of deviancy in these two practices can ultimately lead to a change in the *Ordnung*, as is forecast in the following observations.

"Drinking is outlawed but it has been a problem for a long time. They don't allow drinking but they tolerate it to a certain extent. A few Amish are alcoholics. They know that if they clamp down too much they are liable to lose many of the boys." In Ohio a few Amish members are known to be participants in Alcoholics Anonymous.

"The Amish are tolerating automobiles. Their parents know that they have them, but they are tolerated. This represents a change from ten years ago. They are stringing along with them, but by the time they get married, they are hoping they will settle down."

Parents who have complained to the bishops about the boys owning and driving cars, and who put pressure on them to expel these innovators, have been told by a senior leader that they will have to tolerate the situation. As an outcome a few families who could no longer "stand the situation" sold their farms and moved to Ontario. There are differences of opinion on the question among the bishops. "We have some bishops that just can't contain themselves the way things are going," said one Amish patriarch. But the regular meeting twice each year of the bishops has still kept the Lancaster County Amish from splitting.

### The Strain toward Renewal

As long as the young people accept the values of the adult society, these pattern differentiations do not constitute a direct threat to the culture. But there is one interest group, known as the "Bible study group," which attempts to renew the goals of the Amish society from within. Those young people who do not want to engage in any of the alternatives open to them in the traditional singings or the hoedowns, meet for Bible study and discussion. "There have always been a few," said one young man, "who do not want to go along with the groups that drink, smoke, bundle, and dance." These are dubbed as the "goodie-goodies" or Christians.

A group began meeting for Bible study in Pennsylvania in 1953; some groups began earlier in Indiana, and Ohio. An abortive effort was also begun in Ontario. In Pennsylvania the movement began after a mature young man "decided to become a Christian." He invited friends to his home, where they played games including Bible quiz games, and began to meet on Saturday evening every two weeks for Bible study. The group enlarged very rapidly as the activity became known, and older people also began to attend. After six months the officials ordered the attenders to stop their activity. They were punished for their deviation by getting "set back" from communion. The group was promptly disbanded. Objections raised against the Bible study group were: that each person prayed audibly, after which they talked among themselves as to who had the best prayer, and that one of the group stood up to interpret the Bible to others. The latter, if true, could be taken as competition with the legitimate church.

After several months of inactivity, a few young persons again decided to meet for Bible study. This time the group remained small and was confined to the unmarried. To divert the previous objections, the group decided to meet around a table and dispense with a formal leader. The order of the service, then as now, is: a song, prayer (both silent and voluntary), verse-by-verse reading of passages of the Bible in German, repeating the same passage in English, and discussion of the passage, heavily interspersed with moments of silence and reflection, and a closing hymn. Although one person is responsible for leading the discussion, his role is not obvious and he does not stand before the group. Informal planning and visiting follow the period of study and quietness. The group also visits and sings for old people's homes and conducts a social for the group periodically. Offerings are lifted for support of missionary work. Attendance ranges from thirty to fifty single people.

Absolute secrecy for these meetings has not been realized, and the leaders of the Amish know of the continued activity. Those bishops who feel very strongly opposed to the movement have forbidden their young people to attend, with the threat of excommunication. Other bishops have strongly advised against attending but have not absolutely forbidden any-one. Differing evaluations on the part of the ministers as to the seriousness of the activity gives room for discussion. Since the Bible study group attracts members from a wide area, there is representation from many districts, and transporta-tion constitutes a real problem. But this is overcome by the help of brothers or cousins who are members of the meeting-house Amish Mennonites and own automobiles. English neighbors also transport the single Amish person to the Bible study group for a fee. The distance traveled is, of course, often too great for horse-and-buggy travel.

In Indiana the Bible study group began about ten years earlier. A small group, instead of going to the traditional singing, met to discuss the Bible and to sing. Most of this activity was carried on by single girls, some of them of mature ages. The movement was never extinguished by the church, but had it started other than in the Clinton district, it likely would have been stopped. The Clinton area was in many ways more receptive to change. Here the preachers were open to alternatives for young people who did not want to attend the traditional rowdy singings. As in Pennsylvania, the group at-tracted young people from across the entire settlement as word spread of the new institution. Eventually, the Bible study group was attended by married people. Finally the interest and leadership of the group led to widespread acceptance in one or more church districts, as in the case of Elam Hoch-stetler's district, which later affiliated with the Beachy Amish churches.

It becomes clear that group interest in Bible study leads to a departure from the old institutionalized pattern, but success-ful group change is achieved. Here, one group is pitted against another, rather than an individual against the group. If one or more ministers would become the leader of the Pennsylvania Bible study group, a cleavage would be unavoidable. In Ohio the Bible study movement had a similar influence and it was given impetus by young men who had returned from con-scientious objector service in the war. The activity of the group also led directly and indirectly to the formation of a congregation now affiliated with the Beachy Amish. An informal Bible study group in Ontario, which met in the home of a young couple, was forbidden at the point where it attracted persons of the non-Amish faith. The leadership of the small group in this case was willing to suffer excommunication.

The development of the Bible study group into a possible new type of Amish church is given impetus by two other forces, one positive and the other negative. The members of these groups are of the conforming and obedient type rather than the rebellious kind. They want to obey the church and their parents and kin insofar as possible, and this is even more the case in groups where there is a preponderance of unmarried girls plus a few who have been to college. On the negative side, they are prevented from joining the Mennonites by Amish cultural conditioning in their early training and by their antipathy to the ways of Mennonite young people. "Mennonites are entirely wrong in the eyes of Amish people, in the eyes of my mother. If you weren't born there you have no business going there." This is how one Amish person expressed it.

One young man said of the Mennonites: "I found out that the same fellows who were wanting to convert me were smoking, rough and ready guys. It just upset me so much that I decided to go back to my Amish friends whom I liked better, who were more my stripe and who were not hypocrites." An Ohio lad who was estranged from his home said, "Mennonites contacted me and made efforts to witness to me. They were usually shy, and I just endured their talk until they went their way. I did not resent it, unless I had them sized up as hypocrites." Another said, "When I was nineteen I joined the Mennonites and didn't like it and went back to run with the Amish kids. As a kid I did not like the Mennonites; I had picked that up already in grade school. And this all came back to me when I started running around with all those Mennonite guys with big cars and their Mennonite pride." These attitudes reflect considerable social distance and undoubtedly keep some of the Amish youth from attending the Mennonite services.

## Rowdyism and Stress

Persons who do not wish to sever themselves from the Amish social system find ways of adjusting to the group. These persons are not simply passive conformists. Many of them are very active in their own way. There is a way to have a "wild time" without leaving the Amish culture. Those who remain loyal to the outward symbols deviate in a different manner from those who have intellectual problems of adjustment, such as deep philosophical and religious questions. Those who do cut themselves off from the group appear to leave a certain adverse effect on those who stay. The effect appears to be overconformity in some respects, but also antisocial behavior of certain kinds.

Antisocial behavior and rowdyism are experienced as the community becomes threatened by a large number of its young members' leaving. Young people who cannot follow the example of the ex-Amish person appear to turn to other forms of deviation. Parents tend to be ignorant of the tough behavior of the young people, and their ignorance serves an important social function in maintaining existing patterns of behavior.[2] Knowledge of the facts in many cases would be socially disorganizing and might lead to conditions of anomie.

One form of rowdyism is the custom of "cutting up," associated with a boy's first date with a girl. After the couple leaves the singing and goes to the home of the girl, single boys find their way to the home to disturb the couple or to embarrass the young man. Gangs of boys sometimes enter the home and raid the kitchen. The suitor's horse and buggy are sometimes hidden. The horse may be unhitched and sent home, or the harness may be knotted up or used to tie the yard gate fast. In extreme cases such behavior turns into hos-

[2] Wilbert E. Moore and Melvin M. Tumin, "Some Social Functions of Ignorance," *American Sociological Review* (December, 1949), 788.

tile acts, such as cutting the harness into pieces, or disturbing the parents in their sleep. The extremity of the measures taken depends upon the reputation for "toughness" of the young suitor, and upon the mob psychology of the group. If the suitor is a rowdy himself, he is liable for severe trickery and devilment.

These occasions sometimes form the basis of behavior which does not stop with humor and customary initiation rites. Overindulgence in antisocial acts may bring hostility and revenge from an opposing gang. Also, stealing chickens or grain and selling these goods, or trading them for a dance floor for one night, is not unknown. A juvenile who was a leader of one lively Amish group of boys said, "We used to see who could do the best job of swearing and being the biggest blow gut. If there was anything dared to be done, I had to show the boys I had the nerve to do it."

The preoccupation with filthy stories so frequently mentioned in case histories deserves some explanation. They are typically rural stories, emphasizing excrement and crude sex jokes. The writer can attest to the generality of such talk from his own experience as an Amish youth. This is an area of permissiveness, since talk can be indulged in without the knowledge of parents or elders. Amish youth receive little or no guidance in acquiring a knowledge of human reproduction. With Sunday services long, filled with experiences that are routine and of little variety, and with no planned recreation, subjects of conversation tend to turn inward and to narcissism.

Drinking is another form of behavior that has become problematic in larger settlements. Traditionally the Amish, like Europeans, generally saw nothing wrong with a little wine and often made it for modest use in the home. The old practice is no longer widespread, and drinking is generally taboo. Nevertheless, among the young people drinking has reached intemperate proportions on some occasions. There have been several arrests for violation of the liquor laws in midwestern communities. On complaints from parents, the police conducted raids on Sunday night singings. In some cases officers found from 10 to 13 cases of empty beer bottles on the premises, and several juveniles were arrested for drunkenness. Young men with automobiles were believed responsible for selling liquor to juveniles. When the writer attended a singing in one of these midwestern states, he found only from 8 to 12 persons doing any singing at all. The other 150 to 200 persons were either standing around indoors jostling and smoking, were in the barn, or were scattered about on the grounds. Drinking among the youth is common in all the large Amish settlements, but varies with local rules and folkways. Amish fathers bought out a saloon in one instance in a Pennsylvania location in order to stop the trend toward intoxication.

Boys have been arrested for racing their carriages in a disorderly manner in small villages. Parents are concerned about the mischief of the boys, but seem to be helpless. After one arrest at a singing, an Amish father said, "What can I do? I know it's wrong for minors to drink beer, but the boys would get down on me if I didn't allow it."

Some parents have taken action against those Amish Mennonite, or former Amish boys, who insist on associating with the Old Order Amish young people by driving their automobiles to the singing. In a midwestern community parents began reporting license numbers of vehicles at the singing to the authorities and to the local draft boards. Amish youth who served as "spies" turned this information over to the authorities. For violation of the rule against automobiles, young men could suddenly receive notice that their classification was changed from farm deferment to I-A. One man who experienced this said, "This is dynamite."

Outsiders are not welcome at some of the singings and would be chased off the grounds if an uninvited visit were attempted. One outsider who was a farm hand with an Amish family for several weeks went to a singing. He was surrounded by a score or more of Amish boys and accused of wanting their women and of reporting them to the preachers. The lad obviously had no intentions of this kind. He did not escape without being beaten up. Such behavior is reminiscent of the Bavarian villages, or of the old oligarchies, such as Sparta, which prohibited not only journeys abroad but also visits from strangers. Like the Amish culture as a whole, the young too are suspicious of the stranger. The prospect of new thoughts or an intrusion of the traditional morality, as in preliterate societies, is resented. When certain practices have been followed for centuries, the individual members are confronted with "the impossibility of changing a habit of thought that has become automatic," and the prospect of a new line of thought appears to be antisocial, or even criminal.[3] One wonders how such mental immobility can survive within a modern world that seeks change and discovery for its own sake.

"Conditions among the young people" is a topic that is discussed by Amish preachers and is a major concern. The problems are generally conceived as "drinking, smoking, carousing around, and indulging in immoral courtship." These concerns are expressed in print in Amish writings, both in privately published pamphlets and in periodicals. The ministers generally lay the responsibility with the parents. Parents often indicate that preachers preach only *Attnung* (rules) and not Jesus Christ as a Savior and Lord. Many youth justify their actions by saying that their parents had a "high old time" when they were young.

An effective channel for calling attention to problems in the little community is the weekly newspaper of the Amish. Any writer who wishes may share his concerns or offer his advice. This newspaper, *The Budget*, is also used by ex-Amish persons who write their own views, often unorthodox, in the paper. Former Amish persons, whether excommunicated or not, who may now be missionaries or preachers in other denominations, can in this way "preach" to Amish readers. The Amish have no direct control over the editorial policy. In one sense the paper becomes an instrument of acculturation, exposing the Amish communities not only to new religious

[3] Franz Boas, *Anthropology and Modern Life* (1927), 140.

ideas, but also to new forms of machines, medicines, and services.

Chance, or what might be called accidental happenings, also
have the effect of altering traditional behavior patterns. In
Ohio, two young robbers whose vehicle was stalled in a ditch
entered a farm home after dark on the evening of July 18,
1957, and in the course of events shot the father, Amishman
Paul Coblentz. One of the young men, Cleo Peters, was given
the death sentence. Many Amish people signed petitions urging mercy. Nine hours before he was scheduled to die, Governor William O'Neill commuted the sentence to life im-
prisonment. Some Amish people "became burdened about the
spiritual welfare" of Cleo Peters. They wrote letters to him
and also sent delegations to visit him. Discussions and correspondence followed the conversion of Mr. Peters. The sad
incident was interpreted as an act of God, as stated in a letter
to the prisoner: "We believe that God allowed this to call us
back to Him in the work of winning souls to His Kingdom." [4]

An escaped convict in the midwest was discovered working as an Amish farm hand. Without knowing that he was a
convict, the Amish befriended him and prepared to receive him
into their church by baptism. At this time he confessed his
status. Shortly before baptism, someone reported him to the law
officers, who arrested him. He was returned to prison in the
state where he had been convicted only to be paroled. Members of the Amish church met him as he left the prison and
took him to their community.

An Amish farmer was fatally shot by an "English" boy
following an argument in which the young man had tried to
date the Amish daughter. The young man had attempted to
date the girl for some time, but the parents explained that, for
religious reasons, they did not want their daughter to date
with an outsider. The young man fatally shot the the father,
Joel P. Schwartz, and critically wounded his wife.

Such unstructured incidents, drawn from widely differing
communities, have the effect of evoking new sentiments or

[4] *The Budget* (December 25, 1958).

concerns for the outsider. They force the traditional community into thinking on new courses of action. When taken as "acts of God," new courses of action, which would otherwise be resented, are made legitimate.

The stress problems of the Amish community are not unlike those of other societies who have gone before them. Tensions are manifested in a variety of ways. There are on the one hand those who wish to have the conveniences of the automobile and the ways of middle-class American life but are torn between their desire and their religion, or their nearest of kin. Then there are those who want to be no cause for division, but who wish to study the Bible and express their piety in a way that is different from the quiet, submissive, and humble way of the tradition. Others feel frustrated if they cannot prepare themselves for life by attending college. Those who remain loyal to the outward symbols appear to make a successful adjustment to the little community, but often go through a period of permitted "wildness" before they accept the adult roles of the society. Unusual happenings often believed to be "acts of God" tend to provide alternate courses of action.

In group deviation, the personality tends to be protected somewhat from personal stress and conflict. Group assimilation provides the individual with a cultural matrix and a reference group for self-identification. Pattern differentiation tends to be along the same line as those issues which culminate in a cleavage. Excessive loss of members may lead to a change in the *Ordnung*, which will be taken up in a later chapter.

# CHAPTER 14

# SOCIAL CHANGE AND ILLNESS

SOME SOCIETIES HAVE MANAGED to achieve a flexible adjustment during periods of change and stress while others have not. Even though many groups share the same general culture pattern they respond to stress in very different ways. The Fox Indian tribe, for example, made "a good adjustment" to the American culture, "while the Sauk sank into apathy on a reservation, and the Kickapoo fled the country." [1] One tribe succumbed rapidly to acculturation, one tribe fled to Mexico, and one purchased land as a way out of its difficulty. In the little Amish community it is possible to observe some of these same types of adjustment and maladjustment under stress.

Not all find stability and fulfillment in the Amish community or a satisfactory adjustment to life outside the community. The people in the little Amish community are able to act together in an integrated manner over long periods of time because they have learned meanings and values that are commonly understood and adhered to. As the community becomes larger and more complex not all individuals within the community do what is expected of them, which results in personal and social disorganization. When the members no longer share a significant proportion of values and meanings, and when these no longer guide the behavior of a significant proportion of individuals, then disorganization may be said to prevail. For the individual this may take the form of any number of personal problems such as internal conflict, alienation, and meaninglessness, often manifested in suicide, alcoholism, and various types of neuroses. Individuals may feel helpless to

[1] William Caudill, *Effects of Social and Cultural Systems in Reactions to Stress* (Social Science Research Council, Pamphlet 14, 1958), 12.

control the outcome of their actions, and may manifest power-lessness, suspicion, cynicism, isolation, theft, or gang behavior.

In this chapter we shall consider the effect of social change on the health of the individual. When the individual cannot find fulfillment in life, sickness is one of the many alternating forms of adjustment. Sickness is a socially approved form of deviation in Amish life, as in the great society the "sick role" is increasingly sanctioned as one alternative to the problem of adjustment.[2] Thus the person faced with a stressful situation may become sick and thereby find an advantageous position. It is now generally recognized that the social setting in which people live and the things they believe are correlated with many symptoms of physical and mental illness.

## Health and Medical Behavior

In Amish society both folk and scientific concepts of heal-ing are utilized. When folk and scientific notions come into conflict, a certain amount of maladjustment and stress are evi-denced. The sick person who is caught between contradictory expectations becomes the victim of cultural systems in stress. Cultural stress is perhaps more subtle and less understood than the more obvious forms of personal stress.

Concern for the sick is of major importance in every Amish community. An ill person who is missing at the religious serv-ices is often visited by relatives and friends in the afternoon. Illness also becomes major news in the Amish newspaper.

Since there are no trained physicians among the Amish they patronize the physicians in their locale. There is nothing in Amish religion which forbids the use of modern medical serv-ices, including surgery, hospitalization, dental work, anesthesia, and immunization. While some have been reluctant to accept immunization, the Amish have, in the opinion of one physician, "no objection which persuasion cannot overcome." The bound-

[2] Talcott Parsons, "Illness and the Role of the Physician: A Sociological Perspective," *American Journal or Orthopsychiatry* (July, 1951), 452. Also John A. Clausen, *Sociology and the Field of Mental Health* (1956).

aries that keep out the automobile, radio, and television have no counterpart in the medical field. Health and recovery from illness do not constitute a threat to the community. Any resistance to new forms of medical treatment is not based on explicit religious dogma but on the general tendency to accept the old as the best.

The persistence of medical folk knowledge is reflected in certain attitudes and practices of healing. Illness which is not understood or which does not respond to professional treatment will bring folk cures into the experience of the sick person. Persons who are chronically ill are taken not only to professional medical centers but also to other practitioners who happen to be recommended to them. The following case illustrates the point.

A tumor was observed on the arm of a middle-aged woman; she was taken to the family physician who found more tumors. The specialist wanted to remove one tumor, but the spokesman for the Amish woman said, "We didn't let them as we were afraid it might be cancer. We tried other things for a year, then we had one taken out." Following this she was given the Koch cancer treatment "which didn't do any good." She was then taken to special medical centers in two large cities, and finally to the Hoxsey cancer clinic. To relieve the suffering woman from pain, about 200 tumors were removed from under her right arm, but finding no relief she went to the Mayo Clinic. "They could not help her either. She has been to different chiropractors. She took foot treatments and iodine and all kinds of medicine. She is now taking strong pills which cost a lot." The length to which the Amish will go to find relief from sickness is almost inexhaustible, but they tend to favor quasi-medical cures. "Too many pills" and "strong medicine," according to some Amish people, "are not good for a person."

Amish medical knowledge is nourished by health and patent-medicine advertisements in their newspaper, by rural farm almanacs, and by formulas handed down from the past. The patent names of the remedies advertised in *The Budget* vary through the years, but the ailments they claim to cure remain the same. Remedies for rheumatism and arthritis are most numerous, but there are also testimonials associated with vitamins, tonics, and bitters to cure constipation, to relieve itch, and other ailments. Testimonials from non-Amish are accepted as readily as from Amish persons. An Amish woman who found relief for severe croup, passed on her formula to other readers: "Boil vinegar, and if it is a severe case of croup, hold the child over full steam, enough that the child can breathe easily." For infections, she recommended a poultice of milk and linseed meal. Teas and homemade formulas constitute another source of treatment. "They use all kinds of teas for all kinds of ills," said one physician, "and I don't interfere with it unless I know it to be detrimental."

*Brauche* or sympathy-healing plays a role in Amish life even though some of the more progressive Amish have condemned it as witchcraft. The usual English translation of *Brauche* is "powwowing." The Amish have retained this healing art from the Pennsylvania German culture and most of the forms can be traced to a book by John George Hohman, *Der Lang verborgene Schatz und Haus-Freund* ("Long Lost Friend") published in Reading, Pennsylvania, in 1820. Some of the spells in this collection have been traced back to Albertus Magnus who died in Cologne in 1280, and some are apparently more ancient. There is evidence that the Amish also have borrowed spells and charm from the outside world as some charms in their homes are in the English language. Here as in the ideal-typical folk society there is common practical knowledge but no science and "no systematization of knowledge."[3] The tendency to rely on oral testimony, so pervasive in the whole of Amish life, is specifically manifest in the healing arts.

*Brauche* is performed by some of the older Amish members in the community. They receive no remuneration for their services. The patient does not always need to be present when the actual incantations are performed, but he must believe in the practice to obtain results. One who desires to acquire the skill can obtain it only from an older person of the opposite

[3] Robert Redfield, "The Folk Society," *op. cit.*

sex upon the promise that the formulas will be kept secret. The chief features of *Brauche* are the silent repeating of certain verses or charms at appropriate times.

There are several Amish folk practitioners of varied reputation. One regularly visits Amish communities in several states in the interest of "curing." He claims to possess a special gift of healing, asserting that his practice is neither *Brauche* nor powwowing. His gift of laying on of hands has been supplemented with bonesetting, which he learned from a non-Amish practitioner. Concerning his skill he said: "Of all people who are sick, very few do not have a bone out of joint in their system." Although his work is highly praised by some, he is not receiving general acclaim.

The stress between folk and scientific systems of healing becomes explicit in physician-patient relationships. In the opinion of physicians, the Amish have a higher frequency of certain complaints than non-Amish patients. An opinion survey among 46 physicians reflects some of these different expectations.[4] Some of the most frequently occurring symptoms and complaints are normally associated with conditions of stress and culture change. Conditions believed to occur more frequently among Amish than non-Amish are obesity, chronic bed-wetting, digestive disturbances, and mental disorders.

The physicians with few exceptions rate the Amish as desirable patients. They are "dependable, stable, and appreciative." The peculiar transportation problems of the Amish tend to make it difficult for them to respect the office hours of a small-town physician. The physicians hold that the Amish pay little attention to preventive medicine, which they ascribe to a lack of formal education. They report a tendency to "wait too long to consult a physician, especially for the children." "An Amish man may feel that a chiropractor prevents disease while an M.D. just treats it," said one physician. A trait which appears to be characteristic also is the practice of "changing doctors." If the desired results are not obtained with one doctor, or if his manner or services are not quite

[4] J. A. Hostetler, "Folk and Scientific Medicine in Amish Society," *Human Organization*, Vol. 22 (winter 1963–64), pp. 269–75.

satisfactory, another doctor is summoned. The writer knows of a case where five different physicians were called in during the course of a single illness. That the Amish people are more inclined to use home remedies, chiropractors, and various kinds of practitioners, than are non-Amish patients, is also borne out by the judgment of the physicians. "They will travel great distances for quack cures," said one physician. One state inspector who investigates quasi-practitioners states that he invariably finds Amish patients at these places, and often at distances far from an Amish community. The psychotherapeutic practitioners offer hope that the Amish do not find in the highly rational and scientific institution of modern medicine. Common complaints Amish patients have of physicians is that they give drugs that are "too strong," have little time to talk, and "give little satisfaction." The Amish find no Biblical grounds for opposing modern medicine, blood transfusions, and immunizations. Folk-healing persists in a culture that prizes isolation in general. The old ways are familiar ways and preferred ways in a society that ranks practical knowledge above theoretical knowledge. The advice of a friend concerning a treatment is pitted against the advice of a scientifically trained man in a society that is suspicious of higher learning. For a sudden illness, for broken bones and wounds, or for pregnancy, the physician is consulted first. For nameless pains and longstanding disorders, folk diagnoses and treatments are sought.

The Amish have made a significant contribution to medical genetics in recent years by allowing researchers to study their hereditary problems.[5] Several recessive genetic disorders have been found to have a relatively high occurrence: a rare type of anemia, phenylketonuria, hemophilia, six-fingered dwarfism, and a "new" form of dwarfism affecting the growth of cartilage and hair. Several disorders have been diagnosed for the first time. Because the Amish are a well-defined population and have good family records, it is possible to trace many of the cases to a common ancestor. The Amish are not allowed to marry first cousins, but even though they appear not to marry

[5] See terminal bibliography: Bowman, Cross, Jackson, Juberg, and McKusick.

close, there has been much intermarriage for generations. Marriages are for the most part confined to neighborhoods, with little intermarriage between the Amish of different states and regions. This increases the chances that recessive genes will match up on both sides of a family. More intermarriage between communities would probably diminish the problem.

## Mental Illness

The Amish people are by no means free from mental illness. An investigation of Amish admissions in two Mennonite-operated mental hospitals provides us with some knowledge of this aspect of illness. Brook Lane Hospital, which was opened in 1948 in Maryland, and Philhaven Hospital, started in 1952 in Pennsylvania, operate on a self-sustaining basis, with admission coming from all faiths. Amish and Mennonite admissions are only a small proportion of the total. The capacity of these hospitals is under 40 beds each and they do not retain patients needing care over long periods of time. From their founding date through 1959 these hospitals admitted 64 Old Order Amish members and 504 persons of Mennonite affiliation. Not all Amish who become mentally ill are admitted to these two hospitals, but the Amish now prefer them to state institutions.

Admissions occur at all ages in about the same frequency from ages 15 to 60 (Table 10). Men and women are admitted in about equal proportions. The Mennonite admissions have a higher proportion of women than men. The proportion of the admissions who are married was about the same for both the Amish and the Mennonite groups (Table 11). From the admission records it was also possible to gain some knowledge about the presence of suicidal tendencies. The results are shown in Table 12. Of all Amish admissions 40 per cent had suicidal tendencies, distributed about equally among men and women. The records indicate that Mennonite persons had fewer such tendencies but suicidal tendencies were more pronounced among women.

The diagnoses of all cases at these hospitals are made by

Table 10

Amish and Mennonite Admissions to Mental Hospitals
By Age and Sex, 1948–59

| Age | Amish | | Mennonite | |
|---|---|---|---|---|
| | No. Cases | Per cent Women | No. Cases | Per cent Women |
| 10–14 | – | – | 3 | – |
| 15–19 | 8 | 50% | 23 | 47% |
| 20–24 | 7 | 70% | 60 | 50% |
| 25–29 | 7 | 30% | 64 | 70% |
| 30–34 | 7 | 30% | 70 | 62% |
| 35–39 | 7 | 70% | 66 | 70% |
| 40–44 | 5 | 20% | 35 | 70% |
| 45–49 | 4 | 50% | 36 | 70% |
| 50–54 | 6 | 66% | 26 | 57% |
| 55–59 | 6 | 66% | 29 | 51% |
| 60–64 | 2 | – | 37 | 70% |
| 65–69 | 1 | – | 36 | 72% |
| 70–74 | 2 | – | 8 | 87% |
| 75–79 | 2 | – | 9 | 11% |
| 80 and over | – | – | 2 | – |
| Total | 64 | | 504 | |
| Per cent | | 51% | | 64% |

psychiatrists. Of the 64 Amish cases, none were diagnosed as having brain disorders, while 53 were classed as having psychotic disorders and 11 came under the category of psychoneurotic disorders.[6] It would appear that the disorders are functional rather than organic, that they arise out of individual experience in life without direct physical cause. They are nonetheless potent in affecting the judgmental aspects of personality.

The Amish themselves have developed little explicit therapeutic knowledge to deal with cases of extreme anxiety. Many of the individuals are handicapped in living up to the social

[6] According to *Diagnostic and Statistical Manual, Mental Disorders* (American Psychiatric Association, 1952), 78–85.

Table 11

Amish and Mennonite Admissions to Mental Hospitals
by Marital Status, 1948–59

|  | Number of Admissions | Per cent Who Were Married |
|---|---|---|
| Amish | 64 | 60% |
| Mennonite | 504 | 63% |

Table 12

Suicidal Tendencies of Admissions to Mental Hospitals, 1948–59

|  | Number of Cases | Per cent Having Suicidal Tendencies | Per cent of the Cases Who Were Women |
|---|---|---|---|
| Amish | 58 | 40% | 48% |
| Mennonite | 406 | 26% | 65% |

NOTE: Probability less than 0.001.

expectations of the Amish faith. The concept of "insanity" is not foreign to them but neuroses is more so. The following behavior patterns in the Amish society would appear to indicate neuroses: failure to marry, frequent visits to doctors, failure to find satisfaction in a full day's work, occupation with problems of religious orthodoxy, and rigidity of attitude.

On the other hand, the Amish culture provides "natural" aids to the mentally disturbed. Persons who are considered abnormal are urged to "work, rather than sit around and read too much." Their family and community connections provide a sense of belonging and of being needed. In some instances mentally retarded persons are cared for at home.[7] Visiting and

[7] An aged Amish bishop who cared for his demented daughter at home for years was charged under a criminal code and sent unjustly to a state reformatory. See John Umble, "Justice Fails Again," *Gospel Herald* (February 3, 1948).

travel provide occasions to renew connections with relatives and friends. The sick person is given opportunity to visit as well. Certain tolerance for deviants, especially "sick" persons, is permitted within the society. Special prayer for the sick and confession are perhaps not as well developed and relied upon as in some religious groups.

## Anomic and Suicidal Patterns

One symptom of severe stress is anomie. The term "anomie" was used by Emile Durkheim to refer to a mental state of normlessness, of being without values to guide one's actions.[8] A person in such a situation is without moral guides to action, or if he is aware of such guides, he may be caught between two opposing courses of action, so that he cannot act upon his own volition. The rules of the group have become meaningless to him. He cannot anticipate how others will behave or direct his own behavior since he lacks the needed expectations with which to guide himself. Thus the anomic person lives in a world without direction or purpose; living in mental isolation from others, he is estranged from group membership. Frequently a person suffering from anomie may revert to apathy and despair. One manifestation of anomic tendencies is suicide.

Suicide occurs in all contemporary societies as well as in many folk societies. The rate of suicide has generally increased in those societies which have become urban and industrialized. Suicide rates are generally higher among males than females, they increase with age, and are higher in the cities than in rural areas, higher among Protestants than Catholics, and higher among divorced persons. Married persons rather than single persons have the lowest rates of suicide.[9] A study of suicides in Michigan reported a higher rate of suicide among

[8] Emile Durkheim, *La Suicide* (Paris: Alcan, 1897); English edition (Free Press, 1951).
[9] S. Kirson Weinberg, *Social Problems in Our Time* (Prentice-Hall, 1960), 409.

rural than urban people.[10] This high rural rate was believed to be associated with the many retired farmers who had urban occupations but who resided in rural areas or on the fringe of the urban area. The findings suggest that as urban values and ideals are disseminated in rural areas, there is more intense conflict between the values of urban and rural people. The possibilities for maladjustment and personal disorganization are therefore increased among rural people.

In one Amish community two well-informed Amish persons could recall fifteen suicides, fourteen of whom were males. A young man had attempted suicide at the age of nineteen. He had been regarded as a misfit, and the boys "always made fun of him." His parents were extremely strict, and he "got caught" in a number of things. He worried a lot. He was never accepted well by the group. He was discovered sleeping with a loaded revolver under his pillow and was then admitted to a mental hospital. Another boy of twenty-two shot himself. He was a quiet person and was always very compliant. "He never shared in our devilment," said one informant, "because he was different." He had model parents, a nice home, and was well liked. Such anomic individuals have apparently not been able to internalize the values of their group. Many of these cases appear to be persons who were young men. This age appears to be the most crucial for acceptance or rejection of the basic values of the culture.

Of the three types of suicidal behavior, anomic, egoistic, and altruistic, the first is the most commonly associated with group disintegration, particularly when new meanings do not emerge to take the place of old ones.[11] The following Amish case illustrates the inability of one individual to establish meaningful group relations.

"Dan was very sick as a boy, and he became a hunchback. He and his older sister never got along well and they fought like dogs and cats. The Amish young people called him

[10] W. Widick Schroeder and J. Allan Beegle, "Suicide: An Instance of High Rural Rates," *Rural Sociology* (March, 1953), 45.
[11] Emile Durkheim, *La Suicide*.

'Humpy' and he never liked that. He grew up and never got married. Because Dan had the identical first and last name as his father, who was a bishop, he often opened letters intended for his father. Some of these letters were from unmarried Amish girls who had to make confessions. The letters had an adverse effect on his mind, so that he finally moved away from his paternal home to a small house of his own. One day they found him dead in bed. The doctor said it was heart trouble, but later we found out that he took his life. The doctor only said this for the good of grandmother."

A similar case was that of a teen-age boy, the son of a preacher, who came late in the family. The father was "of the nervous type" and was dubbed a rather uncomplimentary nickname. The boy was an only son in the family, and "the father wanted him to dress just like he had dressed when he was young." The difference in dress made the boy stand out more from others of his age. The father did not realize that the rules had changed a bit from the time when he was a boy. He appeared odd to the boys of his own age. He drew back into a shell because many laughed at him. He imagined that everybody was making fun of him. When the parents went visiting much in the wintertime, the boy would stay at home. He would spend his time alone. He didn't know enough to do any reading that was worthwhile. So, one day they found him hanging from a rope."

Mate selection and marital adjustment appear to have some bearing on suicide. In one suicidal case, a young man of a small splinter group "switched back" to the Old Order church to obtain a wife. "There were so few young people, and no prospective mates at all in his own group. He married and was later ordained to the ministry in the Old Order church. Then one day he hung himself. Just why he did this, we do not know; perhaps he knew that he was wrong in having made the change for a wife against his better knowledge." Another man of about fifty appears to have had difficulty living with his wife. He absented himself from his family on several occasions. "For some reason he had an extraordinary amount of struggles in life. Sometime later he was found in a stream with a stone around his neck." A young man who was married for only a short time took his life. "From the grapevine there are indications that he married a battle-ax. He was a fairly mild man, and I guess it just got the best of him."

Persons who carry heavy responsibility for maintaining the Amish norms are subjected to extraordinary role stress. The strain of strong negative sanctions for deviation or for suggesting alternate courses of action no doubt contributes to anxiety and conflict in persons charged with boundary-maintaining functions. One of the most dramatic instances is that of a prominent leader who hung himself to the surprise of the entire Amish community. Many Amish and non-Amish persons regarded the man as possessing unusual personal abilities. The reason for his very sudden "disgraceful" act remained a mystery to his kin and his close associates. However, in examining the social relationships and circumstances preceding the act, it is clear that the leader was caught between contradictory expectations. As sometimes occurs, his office required temporary oversight of several districts. While all the districts had the same *Ordnung*, they differed in their conformity to the rules. In one district persons were "plainer," had longer hair, and larger brims on their hats, and no young man had a driver's license or an automobile on the sly. In another district, the young men "had cars on the sneak," they played games with instrumental music, and some of the girls had drivers' licenses. Some of the parents brought pressure on the bishop for the irregularities. The leader had been conducting instruction classes for baptism in all districts, consisting of about fifty young people. The situation was a very hard strain on him "because people in these districts didn't co-operate with him for different reasons." Parents had hinted that he was not strict enough.

While each leader is held responsible for the discipline in his own district, his actions and policy with respect to keeping the "old order" are evaluated by older persons. These aged bishops "have a lot of influence, and they are rich. They are feared for some reason, and they tell the preachers what to do." Now it happened that the leader in question was summoned to a meeting of bishops. He had been charged with not being strict enough in his instruction to the classes in baptism. According to people who knew him, "he was one of the few who could tolerate ex-Amish boys," and "he did not lay down the laws as strictly as parents wanted them." The perplexed man decided not to attend the meeting to which he had been summoned. Instead he wrote a note informing them of his decision. He spent that night reading and praying, and the next morning he was found hanging in the barn.

"It was a tremendous shock to our family," said one person. "No one ever talked about it, and I have never heard anyone talk about it. They went to the funeral and came home and said nothing, except that there was practically no one there." Suicide in Amish life is regarded as an act of disgrace, if not treason. Among the young people the bishop had been very well liked and was highly respected. But with his mysterious death, there was no question but that this meant for the applicants of baptism stricter conformity to the rules.

It would appear that among the Amish the rate of suicide is just as high, if not higher, than for the nation. Presently the rate of suicide in the United States is 10.3 per 100,000 persons. At this rate the 50,000 Amish people would need to have but five suicides per year to approximate the rate for the larger society. The frequency of Amish cases appears to be highest among young men, which is generally the age in Amish life when the basic values of the culture are usually accepted or rejected.

# Part IV

# SURVIVAL

# CHAPTER 15

# RESPONSES TO CHANGE

How DOES A SMALL SOCIETY that by charter forbids change finally come to sanction and make legitimate certain innovations? When an automobile for several generations has been the symbol of the "world," what processes are necessary to make it legitimate? In this chapter let us observe how the *Ordnung* is changed and some selected reactions to change. A major change within the society, such as a change in the rules, has a widespread effect on the organization of the group.

Changes may come about in one or all of the following ways. First, the rules are not enforced uniformly for all members: There is differential enforcement for members within a single church district. Second, attitudes of the bishop and the ordained men in a given district may differ from those in other districts. Third, the two aspects of behavior which are most affected by change have to do with economic and religious behavior. An example of economic change is the adaptation from general to specialized farming and of religious change, the development of interest in missionary work, followed by Bible study in English, the organization of Sunday schools, and the erection of meetinghouses. In the fourth place leaders and parents tend to be tolerant of youthful activity (often rowdy in character) because they know that the risk of having children "go English" or "getting their hair cut" is very great.

Sanctions are not always uniformly enforced between old and young members and between persons of different occupations. An old man who was under the strain of having a chronically ill wife and who may have been slightly senile, was in one instance the first to obtain electricity in his house. His argument with the church officials was that he must have a refrigerator to keep medications and dietary preparations for his wife who was under strict observation by the physician. The incident forced a change in the *Ordnung*. Old people are allowed privileges others may not have, such as inside toilets. These exceptions often lead to universal acceptance of the innovation. An old, feeble man who needed to use the bathroom several times a night built a small light fixture and switch into his private bathroom. The source of energy was flashlight batteries. The grandparents of one household who lived a short distance from the main farm house were allowed a primitive "telephone" between dwellings. All of these cases involved people who were generally conforming Amish persons, whose life contribution and character in other respects was beyond question.

Persons who travel from their home community are expected to conform to the rules of their own district, but those who travel far from home, as for example to Florida, where many older Amish persons stay for the winter months, sometimes deviate from the rules of their home church until they return. This temporary relief from the rules has made travel popular and the normal thing for many retired Amish couples. It is now common for the young, both single and married, to also spend some time in Florida.

*Innovations accompanied by economic rewards have greater chance of being accepted than changes of a non-economic character.* Innovations in styles of hair or clothing, or permitting photographs, are of the latter type. Persons who are engaged in non-farming occupations, such as carpentry, masonry, plumbing, contract building, and sawmilling, are engaged in making a living. These occupations require equipment and institutionalized means of communication and travel not allowed by the whole Amish community. The pay-telephone just across the road from the Amish mill and the cabinet shop, are mainly for use by the nearby Amish proprietor. Utility and farm-machine companies who service the general farm population are knowledgeable about Amish rules, and adaptations are made so that benefits may be realized without bringing the sanctions of the church on any specific family. Persons who work in local factories or processing plants travel to and from work with non-Amish means of transportation. These accepted patterns of behavior, which are directly related to economic rewards, tend to become institutionalized. Persons who are striving to make ends meet, who are saving money to make a down payment on a farm, are usually the ones who engage in this form of activity. Their money-making activity is considered by older persons as temporary until they become established on the farm. But all of these diverse occupations are potential sources of change; especially when there is differential enforcement of the *Ordnung*.[1]

Exceptions to the rule have symbolic value to the younger generation. A respected Amish person, "Hay-John" Miller in Iowa, as a young man had attended normal school and was certified to teach earlier in the twentieth century. Today young Amishmen seek to change the rule against going to college by appealing to him as a model for furthering their training.

Finally, it would appear that *agricultural ideas and practices which are not visually perceptible are more likely to be accepted than things which have visual symbolic value.* A new fertilizer or a new hybrid chicken will be more acceptable than a tractor or a farm truck. All of these objects have economic value and no one can object to a crop of hybrid corn as appearing "worldly." When hybrid seed came on the market it did not take the Amish long to adopt it. Contour farming on the other hand, which is clearly visible and has little promise of economic reward, has not been generally accepted.

The rules of a church district are for all members but change occurs when they are not uniformly enforced. The punishment that applies to the baptized member cannot apply to the unbaptized young man who wants an automobile. The only controls that can be brought to bear here are parental sanc-

[1] Gertrude Huntington has observed this change characteristic and many more in her analysis of an Ohio church district: "Dove at the Window" (Ph.D. dissertation, Yale University, 1956).

tions, and these are difficult to enforce with increasing contact with outside influences: the school, the part-time job, revival influences, and access to means of travel. Renters, rather than owners of farms, are the innovators and agitators for the tractor. The well-established, traditional Amish farmer with a large family has less need for a tractor than the young couple faced with problems of help, capital, and of making a financial success. Renters are more inclined to engage in specialized farming, such as raising cash crops and poultry, than are owners. In this way prevailing farm practices and ideas slowly but quietly become accepted as normal.

## Division and Migration

Unfavorable reactions to change are manifested by schisms over what appear to the outsider as trivial and hair-splitting questions, by migration, and by various manifestations of over-conformity. Amish history is a history of divisions. The many divisions are possible because the Amish accept the general American belief in individualism, because of the sacredness with which the Amish consider their mode of life, and the land room and freedom of movement in America. Divisions prevent change in that they keep deviants out of the small in-groups which develop on the basis of these cleavages. A few cases will illustrate how division is a form of adjustment that seeks to prevent change.

Earlier in this book we discussed the Moses Hartz *Meidung* case, which was the first major controversy in Pennsylvania and is still talked about in Amish circles. The son of an Amish preacher had joined the Mennonites since he was engaged in the milling industry. The preacher refused to shun his son, which formed the issue on which the church took sides. "Many people talked about how they were going to withdraw but when the time came there were not many who had the backbone. To withdraw from the *Freundschaft* is hard, and among the Amish this is their life. So there was a group here [1910] without a minister and without communion." This small group, which was not in sympathy with the strict *Meidung*, appealed for ministerial help from "Big Valley" in Mifflin County, where there were three districts of Amish. The bishops here were John Zook, Sam Peachey, and David Peachey. The strict *Meidung* had never been an issue in the Big Valley churches. Bishop Zook thought the defecting Lancaster group should be helped and the three bishops decided to take the *Rat* (counsel) of their congregations on the question. Zook reported a favorable vote from his district, but Peachey reported: "*Mir hen kenn eniger Rote katt.*" (We had no unanimous decision.) Bishop Zook replied: "If you would have taken the vote the way you should have, you would have gotten a favorable decision." Someone had talked to Bishop Peachey before he took the vote of his district, and instead of taking the vote to come in and help the group, he took the vote *not* to come and help. The outcome was the division of the two Big Valley districts into two factions. The Zook group helped the Lancaster sympathizers and the Peachey group did not. Another result was that the strict *Meidung* policy was brought into Mifflin County through the Peachey group.

The question of strict *Meidung* has formed the core of most Amish divisions. Where this doctrine has not been held and practiced there has generally been an acceptance of outside influences and peaceful assimilation. Many divisions are associated with minor issues that tend to disguise the "core" issue of *Meidung*. The Beachy division in Somerset County, Pennsylvania, in 1927, became known as the "automobile Amish church," but the rift was instigated by different opinions on the question of *Meidung*. The John A. Stoltzfus church of Lancaster County affiliated with the Beachy group in 1930, and others who affiliated with the Beachy adherents in Ohio, Virginia, Indiana, and Iowa, severed their connection with the Old Order.

A church can disintegrate on account of division and migration as did one district in southeastern Pennsylvania within the past decade. "They seemed to have two extremes in that church all along. The bishop was very strict and the members could not reason with him. Some of the married men always tried to see what they could get away with. The bishop had to work with these kind of people." Over a dozen families left and joined the Mennonites. Others moved because they did not like the friction. The two or three families that were left went to other Amish districts and the bishop finally moved to a new location. Another contributing influence that hastened the disintegration of this Amish group was a community-wide Mennonite revival campaign.

Some bishops who realize the devastating results of division will use their influence to avoid issues that might develop into one. The question of whether to allow meetinghouses caused considerable tension among the Amish from 1860 to 1890. One region where the Amish built meetinghouses but kept the Old Order way of life in other respects was Somerset County, Pennsylvania, and adjoining Garrett County, Maryland. In 1880 and 1881 the two churches voted favorably on the question. After the meetinghouse was built the question remained of what kind of seats to install. There was a difference of opinion: some thought backless benches were all that was necessary; others felt that the benches should have backs. During the week a few of the carpenters quickly but quietly built seats with backs and put them into the church. When the people arrived on Sunday, an opponent said: "We have to do something." The bishop replied: "Ich denk sie hen uns gebodde." (I think they have beat us to it.)

Aged and financially able members have a great deal of influence in the community. Seldom are the unanimous suggestions of the ordained men overruled by the lay members in council, but it can happen. A member who had been steaming tobacco beds with equipment mounted on a truck had been caught driving the truck when he was supposed to hire a driver for it. When the driver was temporarily absent the owner would sometimes drive it short distances himself. A member complained to the preachers, who in turn recommended excommunication. Other members, many of whom had hired the services of the incumbent member, were opposed to excommunication. The bishop was "very understanding" and the decision was modified from excommunication to confession of a fault. What might have developed into a serious cleavage was thereby forestalled.

One self-educated, mature Amish layman believes that peaceful resolution of differences is possible. He informed me that as the population grows there seem to be more and more people of different opinions. "Some do not understand church matters the same as others; as a result, a minister might draw away from his group and take with him some of the members. In this way a new branch is started, who naturally plan their own rules slightly different. It is my opinion that some divisions may not be exactly harmful, so long as they do not neglect or turn away from the true commandments of the Bible, or so long as they do not get in their heads that they are better than others. There are two extremes. One is to adhere to the old time customs, and the other is to follow the pleasures of this fast-age world. Then there seems to be a middle class among our various churches who have been content. It has been my opinion that the middle class has held our churches together among us." The development of a body of knowledge that advocates "a middle of the road" position, if widely adopted by the leaders, could prevent some divisions which might otherwise slice communities into many factions. When there is unity of opinion among the ordained persons few issues are important enough to threaten cleavage in a given church.

When unanimity cannot be achieved in a local church, migration is another form of adjustment. The opportunity for family heads to move from a district that is "too strict" to one that has less restrictions and/or from one that is "too worldly" to one that is "keeping the old faith," prevents many potential conflicts from arising. If a member has difficulty keeping one aspect of the *Ordnung* he may find conditions easier elsewhere. Ordained leaders have less freedom of movement from one community to another, but some movement cannot be prevented and is often peacefully achieved through consultation with the officials in the recipient community. A stricter-than-ordinary bishop in one settlement was allowed by common consent of the ordained to expand his community geographically in the direction of the non-Amish settlement. In this way the "stricter" family heads moved into his territory, now largely a new settlement.

When Amish migration occurs the outsider is inclined to interpret it as a search for new land where prices are more reasonable. While this may be true, the underlying process is usually the resolution of a religious problem. The recent migrations to Oxford County, Ontario, from Pennsylvania, Maryland, and Ohio were precipitated by disagreements in the large, well-established settlements. In commenting about this movement, a father in Lancaster County said: "Those people want to go back fifty years, but I don't think it can be done." The settlements in Missouri and Tennessee in the past ten years were instigated by conservative-minded elements who were dissatisfied in their home communities, Iowa and Pennsylvania.

Many fathers who realize that the *Ordnung* is "not being kept the way it should" bring pressure to bear on the bishop to excommunicate the offenders. In the case of boys who own automobiles secretly one bishop has taken the position that "we must be patient." The only alternative for those who cannot "have patience" is to move to other communities. Within the three large Amish settlements there is no absolute uniformity of *Ordnung*.

The expanding settlement near the southern part of Lancaster County is predominantly a conservative movement. The Amish group in Elgin County, Ontario, is made up of families from different states who have similar attitudes and interests in re-creating a "clean" Christian community. They have made it clear to other Amish that they wish to get away from smoking, drinking, party games, bed courtship, and want to have a private school for their children, including Sunday school. Yet they maintain a stand against tractor farming and the automobile. Their leaders are aggressive in writing and defending their practices. The Amish in Grey County, On-

B. Hostetler

Leaders in Washington, D.C., seek exemption from government welfare programs. Photograph by World Wide Photos.

When folk and civilized ways clash on the highway
there is tragedy. Photograph by Indiana State Police.

Children examine the vehicle of an outsider. Photograph by Photo Arts.

Goods and services of the great society are within easy reach of
the members. Photograph by U.S. Independent Telephone Assn.

The rule of no electricity is here suspended for
a special occasion. Photograph by Photo Arts.

A horse-drawn hay crimper conforms to the rules of the church, even though a mounted motor is the source of power. Photograph by Robert Frey.

A buggy in Indiana pulling a motorboat. Amish who live around lakes find fishing a natural activity. Photograph by *Goshen News*.

"You are a tourist with a camera. You make us sick." Photograph by *Pittsburgh Press*.

tario, came from the Swartzendruber group in Ohio (in 1955) and wish to take a firm stand against bed courtship. The preachers of this group had taken a firm stand against this aged custom in their home communities and had been "set back" for their views. Over a century ago some Somerset County, Pennsylvania, Amish moved to Iowa for similar reasons.

"I think the Amish should spread out more," said one Amish patriarch in Pennsylvania. "They are too much in one bunch here, and the land prices are too high. If they are to develop spiritually, there just isn't time if they have to work so hard to maintain their high land prices. They are too busy with material things. I had an argument with those who want to move away because things are changing too fast. I told them they can live here and still don't have to change so fast as the rest. But they seem to think that all the rest should do as they say. That won't work. Those who want to keep the older things should be allowed to do so without bothering those who want to be more aggressive, and the other way around. We have some bishops that just can't contain themselves the way things are going."

Without freedom of movement the Amish would be in serious difficulty trying to resolve their individual viewpoints. The decision to sell a farm and relocate is not an easy one, particularly when the farm may be a very productive one and the family may be a large one. My own father's decision to sell his Pennsylvania farm, the home place of my grandfather, and at the age of fifty to move to Iowa did not come without sobs, discomfort, bitter feelings between the relatives, and much gossip. His was an effort to get away from the strict *Meidung* group and to start life over in a community that was free from these heavy restrictions.

### Overconformity and Stricter Rules

Overconformity is an adjustment to change or the threat of change and is expressed in a number of symbolic ways in Amish life. The length of a man's hair is generally a reflection of his degree of conservatism. In districts with short hair we may expect to find more changes and outside influences than in districts with longer hair. An Amish person who overconforms to the rules will let his hair grow longer than the *Ordnung* requires just "to play safe." Older members and ministers frequently adhere to stricter regulations than those required, just for the sake of avoiding any possible criticism. Some of the aged Amish persons of very conservative groups have told me that the hair is worn longer today than it was fifty years ago. If this is the case, we are faced with some very interesting hypotheses concerning social change. The assumption that change is always in the direction of the external world may be false. The most conservative Old Order Amish groups today may in fact be groups who have become more conservative by overconformity through the years, just as other groups have become more progressive. Fathers let their hair grow longer than the boys, and the ministers let theirs grow longer than do the lay members. There is a kind of competition among status seekers to see who can conform most to the rules. All of this tends toward overconformity and stiffening the *Ordnung* or making it stricter than before.

A few life experiences will illustrate this form of behavior. A boy who ran away from home, who had cut his hair, and was converted in a Mennonite group, discovered how the community reacted to his leaving. He said: "The Amish came in large numbers to visit my home. Our house was just filled with people, my brother-in-law told me. He said they just looked at each other, and cried and cried to each other. There was more crying than at a funeral, and it was almost like one." Such abnormally tense periods affect the younger members of the family. Parents become stricter in discipline and make sure that the younger children will not take the same deviant course.

Another young man who had been excommunicated from the church for "a strange belief," for advocating assurance of salvation, remembered that as a young man his mother normally sang gospel songs in English while working at home.

After "all this trouble got stirred up, she cut out all the English singing at home. I was the only boy that had left the Amish church for a long time, and my parents could not stand to think that it was their boy." The parents in this instance avoided all signs of being "English" that might be interpreted by the wayward boy as justification for his interest in non-Amish behavior. The boy also observed that his parents became firm in their relations to other members who had been put under the ban.

A mother whose boy was taking interest in a Bible study group reminded her son of her mental condition. "If you don't care if I go to a mental hospital, go ahead with what you are doing." Another excommunicated boy, the son of a very conformist family, was believed to be sick. "My older sister got the idea that I had sugar diabetes. She took me down to the doctor with the horse and buggy and made me take a physical exam. My parents thought maybe my contrary streak was due to my physical condition. Later I talked to the doctor and he said there was nothing wrong with me." The family had obeyed the *Ordnung* all these years by conforming more than was necessary and went to great lengths to discover the cause of their son's deviation.

A boy checked his Bible after returning home from preaching to see if the preacher had quoted it properly. He said, "I told my mother I did not agree with one point. She said I should not find fault with the sermon. She did not think it right to look it up in the Bible to see if it was true. If the preachers said it, she believed it was true. From that time on, I felt my mother was extreme." Overconformity requires an uncritical attitude toward the preachers as well as toward the traditional Amish practices. I recall that my father was observant in noting incorrectly quoted passages of scripture in the sermon. He also felt that lines of poetry or wise sayings did not have the same validity as Bible passages.

The absence of critical thinking about the goals of the society is one of the distinguishing features of the folk society. In the opinion of one ex-Amish person, "The preachers who do not have very much depth or insight into the Bible make up for it by teaching tradition and *Attnung*. They have to tell the people something, so they tell them what to do. If a man doesn't read and try to develop the spiritual side of himself, he is empty." The block against intellectual development and use of critical powers results in greater emphasis on conformity to the rules.

Ardent conformists in Amish society are frequently the "wild" young people of yesteryear. Many of the older Amish fathers believe that the young "sprouts" who are difficult to deal with will eventually grow up and become conforming members. A young man who was "wild, popular, well accepted and liked," is now a preacher and has become very strict. In his sermons he will relate his transformation from a disobedient young man to his discovery of "peace, happiness, and joy" as he obeys the church. The joy becomes conformity and over-conformity. An Amish person explained that when this man was ordained as a minister "he just gave himself up completely to the rules and regulations of the church, and he found peace. He is living a good life. It gives him satisfaction, but when it comes to a knowledge of the Christian life, I feel he is quite vague. Quite a few ministers go through this kind of experience. They have peace with what they know, but they do not do much studying." Confining knowledge to the traditional norms with little attempt to explore new aspects fosters over-conformity.

Older members of the Amish society, as in American society, find it difficult to adjust to changes, even though they are believed to be reasonable changes. Decisions which are rational and imminent may end in emotional blocks. This is well illustrated in an Amish church which had decided to allow the automobile. One of the participants explained "the automobile seemed progressive to our Old Order thinking. Our older people went along with the decision. . . . Theoretically they could see it, but to be part of it was quite a different thing. It caused quite a stir. Ten years before they resolved within themselves never to be anything but Old Order. They had changed in the meantime; they had to accept the decision, but they didn't want to. The decision was accepted mentally but practically they didn't accept it. They became frustrated. They tried to cover it up, and it made them insecure. They began to put stress on something they had never thought of emphasizing before, like parting the hair, which had not been mentioned for years. The hair must be parted in the middle, not on the side, and they drove this point so hard that it became nauseating." Here concessions in one aspect of the *Ordnung* resulted in overconformity in other aspects.

Privately published tracts, poetry, and warnings seem to be appearing among the Amish with greater frequency during the past decade. Some of these are a condemnation of modern technological progress and of pleasure. Dreams, deathbed warnings, visions, and admonitions are linked with recent human events, indicating how man must turn back to God. All of this is issued in the belief that "it is only the straight and narrow way, the way of the cross which leads towards heaven, and with God's help we can walk on it. It is a seducive time in which we live. Even the chosen people can be deceived if we do not beware." [2]

## Preventing Change

The acceptance of the automobile, as an example of change, must overcome all the inhibitions and rules used earlier to keep it out. The means used for social control and for dealing with offenders range from such informal controls as gossip to the power of *Meidung*. A hierarchy of means used for social control includes the following: (1) Personal inhibitions or conscience which keeps the individual from transgressing the rules of the church. But the person who says "I dress Amish but I sure think different on the inside" is not controlled by this means. (2) Informal talk or gossip is an effective means of controlling behavior. Even though gossip is generally not sanctioned within families, it remains one of the most effective means of control in the small face-to-face Amish community. A former Amish person was of this opinion: "There is nothing

[2] From a tract by "P. Y." of Aylmer, Ontario.

the Amish like better than talking and saying juicy things
about somebody."

When a person is not controlled by conscience or by informal talk, (3) he is admonished by the deacon or a preacher
if he is guilty of an offense. The official will obtain the attitude
of the offender, and if he manifests disobedience and remains
unchanged in his intent, (4) the offender is admonished by
two persons, usually ordained men. For minor offenses (5) the
offender must confess his sins to the church by standing, and
for major offenses by kneeling. As additional warning and
punishment (6) the offender may be asked not to take part
in the coming communion. Major offenses such as adultery,
drunkennness, or buying an automobile or tractor (where forbidden) submit the transgressor to (7) immediate excommunication and *Meidung* (shunning) until a change of attitude is
manifest. Most severe of all is (8) excommunication and shunning for life.

In a small society where virtually everyone is related by
blood and where life is governed by informal rather than
formal organizations, change is slow. It takes a half century
for some changes to take place which in the American society
might occur in one year. It took an Amish church fifty years
from the time it adopted a moderate policy of *Meidung* (by
not shunning members who join other churches) until it
adopted the automobile. Change is slow where members give
common adherence to the core elements of a culture. In folk
cultures "new items do not appear with any great frequency,"
says Linton, and the "society has plenty of time to test them
and to assimilate them to its pre-existing patterns. In such cultures the core constitutes almost the whole." [3]

## *How the* Ordnung *Is Changed*

Changing a major rule requires time in Amish society. It
may take decades, and a half century or more to observe even
the slightest symbolic change. To observe how the boundary

[3] Ralph Linton (1940), *op. cit.*, 283.

mechanisms described above are overcome, let us take the case of a Pennsylvania church which during the past decade, suddenly to the surprise of the wider community, allowed the automobile for its members. Automobile dealers in nearby towns experienced a sudden boom in sales. The news that automobiles "were allowed" soon spread through the entire region and the secular community became accustomed to seeing bearded fathers drive their automobiles on the highways. This Amish church had voted almost unanimously, according to one of its members, to allow automobiles.

Upon closer examination and upon reconstructing the sequence of events in this decision, it was not a decision as easy as taking a vote among the members. A number of events reaching back a half century and also contemporary conditions produced this extraordinary example of systemic linkage, or successful change.[4] This church had already relaxed its rules by making changes from the strictest Amish in the community. This church itself split off around 1911 from the "strict" *Meidung* church, and although it retained the dress and in many respects retained the *Ordnung* generally, slight modifications were made over the years. Men began wearing buttons on work jackets, the hair was cut shorter, single women were permitted to work as cleaning maids for non-Amish people, and tractors were adopted for farming. With the availability of pneumatic tires and improved tractors with higher speeds, the Amish began using them on the road to pull wagons to town, to run errands to neighbors, and for the daily delivery of milk to market. Children and boys became completely familiar with the mechanics and skill of driving a tractor.

It was common for Amish parents to engage licensed cab drivers, often Mennonite neighbors who talked and understood the Amish dialect, to transport them to other states and communities. The Amish drove their carriages to the homes of the drivers to make the appointments. Cab drivers were booked in advance for trips to Ohio, Indiana, Iowa, or even as far west as California and Oregon. Short trips, often of an emer-

[4] Charles P. Loomis (1960), *op. cit.*, 32, 241.

gency nature such as trips to the doctor and hospital or to the county courthouse, were arranged by using the non-Amish neighbor's telephone. Use of the telephone became institutionalized among members of this church. Amish parents whose son (not yet old enough for baptism) had an automobile did not have need of the services of a cab driver. In some instances the young sons who owned automobiles joined nearby Mennonite churches and had no intention of becoming Amish. They could not be punished by *Meidung* for no one can come under this sanction unless he has been a baptized member. Amish fathers who were not inclined to uphold the old norms of behavior helped their sons financially to buy an automobile.

Under the above circumstances the desire for the automobile became very apparent in the church among the young men and the married non-farming men who were employed in such occupations as milling, carpentry, masonry, and butchering. Farm hands ribbed their employers about the inconsistency of hitching up horses for road work when transportation was easier and more efficient with the tractor. Sons complained about the slowness of the horses, that they were too much trouble, and that it was dangerous to drive a carriage on the open highway. This informal conversation and "egging" by younger members to Amish landowners, some of them ministers, over a period of several years appears to have set the stage for a favorable nod in the church. That talk about a forbidden norm was permitted at all was important in creating an atmosphere of discussion.

But no amount of desire or discussion on informal occasions could bring the subject of automobiles up for a vote in church. The rules of the church were clear and there was nothing to discuss. Heretofore the only way to own an automobile was to leave the Amish church and transfer to a Mennonite group. Mennonite churches in the area are made up of persons who were of Amish background, but the younger men in this Pennsylvania church did not want to strain their relationship with their relatives by changing churches. They did not want a different religion, but they wanted an automobile.

The only way the automobile could be discussed in church was if some member violated the rule of non-ownership. Early one spring a young single man, a baptized member of a respected family, purchased an automobile. The youngster had secured a learning driver's permit and drove his new possession to the farm of his parents. The whole family was shocked, especially the father and mother who were interested in maintaining "peace" in the church. Obedience to the church and godliness were more important to the family than any change of traditional norms. The father objected to having the automobile on his property. After much persuasion the son returned the automobile to the dealer with the hopes of regaining it later. The youth was not excommunicated since he acknowledged his transgression of the church rules.

A few days later a married man, employed at the town village, purchased an automobile. He did not make the mistake of driving it to his home on the farm, but kept it at his place of employment. He commuted to and from the village with his farm tractor. The church officials deliberated on a course of action. He was advised to "put it away," meaning to sell it, until the church could come to a unanimous decision. He refused the advice of the assembly and was excommunicated. Meanwhile a third member, a young married farmer, purchased an automobile, but he too was excommunicated. Many members were in favor of automobiles but waited for a change in the *Ordnung*. With these offences committed, the officials had justification for bringing the question of ownership of automobiles before the church. Though the offenders had to be punished for their disobedience, there was still the question of whether or not to allow the automobile. It became obvious to the officials that they must arrive at some recommendation among themselves as to the appropriate action.

In the meantime informal discussions continued among the members during weekdays. Amish fathers conversed with each other informally in homes, sometimes until long into the night. Two of the excommunicated men, in desperation, shared their predicament with the bishop of a nearby Mennonite church.

They applied for membership in the Mennonite church. The bishop advised caution about changing churches and suggested that one of them call an informal meeting of all the members who wanted to have an automobile. The meeting was arranged and about thirty Amish persons came to hear what the Mennonite bishop had to say. The bishop read the Bible and prayed with the group. He then explained that people who join a new church because they want an automobile, "usually do not help the church they jump into." He advised the group of Amish people to take the question to their own ministers to see if they could not come to some solution. The bishop's church was already a large one, and he was weary of having former Amish members who wanted membership for no other reason than having the liberty to own an automobile. The members went home and many of them talked to the Amish ministers. The attitude of the Mennonite bishop undoubtedly caused the Amish officials to make a firm decision. He had helped to crystalize opinions among Amish members which brought pressure to bear on the Amish church.

The six ordained men of the Amish church in the meantime had counseled with each other informally. They were forced to decide on a proper course of action and it was up to the bishop to obtain unanimity among his fellow ordained men. By custom, recommendations brought to the assembled body must have the unanimous backing of all the ordained persons. The bishop in this church had been a middle-aged man with a variety of experiences. When single he had worked as a farm hand in the midwestern states. He had been drafted into conscientious objector service and had been a participant in the camp worship and Sunday school services. All of this experience and exposure to wider society before his ordination to the office of bishop provided him with viewpoints unlike other Amish bishops. The views of his fellow ministers were compatible with his. The six ordained men did not oppose the oncoming automobile issue, and they made their recommendation to the assembly.

Decision-making in the Amish church requires taking the

*Rat* or counsel of the baptized members. This is done by each member voting on the recommendation that is placed before the assembly. As is customary, the two deacons in the said church polled the members' meeting, one taking the nod among the men and the other among the women. Members always remain seated and either affirm the decision of the ministers with a nod of the head, oppose it, or remain neutral on the question. The outcome of the *Rat* is usually expressed as: unanimous, practically unanimous, or not unanimous. The result of the automobile vote was practically unanimous with only four old persons not giving assent, and these soon joined the next most conservative Old Order Amish group in the community. Members were instructed to buy only black automobiles or to have them painted black. Within a few weeks most of the members came to church in automobiles and only a few of the older members came in carriages. Every Sunday from forty to fifty automobiles could be seen around the farm buildings where Sunday services were held. The acceptance of the automobile forced still other changes in this community of Amish. The young people who formerly courted with horse and carriage and in traditional ways now had many alternatives before them. The small community, which was bounded by the horse and carriage, was now expanded to include other Amish communities in and beyond the state. Families and young men may now travel a distance of one to five hundred miles on a weekend to see friends or relatives. One woman who opposed the automobile vote said, "Where will this lead to, if our young people are given the privilege of going wherever they want?" The forces of adjustment that were necessary in this small community within a few weeks, which in the secular society required a half century, gave rise to other intense pressure for accelerated change.

For some time the small Pennsylvania church was uncertain of its standing among other Amish groups. There could no longer be an exchange of preachers with Old Order churches. Finally, this church affiliated with the Beachy Amish group, a loosely affiliated group made up of congregations from

Pennsylvania to Iowa who allow the automobiles. Telephones and a meetinghouse were later approved.

## Conditions Favorable to Change

The automobile was the object forcing a change in the *Ordnung* of the church just described. The adoption of such a change was preceded by a relaxing of discipline in a number of other areas of life, even before the present generation. The idea of farm efficiency prevailing in the general American society found acceptance among the middle-aged farm couples in the need for "tractor farming." The widespread practices of hiring automobiles (with drivers) and the use of tractors on the road were institutionalized before the change came about. Patterns of travel and communication could not be maintained under the old norms. Stress resulted and the rules were violated and finally changed. Change among the Amish is often less dramatic than in this Pennsylvania incident, and it is rather rare that a decision so unanimous is possible. This case illustrates important processes of change as they occur in Amish life.

*A major technological change is preceded by a period of conditioning* in which people of a similar opinion find each other and persons of opposing views seek fulfillment elsewhere. This process is made possible by migration and psychic mobility. Change in the *Ordnung* is possible only as the ordained officials can come to a unanimous opinion. In the case just described the conditions were favorable for change. One influential minister who probably would have opposed the automobile had moved from the community six years earlier over the question of electricity. The community had been conditioned for the unanimous decision by symbolic changes. Amish fathers and preachers who "saw what was coming" had opportunity to move out before there was an issue. Migration in Amish society is a major means of escape from adjustment to changes that are considered too great. An Indiana Amish church that adopted the automobile had also experienced a period of conditioning before the *Ordnung* was changed. "There were a number of people who did not think it wrong to own automobiles, and they knew that some of the ministers did not think it wrong. When a few people bought cars, some of the ministers refused to ask members to make a confession. They were not asked to sell them." This church was made up of many families who had moved into the district from other Amish districts and "who were tired of all the restrictions." Several years of using tractors, of Bible study in the English language, and interest in and support of missionary work preceded the adoption of the automobile.

Change, as we have seen, is inevitable in Amish society. The general influences of American culture, both material and non-material, gradually find their way into segments of the Amish. The methods used to keep the community in bounds, described earlier, are not 100 per cent effective in keeping the outside out. The following changes have occurred in one or more communities: Ball bearings have been adopted on carriage wheels. Dairy barns have been remodeled to conform to standards required for selling fluid milk. The young men have changed from black to brown shoes. Hair is cut shorter than the previous generation. Mothers have changed from cotton to nylon material for some women's garments. Tractors for field work have been allowed. The trend from general to specialized farming is very apparent. Young men and women have become interested in education, in occupations other than farming, and in missionary work. Some Amish districts have gone so far as to allow electricity, ownership of automobiles, and telephones. Kitchens have been modernized with appliances. Bottled gas in lieu of electricity, milking machines run by small gasoline engines, and refrigerators operated with kerosene are still other changes. The adoption of such innovations requires reintegration of culture and reorganization of values.

The social organization of the Amish community has little facility for dealing with change. The general effort to preserve the old and degrade the new is so pervasive that change must occur slowly, by a process of osmosis, and often by strained human relationships. Although individuals may want changes and show remarkable creativity, the authority system has almost no institutional means of making change legitimate.

# CHAPTER 16

# THE FUTURE OF AMISH SOCIETY

THERE ARE MANY SMALL SOCIETIES "not yet swept out by the broom of our industrial and urban civilization," says Everett Hughes. "How long it will take to mop them up, no one knows. The process seems to be going on rapidly now, but it will probably last longer than any of us would predict." [1] Several writers have predicted the absorption of the Amish into the great society in a few decades. Social scientists have urged that their communities be thoroughly studied and documented so that once they are extinct, we shall at least have on record a complete ethnographic account of their society. The question is whether the Amish will be able to continue their separate way of life as they have in the past. On the one hand, this is a naïve question. One may as well ask whether there is a future for any society, anywhere in the civilized world, and whether any cultural group can maintain its distinctiveness. A categorical answer to the future is too simple to yield answers which have significance.

All human communities in the world are changing and the assumption that they do not change is fallacious. Furthermore, social change is not a change in one direction. Change is not unidirectional but multidirectional. Social change does not necessarily proceed from the simple to the complex, nor do all societies go through certain presumed stages in the social evolutionary process. Changes in Amish society are not predestined to proceed from the sacred to the secular. Some aspects of change are quite the opposite. Not only have we found in our observations a number of instances of secularization, but also the process of becoming more and more sacred,

[1] Everett C. Hughes, *Where Peoples Meet* (Free Press, 1952), 25-26.

or what is called "sacralization."[2] "Decay" and "rebirth" occur simultaneously in the same society. From the viewpoint of understanding, it is more fruitful to note the directions of development than it is to make categorical predictions. We may also ask seriously whether the Amish in America will follow the European pattern of assimilation.

If the Amish lived in a single, geographic, local, isolated community, prediction would be less complex. But the Amish live in approximately sixty geographic settlements in North America, and each settlement and each church district within the settlement is different from all the rest. Each is constantly striving to resolve its problems, by means of its local heritage and needs, which accounts for uniqueness and a preferred way of habitually solving its problems and fulfilling its charter. Each community must resolve successfully within the limitations of self-realization, its ongoing, living problematic situation.

There are general directions of development among the Amish in North America from which valid deductions can be made. There is on the one hand a marked increase in group assimilation represented by the number of congregations who no longer consider themselves Old Order Amish. They have been called by many different names, depending on their locale; most but not all are affiliated with the Beachy Amish group. There have been at least thirty-four congregations which have changed their affiliation since the Beachy division[3] in 1927. This development is group assimilation, rather than individual assimilation—the Amish who remained in Europe were generally so assimilated. Among Old Order congregations there is a marked tendency toward more conformity and overconformity to the traditions. This polarization or development in opposite directions may be understood in terms of a typology, the New Order on the one hand and the Old Order on the other. In the analysis which follows, we shall use this

[2] Howard Becker, "Normative Reactions to Normlessness," *American Sociological Review* (December, 1960).

[3] The Beachy group is discussed in Chapter 11, pp. 250–51.

typology. The descriptions may not apply in every detail to any specific community but conform to a type of social organization. Both the New and the Old Order will be discussed in terms of the directions of development in the charter, the community, the concept of the world, and personal involvement.

### The Redefinition of the Charter

The charter was treated earlier in this book under five points: separation, the vow of obedience, the rules for living, the ban, and affinity to nature. Every Amish community faces the problem of reconciling its charter with the practical problems of existence. All human communities must either resolve the question of group self-actualization within their environment, or perish, or move to another locale. Like other communities in all places, the Amish must resolve the dual living problem.[4] On the one hand, the group perceives as its goal eternal life by conformity to the simple, believing, New Testament ideal as understood by the community. On the other, it is faced with the existential problem of a natural existence in time and space, in an environment where temperature, soils, and climatic conditions vary, and in modern society where possession of money is a necessary condition for existence.

*In the Old Order* the doctrine of separation from the world means among other things physical isolation, making a living from the soil, and insofar as possible, keeping the rules of the

[4] In both Old and New Orders we may observe a preferred way of habitually solving problems which has been termed by Laura Thompson as the community's "preferred relationship pattern." See "Perception Patterns in Three Indian Tribes," *Psychiatry,* Vol. 14 (1951), 255–63, and "Core Values and Diplomacy: A Case Study in Iceland," *Human Organization,* Vol. 19 (1960), 82–85. Of course such problem solving operates according to a principle of limited potentialities and possibilities, growth, development, and change within its total geophysical context and human capabilities. See for example A. A. Goldenweiser, "The Principle of Limited Possibilities in the Development of Culture," *Journal of American Folklore,* Vol. 26 (1913), 259, 270–80, and *History, Psychology and Culture* (Knopf, 1933).

past unchanged. The baptismal vow means what it has meant at all times in the past and implies lifetime commitment to the *Ordnung* of the church. Ceremony centers around the meeting in the home, not in the meetinghouse. Excommunication and shunning means what it meant in Jakob Ammann's time: the shunning of all who leave the church to become members of other churches. Nonconformity to the world includes nonownership of tractors, automobiles, electricity, and telephones. In situations where their use cannot be avoided, such uses are not to become habitual and are to be avoided as much as possible. So far as the individual is concerned, his personality is tradition-directed rather than inner-directed.

*In the New Order* the charter is modified and adapted to the emerging patterns of change. The traditional way of solving problems no longer permits community self-actualization. Though the changes may be extremely slow as has been discussed earlier, the tendency is toward conformity to the great society. Separation from the world is interpreted to mean spiritual rather than physical isolation. Where making a living from direct contact with the soil is impossible, the New Order no longer interprets the charter in this manner.

In the New Order the acceptance of the tractor symbolized a significant change from the earlier concept of the charter. Midwestern communities, before others, have tended to permit the tractor for field use; in some districts only steel wheels are allowed, while in others the farmer member may use pneumatic tires. The tractor "brings many things in" which were not allowed before: power take-off equipment, and displacement of horse-drawn machinery in general. Greater capital investment is required. High-speed tractors with trailers soon compete favorably with horses on the hard-surfaced road, and then it is only a question of time until the automobile comes in for discussion.

In the New Order the change from "house" to "church" for Sunday services and ceremonial meetings is another change in charter. There are repeated instances of transferral of entire districts from "House" to "Church Amish." This change usually follows the acceptance of the automobile. The meeting-house symbolizes conformity to progressive developments and has far-reaching social significance. People can travel farther, enlarging the group. Church tends to be held every Sunday. There is no longer a noon meal following the service. The net effect is less time spent in face-to-face contact with other members of the community and more time spent in family and individual interests. The patterns of behavior tend toward conformity to those of the prevailing society. The individual person tends to order his life choices around inner-directed rather than tradition-directed goals.

Distinctive dress and hair styles show marked modification in the New Order. As tractors, automobiles, and meeting-houses are adopted, hair and beards are trimmed shorter and shorter. With the dwindling of the beard an Amishman may no longer identify himself as an Amish person. An Amish boy with a shingled hair cut is almost indistinguishable from the "world." Secularization in apparel appears to be greater among men than women, and more advanced among the young than the old. Men wear broadfall trousers, and there are firms who manufacture broadfall work pants and jackets. Men's Sunday dress suits can be ordered, tailor-made, from stores which specialize in "plain clothes." The outer garments of women are homemade, and the secularization of the woman's apparel is confined largely to what garments she may wear under her traditional Amish dress and whether they are store-bought. Among the young, change is manifest in the wearing of sweaters with buttons and zippers, store suspenders, and boys tending to wear caps with little if any rim just like their non-Amish neighbors.

Fundamental changes in farm interests and social habits are recognized by the natural leaders of both Old and New Orders. "When I was a boy," said Bishop David B. Zook,[5] "we used to work in the barn, sweep it out and keep it clean. Today we see too many cobwebs in the barn and the young people are taking no interest but running away from the farm." While

[5] Interview, New Holland, Pa., July 14, 1960.

the young men turn away from the world of animals, many single women turn to domestic housework in the city. With bus service available and attractive wages as maids in "English" homes, many obtain employment in the villages and towns. Living in with English people during the week is now tolerated whereas earlier girls were excommunicated for doing so. So long as this form of culture contact is mutually advantageous and the marginal persons maintain a symbiotic rather than a social relationship with the "English" people, the direction of development may well be peaceful.

## The Changing Community

Amish communities, like other communities, find themselves in a problematic situation: it is the problem of fulfillment as a human group within the range of limited potentialities and possibilities. The constant striving to resolve the problematic situation by means of available natural and human resources, and by means of its own unique local heritage, accounts for differing perception patterns.[6] In Amish communities, as in others, the capacity for building a community is limited by man's own capacity for integrating experience.[7]

In terms of population, the Amish were a small society a half-century ago when no settlement numbered more than a few hundred people. Many of their settlements are still small and isolated, but their most densely populated regions can no longer be classed as small in terms of maximizing primary relationships. The Amish now number about 50,000 people, and their three largest settlements each number from six to ten thousand persons. While their patterns of anonymity develop along different lines than those of the great society, they are similar in kind. The small Amish settlements have less evidence of delinquency and vandalism than do the large settlements.

The changes in personal relations were already obvious in our previous discussion of reference groups and the emergence

[6] Thompson (1951), *op. cit.*
[7] Baker Brownell, *The Human Community: Its Philosophy and Practice for a Time of Crisis* (Harper, 1950), 41.

of special-interest groups. The large church districts are prevented from developing into unmanageable ceremonial units by dividing the district into two meetings. But even so, remoteness and anonymity develop as the group expands geographically. Adults, to say nothing of the young, cannot know all other Amish persons in primary, face-to-face relations, just from the standpoint of sheer numbers. Intimacy gives way to cosmopolitanism and to indifference toward those one does not know. A knowledge of others cannot be maintained except by the kinship system. Those who are not in the *Freundschaft* are least well known, and in some cases altogether unknown.

Land room becomes a problem for the expanding Old Order settlement in a way that is not experienced by the New Order. The over-all problem of acquiring land is not acute, for a great deal of land in this country can be purchased, and much of it is going into forestry and pasture. The problem for the Old Order is to acquire the land in places where they want it. There are few places where solid blocks of land are owned by the Amish, but this does hold true for a few church districts. The Amish tend to buy land adjacent to their settlement as it becomes available from non-Amish farmers around them. In areas where the value of land is high because of rapidly expanding urban areas and the many non-agricultural uses of land, the Amish must pay exorbitant prices. In Lancaster County they are able to do so by raising cash crops, for instance, tobacco.

*The Old Order* members know intuitively that if they lose their agricultural base, they will lose to a large extent the qualities which go into the making of an Amish community. They do not need the knowledge or tools of science on which to base their conclusions. To them, the small farming community is the most promising setting within which to carry out the ultimate goals in life. To the Amish leaders who have themselves experienced the good will, mutual respect, and the sharing of risks and experience, the community is an expression of supreme worth. The loss of an agrarian base is reason for grave concern to them.

In Old Order communities there is a tendency to migrate

in order not to perish. Migration permits renewed attempts at isolation as families move from densely populated settlements to small settlements and to rural areas where no Amish have previously lived. The traditional Amish community is a small community where primary relations are maximized.

The formation of new settlements is not simply a solution to land room but usually occurs in conjunction with other group needs, such as working toward a new consensus of *Ordnung*. In other words, there is usually a reformulation of the leadership patterns and of community reorganization. Two basic requirements in forming a new settlement are to have sufficient consensus of the rules and a large enough group to make possible marriages within the same settlement. Many attempts at settlement have been unsuccessful due to the absence of one or more of these elements. But the presence of extinct communities does not mean that they have disintegrated, failed, or were assimilated. The Amish take their social institutions with them wherever they go. In most cases it means that the space dimension of community has not been resolved in relation to the needs.

One of the obvious hazards between an expanding Amish community and the American society is the many clashes of automobiles with buggies on the highway. The horse and buggy has become a nuisance, if not a peril at night, on the modern highway. In some areas, Amish farmers have applied for liability insurance policies on their vehicles. Several states have made laws requiring not only lights in the front and rear, but also red flashing lights and turn signals. This forced mechanization is quietly understood by the Old Order people. While it represents a significant change, we may note that it is change within limits, or controlled acculturation.

Travel becomes a crucial problem in a geographically expanding settlement. A horse is no longer capable of meeting the demands and needs. For the ceremonial occasion, a horse is sufficient. But for visiting relatives and meeting the needs which emerge beyond the church district, it is necessary to use public transportation—rail, bus, taxi—or sometimes to hire a neighbor with his automobile. Thus the members of the little community are less able to live their lives within their own preferred culture that is partially sheltered from the influence of the great society. Under such conditions, contradictions become apparent.

Density of population not only brings members into closer contact with many more Amish persons, but also with outsiders. The young married couple faced with the problem of farm ownership and of acquiring sufficient capital sees and covets the short cuts of middle-class American farm families. The advantages of electricity and of tractor farming become obvious to them. Amish people who rent farms from non-Amish owners in some areas use these conveniences, particularly if they reside on the fringes of the large settlements. The owner may not want the electricity removed from his farm or have the electric motors and other power-operated machines replaced. These Amish renters become accustomed to otherwise forbidden uses and find it inconvenient to "put away" lights and electricity.

With the emerging larger community, the Amish are realizing the loss of social control in the family and in the church. Not only is there a loss of kinship obligations in favor of economic considerations, but the strongest means of control, *Meidung*, is also weakened as growth is experienced. The defecting member may, due to easy means of travel and personal knowledge of outsiders, and through self help, readily escape his punishment by finding fulfillment in the great society. *Meidung* in such cases brings him not to shame and remorse but drives him right out of his little community.

*The New Order* strives to solve its community expansion problem by adaptation within redefined limits. Instead of staying with the hazardous buggy on the highway, it adopts substitutionary modes of travel which lead to the automobile. Another adaptation is specialization in occupations. While general farming is the traditional and basic form of subsistence, other means of making a living emerge such as carpentering, cabinetmaking, watch repairing, masonry, sawmilling, butchering, working in a factory, or on the railroad. Mass production of turkeys, broilers, and milk as well as cash crops such as peas, tomatoes, and mint (varying with regions) are concessions to market demands in the great society. Once these special types of farming are adopted, there is no turning back to the simple self-contained farm. The competition for economic ends tends to outweigh other considerations. The Amish farmer is forced to enlarge his income even more when he must consider the price of the land he wants to obtain to keep his marriageable sons and daughters on the land.

## The Changing Conception of the World

The view of the world held by any group is internal and not subject to change by direct pressure from the outside. The changing conception of the world constitutes an important equation in the achievement of community self-realization. A change in perception of the world is a necessary condition to the community's effort to achieve harmonious, balanced, and consistent attitudes toward life.[8]

*The Old Order* has maintained a dualistic conception of reality that approximates a fixed position; that is, sharp cultural definitions of church and "world." Man was created and placed in the garden to care for the created world of God, albeit through the fall he is now living in a wilderness under evil influence. The members view themselves as separate from the world not only in life goals, but also in fashion and in material possessions. The community (*Gemeinschaft*) is looked upon as a separate entity living in but "not of the World." The will of God for his people is that they be "not conformed to this world," and "not unequally yoked with unbelievers," but "a peculiar people." [9]

[8] The conception of the world here means the institutionalized concept of the nature of the world, of man, animals, plants, of the self, and of all these categories as they relate to the Kingdom of God and the powers of evil. Robert Redfield in *The Little Community* (1955), stresses the concept of wholeness, as does Laura Thompson (*Toward a Science of Mankind*, McGraw-Hill, 1961, 10).

[9] Such quotations from the Bible constitute a significant core value of Amish culture. The passages are all found in the New Testament respectively in: John 17:16, Romans 12:2, II Corinthians 6:14, and Titus 2:14.

The world is progressing in the view of the Old Order and progress means worldly wisdom and forsaking God. As individuals fall prey to the temptations of the world, or turn to more worldly churches, the Old Order mends its "fences" and attempts to withdraw even deeper from the world. Symptoms of neurotic overconformity and depravity appear to develop. Instead of serving on local public school boards as was common practice years ago, Amish fathers are now forbidden to hold these positions. Instead of sending their children to the one-room public school as was the practice earlier, they now attend their own church-supported small schools. Attendance at consolidated public schools is forbidden, and Amish children are instead taught by Amish members who have frequently no training beyond the elementary grades. Amish men were always required to wear long hair, but during the past fifty years it has gotten even longer in some of the more reactionary groups of Old Order. The effect of such withdrawal is not only a change toward a more restricted view of the world, but also intellectual impoverishment.

"The effect of extreme formalism on personality," says Cooley, "is to starve its higher life and leave it the prey of apathy, self-complacency, sensuality, and the lower nature in general." "A formalized religion and a formalized freedom," he says, "are, notoriously, the congenial dwelling place of depravity and oppression. . . ."[10] The ruling patriarchs cannot promote change and it is psychically impossible that they do so. Their complete identification with the traditional system renders them incapable of abandoning the old as anything but catastrophic.[11]

Greater ethnocentrism develops where change is psychologically at a standstill. Some Amish persons in the past have held that Jesus Christ was an Amishman, that he spoke German, and that the earth was flat rather than global. Many persons in other societies have held to such narrow wishes and they still persist where such "pockets" have not been

[10] Charles H. Cooley, *Social Organization* (Scribners, 1909), 432–45.
[11] L. L. Bernard, discusses this "dilemma in revolution" in *Social Control in its Sociological Aspects* (Macmillan, 1939), 340–43.

displaced by other knowledge. The feeling that "we are a people, a chosen people, apart from all other people," can be retained best under conditions of limited contact with outside groups.

*In the New Order,* by contrast, the view of the world is conditioned by greater contact with out-groups, by awareness and concern for others outside the "fence." The charter is modified from conforming to tradition to a renewed study and interpretation of the Bible. With a change in world view comes greater personal freedom and opportunity for intellectual activity, as well as physical mobility. The Amish people, according to this view, are not by tradition "a chosen people" but are little different from any other people.

Among the developing New Order, there emerges a climate of critical thinking. Tradition is viewed as a block to progress. Capacity for self-evaluation and self-criticism emerges as marginal groups develop, such as the Bible study renewal groups. There are two kinds of internal critical groups. The one is a renewal effort hoping to retain its identity and good graces within the culture and by slow osmosis to alter the dead mechanisms of the society. The other is the self-hate group which seeks to demoralize and abolish the traditional system, but such efforts are usually individualistic and less well organized. Reactionary individuals tend to leave the formalistic group entirely.

The New Order shifts in the direction of modern Mennonitism and Protestantism in its view of reality. Concern for "lost souls" emerges along with individual "assurance of salvation" and missionary activity. The Old Order is regarded by the New as "a prospective mission field to whom the Gospel should be preached." One Mennonite pastor cautioned his fellow pastors not to receive Amish applicants too hastily, advising that "pastors should thoroughly indoctrinate them in the plan of salvation, of the grace of God, of faith and the Christian life, and root out the legalistic and negative thinking that has resulted from being under Amish discipline."

This antagonism lies deeper than contemporary so-called "errors in theology." The Amish have simply perpetuated the forms of Anabaptism with a definition of salvation as obedience to community as rooted in the Gospel accounts. Contemporary Mennonites who are descendents of the Anabaptists have drifted from their founders toward Protestantism with its emphasis on individual salvation epitomized in the writings of the Apostle Paul. Thus a Mennonite pastor may feel that Mennonites have more in common with evangelical Protestants than with the Amish. The question is well stated by Friedmann: "Is the Gospel to be understood through Paul, or is Paul to be understood through the Gospel?"[12] The Amish simply understand *Nachfolge* (discipleship) as commitment to the love community, while the view of Paul and much of Protestantism starts with sin and the experience of individual justification. The one stresses personal enjoyment and the other suffering. Both emphases "should meet each other frequently," says Friedman, but this antipathy explains one of the underlying diversities in world view between Protestants and the Old Order Amish.

A changing world view is reflected in sermon delivery. The New Order type of delivery is a reaction to the singsong sermon. Instead of secluded eyes and a rhythmic pattern, the New Order preacher faces his audience and the individuals within the audience eye to eye. He is forceful in his delivery. He wanders from his standing position as much as from four to eight feet for the sake of emphasis. He may step forward or backward, or place his hands on the shoulder of a brother seated nearby. He is more inclined to use illustrations from contemporary life than is the Old Order, which limits its illustrations to the Bible. His quotations of Bible verses are given in full. He appears confident of himself, and many more English and mixed words creep into his delivery.

The tendency to use the English language develops with a changing world view. English words and phrases are adopted in sermons and ceremonial occasions, but it is essentially an outgrowth of usage in domestic relations. The problem is twofold: It is hard for the minister to put new ideas in old

[12] Robert Friedmann, *Mennonite Piety Through the Centuries* (Mennonite Historical Society, 1949), 85.

forms, and the decreasing familiarity with the German makes it hard for the member to grasp the meaning. Dialect words are at first substituted in sermons for English ones, such as: surely, accident, condition, peaceful, absolutely, flood, judgment, chance, and disappointment. English words are also used with a German prefix or suffix, as: *Er hat unser sins aus [ge] blot* (He hath blotted out our sins), and *Noah hat Gott nicht [aus] figur [a] kenna aber war gehorsum* (Noah could not figure out God but was obedient). The inability to use either standard German or English in its entirety introduces not only linguistic stress but also human stress and an element of personal instability necessary for effective communication. When the language of the world is used to express sacred concepts there has been an almost complete symbolic reorganization. The absence of formal German schools for the young and the inability of the family to impart this knowledge complicate the task of indoctrinating the young in the traditional world view.

## Changing Patterns of Involvement

The changing conceptions of the charter, of the community, and of the world explain the changing behavior of the members of the community. An understanding of interpersonal relations is possible in the context of culture viewed as a whole, including the actual difficulties and threats in the community's problematic living situation. Anxieties and fears, real or imaginary, are expressed in the social and ceremonial institutions, and in personality structure such as neurotic anxiety or meaningful existence. Behavior is expressed by conformity or nonconformity to the traditional or expected patterns. The traditional patterns of non-involvement in the world outside the little community change as conceptions of the world are changed. Patterns of involvement show a greater range of permissive behavior in, for example, socio-economic activity outside the community.

Participation (1) in economic affairs and (2) in benevolent

causes outside the local Amish community are two principal ways in which the members have become involved in the world beyond the community. There are other altered behavior patterns but our discussion of these two will illustrate the principle.

*The Old Order* has curbed with greatest success the participation of its members in all affairs outside the little community. This has been done by consistent perception of the traditional charter; i.e., of the doctrine of nonconformity to the world, or of the unequal yoke, and by the severe punishment of offenders.

The economic goals of the great society are avoided as much as the living, problematic situation will permit. Resources are important to the Old Order for the achievement of community goals; hence some involvement is necessary. Greater dependence on outside resources and services changes the habits of buying and selling, of interpersonal relations in the community and domestic life, and in handcrafts. Change is slow, often dreaded, but nevertheless inevitable and tends toward the direction of the technological ways of the great society.

The Old Order has had to work out its symbiotic relations in the face of the enormous world revolution of mass production, mass consumption, and mass leisure. "The world revolution of our time," according to one source, "is 'made in U.S.A.' . . . Nothing ever before recorded in the history of man equals, in speed, universality and impact, the transformation this principle has wrought in the foundations of society in the forty years since Henry Ford turned out the first Model T. . . ." [13] The sweep of this revolution has undermined small societies which have no resistance to the new forces, no background or habit pattern of industrialized life to "cushion the shock." Self-sufficiency vanishes, and with it a way of life. The countryside is subjected to the rule of the cities, which have grown enormously. Agricultural workers have been re-

[13] Peter F. Drucker, *The New Society: The Anatomy of the Industrial Order* (Harper, 1949), I.

duced to a small figure of the total population. After the work of this mass revolution the Old Order members stand out as conspicuous, living museums, and as reminders of preindustrialized, frontier America.

Yet, the Old Order folk are not really representative of frontier America, despite the fact that the cosmopolitan American city-dweller may look upon them as islands of sanity. The differences between Old Order and other farm practices have been leveled to distinctions in technological folkways. If we observe, for example, a prosperous Old Order Amish farm in the Midwest, we find there are neither electric lights, rubber-tired farm implements, nor a telephone. By avoiding them, the Amishman abides by the rules of his church. But there is a propane gas installation on his farm. His wife uses the latest-style gas range, a kerosene-burning refrigerator, and an automatic, gas water-heater with a gasoline engine to keep up the water pressure. Upstairs is a fully equipped bathroom with toilet, lavatory, and shower. The kitchen contains the latest-style sink and work table. The lighting in the house is by gasoline mantel lanterns. This prosperous Amish farmer has no automobile, but his Amish-Mennonite neighbor lives nearby and may be summoned any time, day or night, as may be necessary.

Although this Amish farmer (typical of many) is abiding by the rules of his church, he has drifted far from the behavior patterns of a generation ago. His farm operations have been revolutionized, and he depends upon the great industrialized society for his markets and his developing standard of living. In order to sell Grade A milk, he has had to alter his barn, milk house, water supply, and his habits of working with farm animals. To meet the requirements of sanitation, he had to think like the outsider. His milk is collected by a company truck; eggs, produce, and livestock are transported to market by the city people. Butter, bread, and groceries are also delivered to this and many Amish farms on a weekly schedule.

The curiosity and demand of the tourist for earmarks of Amish products, whether for antiques, baked goods, or handcrafts has led to the creation of meaningful market associations with out-groups. The realization that goods can be sold for needed cash has caused many Amish households to sell these products. Art experience and expression is also changing. Traditional, decorative art in homes was usually modest but evident in needlecraft, penmanship, and family records. Designs on chair cushions or on furniture today lack the dignity of their earlier traditional motifs. Antiques are frequently sold. In Amish corner cupboards or open shelves gayly colored show china from the dime store is mingled with family heirloom pieces a century or more old. The lust of the eye, it would appear, has deceived them in knowing what is traditional and in keeping with their otherwise nonconformed culture.

Improvements on farm implements, soil science, and farm-management practices are developments that will change with time and with still further inventions in the great society. Some of the new farm supplies and equipment often sold by the Amish themselves or used among them, are diesel engines, buzz chain saws, oil heaters, rubber buggy tires, hybrid seed corn, vitamins and minerals, cleaning agents, kerosene refrigerators, septic tanks, sewing machines, buggies and their accessories. The Old Orders tend to adopt many farm implements and practices as they become obsolete on the modern American farm. Thus direct involvement and identification with outside symbols and persons are avoided.

The goal of agriculture production among the Old Order does not conflict with that of the great society. The goals are compatible but the means differ. When government officials advised the Amish during World War II to scrap their horses so they could produce more farm products, the Amish replied that farming with horses was giving the country the highest possible output. There is a limit to which the Amish accept the economic goals of the great society. They have not transformed human relationships into exchange value, nor have they allowed economic considerations to tear asunder the ties that bind man to man. Naked self-interest, shameless, direct and brutal exploitation are tempered by their charter.

While economic practices change under the pressure of the problem of existence, there is no comparable change in intellectual interests. Many Old Order communities provide gifts in kind and contribute cash toward foreign relief but stop short of personal or administrative involvement.

*The New Order*, on the other hand, is involved in farming and economic activity that is no different from the typical American farmer. Involvement tends to take on concern and responsibility for the world outside the community, including the attempt to convert the outsider not to the traditional Amish patterns but to the general Protestant-Christian faith.

Concerns for other professing Christians outside the local community, and for poor and underprivileged persons, requires organization and co-operation with outside agencies. Young men who are drafted and given conscientious-objector status enter approved service institutions, many of them humanitarian or church-related. In the New Order type, there is the beginning of foreign service in relief and missionary work, interest in publication in both the German and English language, and limited interest in education. Members frequently find fulfillment of these interests in Mennonite institutions or in close association with this group.

In the future, outsiders will want to join the Amish society more frequently than was true in the past. Even though the Old Order has no regular way to accept new members from the outside, new family names have been introduced through what might be termed as "accidental" or chance factors. Nontraditional Amish family names like Huyard, Jones, and Carter were introduced through childhood adoptions or by farm hands who joined and married Amish girls. In recent years, several young men of non-Amish birth were received into membership by baptism. They were all single, formerly loosely affiliated with Protestant churches, of rural background with a love for farming, and at least two had been graduated from high school. They were attracted to the Amish, in differing localities, largely because of the "plainness" and the uncompromising position of the Amish in maintaining a simple life. "Although the older Amish people were not unanimous in giving their consent for my baptism," says one young man, "the preachers were all on my side. My parents thought I was crazy, and they wanted me to go to see a psychiatrist," he said. An increasing number of letters expressing admiration and respect for the Amish people have come to the writer. As the urban world becomes more hazardous, stressful, and complex, there are those who will be attracted to a simpler way of life.

We have observed that the Amish society is faced with the problem of community self-realization and personal fulfillment for the members in each new generation. The constant striving to achieve these ends has given rise to two general types of social organization, the Old and the New Order. Each is characterized by a unique set of attitudes and practices as reflected in the possibilities and potentialities of their ongoing problem-solving processes and perception patterns. We have observed directions of development in both of the types with respect to the reformulation of the charter, the changing community, the view of the world, and the rules which allow personal involvement in out-groups. Stress problems are apparent in both types, and they differ in kind and intensity with each community. We have observed the manner in which communities resolve or fail to resolve their living problems. The Amish society will thrive or perish to the degree that it can provide community and personal fulfillment for the children raised in Amish homes.

# BIBLIOGRAPHY

The Old Order Amish are the subject of a maze of books, pamphlets, and articles. Seventeen books exclusively on the Amish have appeared in print from 1894 to the present. Thirty additional books devote a section to the Amish; there have been at least six novels, nine children's books, many master's theses and doctoral dissertations, and hundreds of articles in over eighty national magazines.

The first book was written by Barthinius L. Wick with the title *The Amish Mennonites* and was published by the State Historical Society of Iowa in 1894. The second was the *Amishman* by Clyde Smith, published by Briggs Company of Toronto in 1912. The first is a historical descriptive study and the second a narrative of the human-interest type. Melvin Gingerich's *The Mennonites in Iowa* (1939) devotes extensive space to the Amish. Joseph W. Yoder's *Rosanna of the Amish* appeared in 1940. Yoder's sympathetic narrative found widespread acceptance and provoked further literary and scientific interest. Both Calvin Bachman's *The Old Order Amish Of Lancaster County* and Walter M. Kollmorgen's monograph on the same community appeared in 1942. The latter was published by the United States Department of Agriculture as one of six communities studied analytically and is widely quoted in scientific literature. Also in 1942 Yoder published his second book, *Amische Lieder*, a compilation of oral hymn tunes that he reduced to musical scores. H. M. J. Klein's attractive *History and Customs of the Amish People*, a small book of limited edition, appeared in 1946, and the first photographic study, *Meet the Amish*, by John B. Shenk and photographer Charles S. Rice, appeared in 1947. Yoder produced *Rosanna's Boys* in 1948 and *Amish Traditions* in 1950.

As an outgrowth of classroom contact and tutorship with two veteran scholars of Amish life, John Umble and Harold Bender, the author compiled *An Annotated Bibliography on the Amish* (1951). The art and drawings of Kiehl and Christian Newswanger appeared in 1954 in a book entitled *Amishland*. A second book of photographs, *The Amish Year*, by Charles S. Rice with journalistic treatment by Rollin Steinmetz, was issued in 1956. The largest body of newly discovered historical materials found its way into *The Mennonite Encyclopedia* (4 vols., 1956–59), which contains hundreds of articles topically arranged. Elmer Smith's *The Amish People* appeared in 1958 and was followed by *Studies in Amish Demography* in 1960 and *The Amish Today* in 1961. In 1962 William Schreiber's *Our Amish Neighbors* was published. At least twenty-four, if not more, pamphlets have appeared on the Amish. In his monumental history *The Pennsylvania Germans 1891–1965* (1966) Homer Rosenberger includes a section on "Popularization of the Amish" where he has compiled a partial list of national magazines featuring the Amish. Scholarly treatments have been largely of the natural-history type, or of specialized subjects such as educational problems. The major exceptions are the publications of Charles P. Loomis. He has utilized Amish cultural materials in the presentation of sociological theory.

The bibliography that follows is limited to the sources which are cited in the footnotes or text or are directly relevant to social change in Amish society. It includes both scientific and in-group sources utilized in treating the Amish community under conditions of change and stress. The historical collection in the Mennonite Historical Library at Goshen College, Goshen, Indiana, is the most comprehensive of several fine collections of materials in Mennonite colleges and regional historical societies. The following bibliographical entries are arranged alphabetically; when there is more than one title by the same author, the entries for the author are arranged chronologically.

ADAMS, W. MELVIN. "The Real Question in Iowa," *Liberty* (May–June, 1966).

AMERICAN PSYCHIATRIC ASSOCIATION. *Diagnostic and Statistical Manual, Mental Disorders.* Washington, D.C., 1952.

*Artikel und Ordnungen der Christlichen Gemeinde in Christo Jesu.* Mennonite Publishing Company, 1905.

*Ausbund, Das ist: Etliche schöne christliche Lieder.* First edition, 1564.

BACHMANN, CALVIN GEORGE. *The Old Order Amish of Lancaster County, Pennsylvania.* Pennsylvania German Society, 1942. Reprinted 1961.

BAEHR, KARL H. "Secularization Among the Mennonites." B.D. dissertation, University of Chicago, 1942.

BAIN, READ. "Our Schizoid Culture," *Sociology and Social Research* (January–February, 1935).

BATES, MARSTEN. *The Forest and the Sea. A Look at the Economy of Nature and the Ecology of Man.* Random House, 1960.

BEACHY, ALVIN J. *The Amish of Somerset County, Pennsylvania: A Study in the Rise and Development of the Beachy Amish Mennonite Churches.* Hartford Seminary Foundation, 1952.

BECKER, HOWARD. "Normative Reactions to Normlessness," *American Sociological Review* (December, 1960).

———, and BARNES, HARRY ELMER. *Social Thought from Lore to Science.* 3 vols. Dover Publications, 1961.

BECKER, KARL AUGUST. *Die Volkstrachten der Pfalz.* Verlag der Pfälzischen Gesellschaft zur Forderung der Wissenschaften, Kaiserslautern, 1952.

BEILER, AARON E. *Backgrounds and Standards of the Old Order Amish Church School Committee.* Route 1, Gap, Pa. 1937. Reaffirmed 1961.

BENDER, HAROLD S. "The First Edition of the Ausbund," *Mennonite Quarterly Review* (April, 1929).

———. "An Amish Church Discipline of 1781," *Mennonite Quarterly Review* (April, 1930).

———. "Some Early American Amish Mennonite Disciplines," *Mennonite Quarterly Review* (April, 1934).

———. "An Amish Church Discipline of 1779," *Mennonite Quarterly Review* (April, 1937).

———. "The Anabaptist Vision," *Church History* (March, 1944). Reprinted in *Mennonite Quarterly Review* (April, 1944).

———. "The Minutes of the Amish Conference of 1809 Probably Held in Lancaster County, Pennsylvania," *Mennonite Quarterly Review* (July, 1946).

———. *Conrad Grebel c. 1498–1526, The Founder of the Swiss Brethern Sometimes Called Anabaptists.* Mennonite Historical Society, 1950.

———. "The Zwickau Prophets, Thomas Muntzer and the Anabaptists," *Mennonite Quarterly Review* (January, 1953).

BERNARD, L. L. *Social Control in Its Sociological Aspects.* Macmillan, 1939.

BIERSTEDT, ROBERT. *The Social Order.* MacGraw-Hill, 1957.

BIRD, JOHN. "The Unyielding Amish," *The Saturday Evening Post* (July 17, 1967).

*Blackboard Bulletin, The.* Aylmer, Ontario. A periodical published by the Pathway Publishing Corporation in the interest of Amish schools. Founded 1957.

BOAS, FRANZ. *Anthropology and Modern Life.* 1927. Revised edition, 1932.

BOWMAN, HERBERT S., and PROCOPIO, FRANK. "Hereditary Nonspherocytic Anemia of the Pyruvate-kinase Deficient Type," *Annals of Internal Medicine,* Vol. 58, No. 4 (April, 1963).

BRAGHT, THIELEMAN J. VAN. *Het Bloedigh Tooneel der Doops-Gesinde en Weereloosen Christenen.* Dordrecht, The Netherlands, 1660. [English title: *The Bloody Theatre or Martyrs Mirror of the Defenseless Christians Who Baptized Only Upon Confession of Faith, and Who Suffered and Died for the Testimony of Jesus, Their Saviour, From the Time of Christ to the Year A.D. 1660.* Published by Mennonite Publishing House, 1950. Reprinted 1953.]

BRANSON, V. K. The Amish of Thomas, Oklahoma: A Study in Cultural Geography. M. S. Thesis, University of Oklahoma. 1967.

BROWNELL, BAKER. *The Human Community: Its Philosophy and Practice for a Time of Crisis.* Harper, 1950.

BUCHANAN, FREDERICK S. "The Old Paths: A Study of the Amish Response to Public Schooling in Ohio." Department of Education, The Ohio State University. Ph.D. dissertation. June, 1967.

*Budget, The.* Sugarcreek, Ohio.

BUFFINGTON, ALBERT F. "Pennsylvania German: Its Relation to Other German Dialects," *American Speech* (December, 1939).

BURKHART, CHARLES. "The Music of the Old Order Amish and the Old Colony Mennonites A Contemporary Monodic Practice." M.A. thesis, Colorado College, 1952.

BYLER, URIA R. *Our Better Country.* Old Order Book Society, Gordonville, Pa., 1963.

CAUDILL, WILLIAM. *Effects of Social and Cultural Systems in Reactions to Stress.* Social Science Research Council, Pamphlet 14, 1958.

CLARK, ELMER. *The Small Sects in America.* Abington, 1949.

CLAUSEN, JOHN A. *Sociology and the Field of Mental Health.* Russell Sage Foundation, 1956.

CLINARD, MARSHALL B. *The Sociology of Deviant Behavior.* Holt, Rinehart and Winston, Inc., 1963.

COOLEY, CHARLES H. *Social Organization.* Scribners, 1909.

CORRELL, ERNST. *Das Schweizerische Täufermennonitentum.* Mohr, Tübingen, 1925.

CROSS, HAROLD E. "Genetic Studies in an Amish Isolate." Ph.D. dissertation. Johns Hopkins University, 1967.

DAWSON, CARL A., and GETTYS, WARNER E. *An Introduction to Sociology.* Ronald Press, 1948.

DeWIND, HENRY A. "A Sixteenth Century Description of Religious Sects in Austerlitz, Moravia," *Mennonite Quarterly Review* (January, 1955).

DILLING, W. R. "Religion Boosts Domestic Swiss Cheese Output," *American Butter Review* (April, 1950).

DRUCKER, PETER F. *The New Society: The Anatomy of the Industrial Order.* Harper, 1949.

DURKHEIM, EMILE. *La Suicide.* Alcan (Paris, 1897). [English edition 1951, Free Press.]

————. *The Elementary Forms of Religious Life.* Translated by J. W. Swain. Allen and Unwin, 1915.

EATON, JOSEPH W. "Controlled Acculturation," *American Sociological Review* (June, 1952).

————, and MAYER, ALBERT J. *Man's Capacity to Reproduce: The Demography of a Unique Population.* The Free Press, 1954.

EGELAND, JANICE A. "Belief and Behavior as Related to Illness: A Community Case Study of the Old Order Amish." Yale University, New Haven, Connecticut. Unpublished Ph.D. dissertation (2 vols.), 1967.

*Eine schädliche Uebung: Eine Erklärung uber eine untugendliche Gewohnheit oder Gebrauch.* Von einem Liebhaber der Wahrheit. (n.d., n.p.)

ERICKSON, DONALD E. "The Plain People vs. the Common Schools," *Saturday Review* (November 19, 1966).

————. "Showdown at an Amish Schoolhouse," Background paper No. 3, *Freedom and Control in Education,* National Invitational Conference on State Regulation of Nonpublic Schools. University of Chicago, 1967.

————. "Freedom's Two Educational Imperatives," National Invitational Conference on State Regulation of Nonpublic Schools. University of Chicago, 1967.

*Ernsthafte Christenpflicht, Die.* First known edition 1739.

EVERETT, GLENN D. "One Man's Family," *Population Bulletin* (December, 1961).

*Family Life.* Amish periodical published monthly. Volume I, No. 1. January, 1968. David Wagler, editor. Pathway Publishing Corporation, Aylmer, Ontario.

First Presbyterian Church. *Kishacoquillas Valley Cook Book.* Belleville, Pennsylvania, 1950.

Frank, Lawrence K. *Society as the Patient.* Rutgers University Press, 1949.

Fretz, Joseph Winfield. "Mennonite Mutual Aid." Ph.D. dissertation, University of Chicago, 1941.

———. "The Growth and Use of Tobacco Among Mennonites," *Proceedings of the Seventh Annual Conference on Mennonite Cultural Problems* (1949).

Frey, J. William. "Amish Triple-Talk," *American Speech* (April, 1945).

———. "Amish Hymns as Folk Music," in George Korson, *Pennsylvania Songs and Legends,* University of Pennsylvania Press, 1949. Reprinted by The Johns Hopkins Press, 1961.

Friedmann, Robert. *Mennonite Piety Through the Centuries.* Mennonite Historical Society, 1949.

Gasho, Milton. "The Amish Division of 1693–1697 in Switzerland and Alsace," *Mennonite Quarterly Review* (October, 1937).

Gehman, Richard. "Amish Folk," *National Geographic* (August, 1965).

Gennep, Arnold van. *Les rites de passage.* Nourry, Paris, 1909.

Getz, Jane C. "Religious Forces in the Economic and Social Life of the Old Order Amish in Lancaster County, Pennsylvania." M.A. thesis, American University, Washington, D.C., 1945.

Gingerich, Melvin. *Mennonites in Iowa.* Iowa Historical Society, 1939.

———. "Custom Built Coffins," *The Palimpsest* (December, 1943).

Goldenweiser, A. A. "The Principle of Limited Possibilities in the Development of Culture," *Journal of American Folklore,* Vol. 26 (1913).

———. *History, Psychology and Culture.* Knopf, 1933.

Gratz, Delbert. "The Home of Jacob Ammann in Switzerland," *Mennonite Quarterly Review* (April, 1951).

Gross, Neal. "Cultural Variables in Rural Communities," *American Journal of Sociology* (March, 1948).

———. "Sociological Variation in Contemporary Rural Life," *Rural Sociology* (September, 1948).

Gutkind, Peter C. W. *Secularization Versus the Christian Community: Problems of an Old Order House Amish Family in Northern Indiana.* Department of Anthropology, University of Chicago Press, 1952.

Hallowell, A. I. "Social Psychological Aspects of Acculturation," in Ralph Linton (ed.), *The Science of Man in the World Crisis.* Columbia University Press, 1945.

HARTZ, AMOS and SUSAN. *Moses Hartz Family History 1819–1965.* Elverson, Pa., 1965.

HEBERLE, RUDOLPH. *Social Movements.* Appleton-Century-Crofts, Inc., 1951.

HENRY, JULES. *Culture Against Man.* Vintage Books, Random House, 1963.

HERBERG, WILL. *Protestant, Catholic, Jew.* Anchor Books, 1960.

HERSHBERGER, HENRY J. *Minimum Standards for the Amish Parochial or Private Elementary Schools of the State of Ohio as a Form of Regulations.* Compiled and Approved by Bishops, Committeemen, and Others in Conference. n.d. (Route 2, Apple Creek, Ohio.)

HERSHBERGER, JACOB J. (compiler). *Our Youths: A Collection of Letters Pertaining to the Conditions Among Our Youth, The Amish Mennonites.* Lynnhaven, Virginia, 1955.

HOFFER, ERIC. *The True Believer.* Harper and Brothers, 1951.

HOHMANN, RUPERT K. "The Church Music of the Old Order Amish of the United States." Ph.D. dissertation, Northwestern University, 1959.

HOMANS, GEORGE C. "Anxiety and Ritual: The Theories of Malinowski and Radcliffe-Brown," *American Anthropologist,* XLIII (1941).

HOSTETLER, HARVEY. *Descendants of Jacob Hochstetler, the Immigrant of 1736.* Brethren Publishing House, Elgin, Illinois, 1912. (Reprinted in 1962 by Noah Wengerd, Meyersdale, Pa.)

———. *Descendants of Barbara Hochstedler and Christian Stutzman.* Mennonite Publishing House, 1938.

HOSTETLER, JOHN A. "The Life and Times of Samuel Yoder, 1824–1884," *Mennonite Quarterly Review* (October, 1948).

———. "The Amish in Gosper County, Nebraska," *Mennonite Historical Bulletin* (October, 1949).

———. *Annotated Bibliography on the Old Order Amish.* Mennonite Publishing House, Scottdale, Pennsylvania, 1951.

———. "The Amish Family in Mifflin County, Pennsylvania." M.S. thesis, The Pennsylvania State University, 1951.

———. *The Sociology of Mennonite Evangelism.* Herald Press, 1954.

———. "Old World Extinction and New World Survival of the Amish," *Rural Sociology* (September–December, 1955).

———. "Folk and Scientific Medicine in Amish Society" (unpublished, 1963).

———, and HUNTINGTON, GERTRUDE ENDERS. *The Hutterites in North America.* Holt, Rinehart and Winston, Inc., 1967.

HOUGHTON, ARTHUR V. "Community Organization in a Rural Amish Community at Arthur, Illinois." M.A. thesis, University of Illinois, 1926.

HUGHES, EVERETT C. *Where Peoples Meet.* Free Press, 1952.

HUIZINGA, JOHAN. *The Waning of the Middle Ages.* Reprinted by Doubleday Anchor Books, 1924.

HUNTINGTON, GERTRUDE ENDERS. "Dove at the Window: A Study of an Old Order Amish Community in Ohio." Ph.D. dissertation, Yale University, 1956.

INDIAN EDUCATION RESEARCH STAFF. "Field Guide to the Study of the Development of Inter-Personal Relations." Committee on Human Development, University of Chicago, Chicago, 1942. Mimeographed.

JACKSON, C. E. *et al.* "Progressive Muscular Distrophy: Autosomal Recessive Type," *Pediatrics* (1961), 28: 77

JACKSON, GEORGE PULLEN. "The American Amish Sing Medieval Folk Tunes Today," *Southern Folklore Quarterly* (June, 1945).

———. "The Strange Music of the Old Order Amish," *The Musical Quarterly* (July, 1945).

JOHNSON, BENTON. "A Critical Appraisal of Church-Sect Typology," *American Sociological Review* (February, 1957).

JUBERG, R. C. *Selection in the ABO, Rhesus and MNSs Blood Group Polymorphisms in an Amish Isolate of Northern Indiana.* Ph.D. dissertation, University of Michigan. 1966.

KELLEY, DEAN M. "Is There Room for the Amish?" *Town and Country Church* (May–June, 1966).

KEPLER, LUTHER F., JR., and FISHER, ANNE KEPLER. "The Nebraska Old Order Amish," *Mennonite Life* (July, 1961). Illustrated.

KHALDUN, IBN. *An Arab Philosophy of History, Selections from the Prolegomena of Ibn Khaldun of Tunis* (1332–1406). Translated by Charles Issawi. Published by John Murray, London, 1950.

KING, C. WENDELL. *Social Movements in the United States.* Random House, 1956.

KOLLMORGEN, WALTER M. *Culture of a Contemporary Community: The Old Order Amish of Lancaster County, Pennsylvania.* Rural Life Studies: No. 4, United States Department of Agriculture, 1942.

———. "The Agricultural Stability of the Old Order Amish Mennonites of Lancaster County, Pennsylvania," *American Journal of Sociology* (November, 1943).

KUHN, MANFORD H. "Factors in Personality: "Socio-Cultural Determinants as Seen Through the Amish," in F. Hsu (ed.) *Aspects of Culture and Personality*, Abelard-Schuman, Inc., 1954.

LANDING, JAMES E. "The Spatial Development and Organization of an Old Order Amish-Beachy Amish Settlement: Nappanee, Indiana." Ph.D. dissertation. The Pennsylvania State University, Department of Geography. 1967.

LANGER, SUSANNE K. *Philosophy in a New Key: A Study in the Symbolism of Reason, Rite and Art.* Harvard University Press, 1960.

LANSBERRY, THOMAS F., BOLLA, ELMER T., and McKEEN, CHIDSEY T. *Record, In the Superior Court of Pennsylvania, Western District, Nos. 129, 130, 131, 132 (April Term 1949). Commonwealth of Pennsylvania v. Jonas Petersheim, v. Menno G. Brenneman, v. Amos J. Yoder, v. Enos Mast.* Harrisburg, Pennsylvania, 1949.

LEE, DOROTHY. *Freedom and Culture.* Prentice-Hall, 1959.

LINDHOLM, WILLIAM C. "Religious Liberty Defined, Observations of a Clergyman." East Tawas, Michigan. Unpublished. (1966).

LINTON, RALPH. *Acculturation in Seven American Indian Tribes* D. Appleton-Century Company, 1940.

———. "Nativistic Movements," *American Anthropologist* (April–June, 1943).

LITTELL, FRANKLIN H. *The Anabaptist View of the Church.* Beacon Press, 1958.

———, "Sectarian Protestantism and the Pursuit of Wisdom," Address at the National Invitational Conference on State Regulation of Non-public Schools, University of Chicago. 1967.

LOOMIS, CHARLES P. "Farm Hand's Diary." Unpublished, 1940.

———. *Rural Sociology.* Prentice-Hall, 1957.

———. *Social Systems: Essays on Their Persistence and Change.* D. Van Nostrand Company, 1960.

———, and BEEGLE, J. ALLAN. *Rural Social Systems*, Prentice-Hall, 1951.

———, and JANTZEN, CARL R. "Boundary Maintenance vs. Systemic Linkage in School Integration: The Case of the Amish in the United States," *The Journal of The Pakistan Academy for Village Development* (Comilla, East Pakistan), Vol. III, No. 2 (October, 1962), 1–25.

———, and LOOMIS, ZONA K. *Modern Social Theories.* D. Van Nostrand Company, 1961.

McKUSICK, VICTOR A. *et al.* "Genetic Studies of the Amish: Background and Potentialities," *Bulletin of the Johns Hopkins Hospital*, 115 (1964): 203–22.

———. "Dwarfism in the Amish: I. The Ellis–van Creveld Syndrome," *Bulletin of the Johns Hopkins Hospital*, 115 (1964): 305–36.

——. "Dwarfism in the Amish: II. Cartilage-hair Hypoplasia," *Bulletin of the Johns Hopkins Hospital*, 116 (1965): 285–326.

——. "The Distribution of Certain Genes in the Old Order Amish," Cold Spring Harbor Symposia on Quantitative Biology, 29 (1964): 99–114.

MALINOWSKI, BROMISLAW. *A Scientific Theory of Culture*. University of North Carolina Press, 1944.

——. *Magic, Science, and Religion*. Free Press, 1948.

——. *The Dynamics of Culture Change*. Yale University Press, 1961.

MAST, JOHN B. (ed.). *Eine Erklärung über Bann und Meidung Geschrieben zur Zeit der Amisch Spalt von 1693–1711*, 1949.

——. *The Letters of the Amish Division*. Published by Christian J. Schlabaugh, Oregon City, Oregon, 1950.

MEAD, MARGARET. *Culture Patterns and Technical Change*. Mentor Books, 1955.

*Mennonite Encyclopedia, The*. Published by the Mennonite Publishing House, Scottdale, Pennsylvania, the Mennonite Brethern Publishing House, Hillsboro, Kansas, and the Mennonite Publication Office, North Newton, Kansas. 4 vols. 1956–59.

*Mennonite Yearbook and Directory*. Mennonite Publishing House, Scottdale, Pennsylvania, 1905–.

MERTON, ROBERT K. *Social Theory and Social Structure*. Free Press, 1957.

MILLER, D. PAUL. "Amish Acculturation," M.A. thesis, University of Nebraska, 1949.

MILLER, ELIZABETH. *From the Fiery Stakes of Europe to the Federal Courts of America*. Vantage Press, New York. 1963.

MILLER, HARVEY J. "Proceedings of Amish Ministers Conferences 1826–31," *Mennonite Quarterly Review* (April, 1959).

MILLER, L. A. (ed.). *Handbuch für Prediger*. Arthur, Illinois, 1950.

MILLER, WAYNE. "A Study of Amish Academic Achievement," Ph.D. dissertation. School of Educational Administration, University of Michigan. 1968. In process.

MINER, HORACE. "The Folk-Urban Continuum," *American Sociological Review* (October, 1952).

MOOK, MAURICE A. "The Amish Community at Atlantic, Pennsylvania," *Mennonite Quarterly Review* (October, 1954).

——. "The Number of Amish in Pennsylvania," *Mennonite Historical Bulletin* (January, 1955).

——. "A Brief History of Former, Now Extinct, Amish Communities in Pennsylvania," *Western Pennsylvania Historical Magazine* (Spring–Summer, 1955), 33–46.

———. "An Early Amish Colony in Chester County," *The Morning Call* (February 26, and March 5, 1955).

———. "Nicknames Among the Amish," *Mennonite Life* (July, 1961).

———. "The Nebraska Amish in Pennsylvania," *Mennonite Life* (January, 1962).

MOORE, WILBERT E., and TUMIN, MELVIN M. "Some Social Functions of Ignorance," *American Sociological Review* (December, 1949).

NISLEY, JONAS. *Children's Read, Write, Color, Book*. Baltic, Ohio, 1965.

*Ohio Amish Directory*. Millersburg, Ohio, 1959, 1960, 1965.

Ohio Legislative Service Commission. *Sectarian Amish Education*. Research Report No. 44. December, 1960.

Old Order Map Committee. *Amish Farm and Home Directory of Lancaster & Lebanon Districts, Penna*. First edition, 1965. Printed by A. S. Kinsinger, Gordonville, Pa.

PARSONS, TALCOTT. *The Social System*. Free Press, 1951.

———. "Illness and the Role of the Physician: A Sociological Perspective," *American Journal of Orthopsychiatry* (July, 1951).

———. *Working Papers in the Theory of Action*. Free Press, 1953.

———, and Others (eds.). *Theories of Society: Foundations of Modern Sociological Theory*. 2 vols. Free Press, 1961.

PEACHEY, JOSEPH N. and SYLVIA. *Favorite Amish Family Recipes*. Pathway Publishing Corporation, Aylmer, Ontario, 1965.

PEACHEY, PAUL. *Die Soziale Herkunft der Schweizer Täufer*. Karlsruhe, 1954.

Pennsylvania, Commonwealth of: Department of Public Instruction. "Policy for Operation of Home and Farm Projects in Church-Organized Day Schools." October 5, 1955.

PETERS, FRANK C. "The Ban in the Writings of Menno Simons," *Mennonite Quarterly Review* (January, 1955).

RABER, J. A. (ed.). *Der Neue Amerikanische Calendar*. Baltic, Ohio, 1930.

RADCLIFFE-BROWN, A. R. *Taboo*. The Frazer Lecture, Cambridge, 1939.

REDEKOP, CALVIN WALL. "The Sectarian Black and White World." Ph.D. dissertation, University of Chicago, 1959.

REDFIELD, ROBERT. *Tepoztlan: A Mexican Village*. University of Chicago Press, 1930.

———. *Chan Kom, A Maya Village*. Carnegie Institute of Washington, 1934.

———. "The Folk Society," *American Journal of Sociology*. (January, 1947), 292-308.

———. *The Folk Culture of the Yucatan.* University of Chicago Press, 1949.

———. *A Village That Chose Progress: Chan Kom Revisited.* University of Chicago Press, 1950.

———. *The Little Community.* University of Chicago Press, 1955.

———. *Peasant Society and Culture.* University of Chicago Press, 1956.

ROSENBERGER, HOMER TOPE. *The Pennsylvania Germans 1891–1965.* The Pennsylvania German Society, 1966.

SCHROEDER, W. WIDICK, and BEEGLE, J. ALLAN. "Suicide: An Instance of High Rural Rates," *Rural Sociology* (March, 1953).

SERVICE, ELMAN R. *Profiles in Ethnology.* Harper & Row, 1963.

SHOEMAKER, ALFRED L. "Studies on the Pennsylvania German Dialect of the Amish Community in Arthur, Illinois." Ph.D. dissertation, University of Illinois, 1932.

SHOWALTER, MARY EMMA. *Mennonite Community Cookbook.* Winston, 1950.

SIMMONS, LEO W. *The Role of the Aged in Primitive Society.* Yale University Press, 1945.

SIMONS, MENNO. *Opera Omnia Theologica.* Amsterdam, 1681. [English edition: *The Complete Writings of Menno Simons c. 1496–1561.* Translated by Leonard Verduin and edited by John Christian Wenger. Herald Press, Scottdale, Pennsylvania, 1956.]

SMITH, C. HENRY. *The Mennonites in America.* Goshen, Indiana, 1909.

———. *The Education of a Mennonite Country Boy.* Mimeographed. Bluffton, Ohio, 1943. [Published in 1962 by Faith and Life Press, Newton, Kansas, as *Mennonite Country Boy;* the early years of C. Henry Smith.]

SMITH, ELMER LEWIS. "A Study of Acculturation in an Amish Community." Doctor of Social Science dissertation, Syracuse University, 1955.

STOLL, JOSEPH. *The Challenge of the Child.* Pathway Publishing Corporation, Aylmer, Ontario. 1967.

———. *Who Shall Educate Our Children?* Aylmer, Ontario, 1965.

———. *The Lord is My Shepherd. The Life of Elizabeth Kemp Stutzman.* Pathway Publishing Corporation, 1965.

STOLTZFUS, GRANT M. "History of the First Amish Communities in America." M.A. thesis, University of Pittsburgh, 1954.

STONEQUIST, E. V. *The Marginal Man.* Charles Scribner's Sons, 1937.

STROUP, J. MARTIN. *The Amish of Kishacoquillas Valley.* Mifflin County Historical Society, 1965.

STUTZMAN, D. J. *A Call to Repentance*. Millersburg, Ohio, n.d.

SUMNER, WILLIAM G. *Folkways*. Ginn and Company, 1906.

THOMAS, WILLIAM I., and ZNANIECKI, FLORIAN. *The Polish Peasant in Europe and America*. Knopf, 1927.

THOMPSON, LAURA. "Core Values and Diplomacy: A Case Study of Iceland," *Human Organization*, Vol. 19 (1960), 82–85.

———. "Perception Patterns in Three Indian Tribes," *Psychiatry*, Vol. 14 (1951), 255–63.

———. *Toward a Science of Mankind*. McGraw-Hill Book Co., 1961.

TOENNIES, FERDINAND. *Gemeinschaft und Gesellschaft*. Fues' Verlag, Leipzig, 1887. [English edition: *Community and Society*. Translated by Charles P. Loomis. Michigan State University Press, 1957.]

TROELTSCH, ERNST. *The Social Teachings of the Christian Churches*. Translated by O. Wyon. Macmillan, 1931. [New edition in 2 vols., Free Press, 1949.]

TURNER, RALPH H., and KILLIGAN, LEWIS M. *Collective Behavior*. Prentice-Hall, 1957.

UMBLE, JOHN. "The Amish Mennonites of Union County, Pennsylvania, Part I, Social and Religious Life," *Mennonite Quarterly Review* (April, 1933). "Part II, A History of the Settlement," (July, 1933).

———. "The Old Order Amish, Their Hymns and Hymn Tunes," *Journal of American Folklore*, Vol. III (1939).

———. "Why Congregations Die," *Mennonite Historical Bulletin* (October, 1947).

———. "Justice Fails Again," *Gospel Herald* (February 3, 1948).

———. "Factors Explaining the Disintegration of Mennonite Communities," *Proceedings of the Seventh Annual Conference on Mennonite Cultural Problems* (1949).

*United States Census of Population, 1960. General, Social and Economic Characteristics, Series PC (1)–1C.*

WAGLER, DAVID. *The Mighty Whirlwind*. Aylmer, Ontario. 1966. Pathway Publishing Corporation.

WARREN, ROLAND L. "German Parteilieder and Christian Hymns as Instruments of Social Control," *Journal of Abnormal and Social Psychology*, Vol. 38 (1943).

WEBER, MAX. *Gesammelte Aufsätze zur Religionssoziologie*. 3 vols. Mohr (Siebeck), Tübingen, 1922.

———. *From Max Weber, Essays in Sociology*. Translated and edited by Hans H. Gerth and C. Wright Mills. Oxford University Press, 1946.

———. *The Theory of Social and Economic Organization*. Translated by A. M. Henderson and Talcott Parsons. Free Press, 1947.

————. *Rational and Social Foundations of Music.* Translated and edited by J. Riedel and Don Martindale. Southern Illinois University, 1958.

WEINBERG, S. KIRSON. *Social Problems in Our Time.* Prentice-Hall, 1960.

WELLS, RICHARD D. Articles of Agreement Regarding the Indiana Amish Parochial Schools and the Department of Public Instruction. Indiana Department of Public Education. 1967.

WENGER, JOHN C. *The Doctrines of the Mennonites.* Mennonite Publishing House, 1958.

————. *The Mennonites in Indiana and Michigan.* Herald Press, 1961.

WILLIAMS, GEORGE H. *The Radical Reformation.* Westminster Press, 1962.

WILSON, BRYAN. "An Analysis of Sect Development," *American Journal of Sociology* (February, 1959).

WOOD, RALPH. *The Pennsylvania Germans.* Princeton University Press, 1942.

YODER, JOHN H. "Mennonites in a French Almanac," *Mennonite Life* (October, 1954).

YODER, JOSEPH W. *Rosanna of the Amish.* Yoder Publishing Company, 1940. Reprinted by Herald Press.

————. *Amische Lieder.* Yoder Publishing Company, 1942. After 1961 by Herald Press, Scottdale, Pennsylvania.

YODER, SANFORD C. *The Days of My Years.* Herald Press, 1959.

ZOOK, NOAH. *Seeking a Better Country.* Old Order Book Society, Gordonville, Pa., 1963.

# INDEX